Hiking through History
San Francisco Bay Area

Hiking through History
San Francisco Bay Area

41 Hikes from Lands End to the Top of Mount Diablo

Tracy Salcedo

FALCONGUIDES

GUILFORD, CONNECTICUT
HELENA, MONTANA

In memory of my grandparents,
Petra and Antonio Salcedo
Muriel and Howard Blakiston

FALCONGUIDES®

An imprint of Rowman & Littlefield
Falcon, FalconGuides, and Make Adventure Your Story are registered trademarks of Rowman & Littlefield.

Distributed by NATIONAL BOOK NETWORK

Copyright © 2016 by Rowman & Littlefield
Maps: Alena Pearce © Rowman & Littlefield

British Library Cataloguing-in-Publication Information Available

Library of Congress Cataloging-in-Publication Data

Names: Salcedo-Chourre, Tracy.
Title: Hiking through history : San Francisco Bay Area : exploring the region's past by trail / Tracy Salcedo-Chourre.
Description: Guilford, Connecticut : FalconGuides, [2016] | "Distributed by NATIONAL BOOK NETWORK" —T.p. verso. | Description based on print version record and CIP data provided by publisher; resource not viewed.
Identifiers: LCCN 2016004081 (print) | LCCN 2015050610 (ebook) | ISBN 9781493017973 (e-book) | ISBN 9781493017966 (paperback : alk. paper)
Subjects:LCSH:Hiking—California—SanFranciscoBayArea—Guidebooks.|Trails—California—SanFrancisco Bay Area—Guidebooks. | San Francisco Bay Area (Calif.)—Guidebooks.
Classification: LCC GV199.42.C22 (print) | LCC GV199.42.C22 S2368 2016 (ebook) | DDC 917.94/604—dc23
LC record available at http://lccn.loc.gov/2016004081

♾™ The paper used in this publication meets the minimum requirements of American National Standard for Information Sciences—Permanence of Paper for Printed Library Materials, ANSI/NISO Z39.48-1992.

Contents

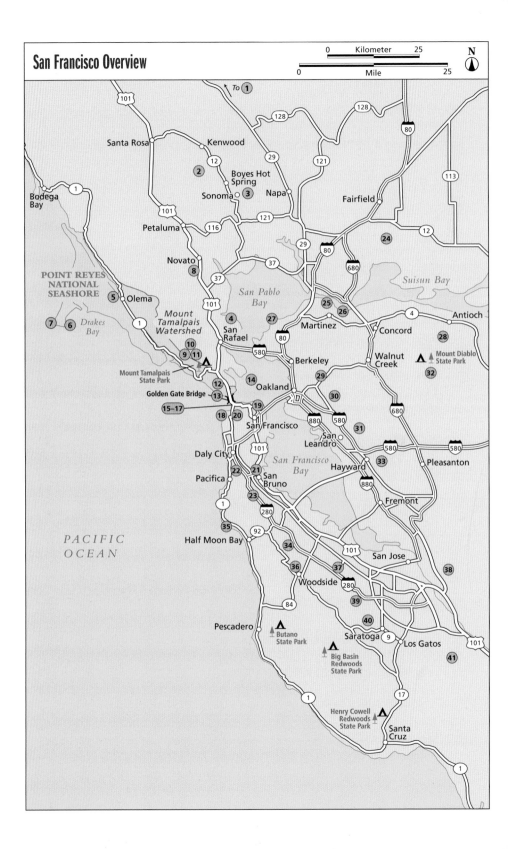

San Francisco Overview

Acknowledgments

The sources I pulled from to write this guide are so numerous that to lay them out in detail would constitute another book-length tome. Suffice it to say that without the work of an army of Bay Area historians, whose research has been compiled in books, park brochures, pamphlets, historical walking guides, and online in blogs and on websites for the various parks, cities, and towns discussed herein, this guide would not have been possible. Likewise, I am indebted to state, regional, and national park officials and volunteers throughout the region. Without their foresight in conservation and hard work in preservation, these trails and the historic landscapes would not exist.

My family's long history in San Francisco, spanning six generations on my mother's side and a scant but equally story-full two on my father's, has been my backbone in this endeavor. I thank my entire family, including those far away (Uncle Walter, Denise Jackson, and Jan Juliann Leitch among them), for the tales they've told and the support they've provided.

I'm lucky that my writers' group includes two historians and a journalist, whose support of my work has been invaluable. Thank you to Ann Peters, Arthur Dawson, and Jim Shere.

Thanks too to my coworkers at Streetwise Reports, who not only support my "side job" but also suppress their snickers when, after a long weekend on the trail, I hobble stiffly around the office.

Thanks to my sturdy, patient companions on the trail: Bettina "That's the Golden Gate Bridge. Shouldn't you make a note?" Hopkins, Kerin McTaggart, Julianne Roth, and Patrice Fusillo.

A huge thank-you is due the editors, mapmakers, and designers who put Falcon-Guides together. I am forever grateful for the work you do to make the guides I write the best they can be.

Finally, my everlasting love and gratitude to my sons, Jesse, Cruz, and Penn.

Introduction

Standing on a trail on the slopes of Mount Tam, I watched the fog do what it always does under a summer sun: burn back to sea. It floated like an old gray quilt on the Pacific, fraying on the edges as it slipped through wooded ridgelines, slowly revealing the arc of Stinson Beach far below.

On another trail, the shocking orange of a tiger lily flashed amid ferns next to a waterfall that ran even in a drought.

And on another, I stepped into the slot between two massive redwoods, steadied myself with a hand on each trunk, and looked up at the impossible straightness.

On other paths, I slipped my hands through blooming sage and lupine to scent myself with their perfume. I walked labyrinths. Made way for lizards. Straddled fault lines. Peered into mine shafts. Walked through hand-hewn tunnels. Waited for cattle to cross. Waited for newts to cross. Listened to eucalyptus creak and moan. Peered into a Fresnel lens. Pressed my palms against the mossy stonework of a dead author's ruined home. Held my breath as a hawk with a king snake in its talons swooped low over the trail and then dropped the twisting serpent into thick brush, then tiptoed as I carried on, expecting the wounded reptile to slither out of the grass underfoot.

These are not traditionally historic things, but they are part of the history of any experienced hiker in the Bay Area. As for "real" history—well, that is as abundant

Lupine and the long stretch of South Beach on Point Reyes

1

Steps lead up to the parapet overlook at Sutro Heights.

along the region's trails as oak trees and sword ferns. No point in lingering on the specifics here, as the stories of explorers, gold miners, ranchers, soldiers, padres, and empire builders are better told in the context of the treks described in this guidebook.

But as you climb these hills and delve into these valleys, consider the untold stories. Consider that San Francisco's Mission Dolores was established in the same year that the United States declared its independence. Written history in the Bay Area goes back only that far. Behind, the region's history is unwritten, the stories disappearing as the native storytellers have passed away, their thousand voices speaking in hundreds of languages lost.

The stories we create ourselves as we walk along the seashore, or among the redwoods, or down San Francisco's busy Embarcadero, may fall away as well, unless we share them. That's what this guide, hopefully, will do best: provide a deeper context for your personal tale of the trail.

Tips and Courtesy

Trails throughout the Bay Area have become more congested in recent years. To mediate some of the problems that come with crowds, please be courteous and thoughtful.

- To avoid traffic snarls and increase your odds of finding parking in designated lots, shoot for the proverbial "alpine start." The earlier you get to the trailhead, the better chance you have of getting a good parking place and a reasonably uncrowded hike.

- If you must park outside designated lots, be sure to choose a space that's safely off access roads and that doesn't block access to driveways, fire hydrants, gates, and public walkways.

- If you are hiking in a group, please make way for hikers coming in the opposite direction. On a narrow trail that means hiking single file. This is about safety as well as courtesy: If the trail has a dropoff, forcing hikers walking the opposite direction to hug the edge can be dangerous.

- Use your earbuds if you choose to listen to music on the trail. No matter how fabulous your music selection, others shouldn't be forced to listen.

- Put your cell phone on vibrate, and then tuck it deep into your pack so you aren't tempted to use it. It's nice to have a phone for an emergency, but using it on the trail, particularly on speaker, to discuss business or personal affairs can wait.

Hiking Essentials

While all of these excursions are day hikes and generally well traveled, no matter the length of your hike, you should be prepared.

For starters, every hiker should carry survival and first-aid materials, layers of clothing for all kinds of weather, a compass, and a good topographic map—and know how to use them.

The next best piece of safety advice is to hike with a partner or a party. If you choose to hike alone, tell somebody where you're going and when you plan to return.

Before you set out on any hike, consider physical conditioning. Being fit makes wilderness travel more fun and much safer.

Here are a few more tips:

- Check the weather forecast. Be careful not to get caught at high altitude in a bad storm or along a stream in a flash flood. Watch cloud formations so you don't get stranded on a ridgeline during a lightning storm. Avoid traveling during prolonged periods of cold weather.

- Keep your party together; move only as fast as your slowest companion.

- Before you leave for the trailhead, find out as much as you can about the route, especially the potential hazards.

- Don't wait until you're confused to look at your maps. Follow them as you go, maintaining a continual fix on your location.

- If you get lost, don't panic. Sit down, relax, check your map, and get your bearings. Confidently plan your next move. If necessary, retrace your steps until you find familiar ground, even if you think that might lengthen your trip. If you calmly and rationally determine a plan of action, you'll be fine.

- If you are genuinely lost, stay put.

- Your pack should contain backcountry essentials, including water, an emergency blanket, and an emergency whistle, which will help ensure your safety if you become lost or can't make it back to the trailhead for another reason.

- Stay clear of all wild animals. Make sure you know how best to deal with encounters with a black bear, mountain lion, or other wild creature in the backcountry.

Play It Safe

Hiking is generally a safe endeavor, but common sense dictates that when venturing into the wild, travelers should take precautions. Education is the best protection, but a day pack loaded with everything you need to stay safe if you get held up, for whatever reason, on the trail is good insurance.

Carry a good first-aid kit that includes, at a minimum, aspirin or over-the-counter pain reliever, antibacterial ointment, antiseptic swabs, butterfly bandages, adhesive tape, adhesive strips, two triangular bandages, two inflatable splints, moleskin or Second Skin for blisters, 3-inch gauze, CPR shield, rubber gloves, a snakebite kit, a sewing needle and thread, and lightweight first-aid instructions.

Pack a survival kit that includes, at a minimum, compass and map (a GPS unit will do, but be sure to carry extra batteries), whistle, matches in a waterproof container, cigarette lighter, candle, signal mirror, flashlight, fire starter, aluminum foil,

The "hanging tree" in Almaden Quicksilver County Park

water purification tablets, space blanket, and flare. Do not use matches, lighters, fire starters, or flares when fire conditions are high.

Critters

Hiker share most trails in Northern California with a variety of wild creatures, many of which go unseen and undetected. Some will come right up to you, including that adorable ground squirrel that wants to share your granola bar. Some will pester you, including horseflies, bees, and wasps. Some you may only catch fleeting glimpses of, such as mule deer and pileated woodpeckers. And some you may only encounter by way of what they leave behind: footprints and scat.

For the most part, animal encounters on the trail are benign. Abide by two basic rules for both your safety and that of the animals:

- Do not feed any wild animal, no matter how cute or how much it begs. Acclimating birds, chipmunks, deer, and larger mammals like bears is not only dangerous for humans but also reduces the animals' ability to survive when the humans have gone home.

- Keep your distance. Approaching a wild creature not only increases the chance that you might get bitten (or worse), it also increases anxiety levels for the animals.

Mountain Lions

Mountain lion sightings are relatively rare, and attacks on humans are extremely rare, but it's wise to educate yourself before heading into mountain lion habitat—which includes most of the territory covered in this guide.

To stay as safe as possible when hiking in mountain lion country, follow this advice:

- Travel with a friend or in a group, and stay together.
- Don't let small children wander away by themselves.
- Avoid hiking at dawn and dusk, when mountain lions are most active.
- Respect any warning signs posted by agencies.
- Know how to behave if you encounter a mountain lion. If a mountain lion is more than 50 yards away and directs its attention to you, it may be only curious. Back away, keeping the animal in your peripheral vision. If the lion is crouched less than 50 yards away and staring at you, it may be assessing the chances of a successful attack. Slowly back away, but maintain eye contact. Do not run; running may stimulate a predatory response. Make noise, talking and yelling loudly and regularly. Raise your arms above your head and make steady waving motions, or raise your jacket or another object above your head to make yourself appear larger. Do not bend over, as this will make you appear smaller and more prey-like. If you are with small children, pick them up without bending over. If you are in a group, band together.
- If a mountain lion attacks, fight back. Try to remain standing. Do not feign death. Pick up a branch or rock; pull out a knife, pepper spray, or other deterrent

device. Individuals have fended off mountain lions with rocks, tree limbs, and even cameras.

- Teach others in your group how to behave in the event of a mountain lion encounter. Report encounters, including location, to park rangers, who may want to visit the site and, if appropriate, post education/warning signs.
- If physical injury occurs, leave the area. Do not disturb the site of an attack. Mountain lions that have attacked people must be killed, and an undisturbed site is critical for effectively locating the dangerous mountain lion.

Rattlesnakes

Much of the Bay Area, especially inland, is rattlesnake country. Sightings are relatively rare, and the snakes are an important component of the ecosystem. Rattlesnakes typically are not aggressive toward humans—we are simply too big to be prey. Most snakebites occur when hikers startle or attempt to handle a rattlesnake. To avoid a nasty encounter, watch where you put your hands and feet when you are stepping over logs or climbing on rocks. If you see rattler on or beside a trail, back away and let it move on.

Ticks

Ticks are most prevalent during California's rainy season. Though not all species are carriers, some ticks can transmit Lyme disease if they latch onto a human. After traveling through brush, check your clothing for the arachnids. If one latches on, remove it carefully, making sure to get the mouthparts. You can have the creature tested to see if it might have transmitted the disease.

Weather

Weather in the Bay Area is typically mild year-round, but it is variable. On Mount Tamalpais, for example, hikers can start near the base in shorts-and-T-shirt weather and end up at the summit needing expedition-weight polar fleece to insulate against the fog-born wind and cold. Insulate yourself from the potential consequences of weather extremes by staying properly hydrated, carrying high-energy snacks, wearing a hat, applying sunscreen, and packing layers of clothing that you can add or shed depending on the conditions.

Hypothermia

Hypothermia is a condition in which the body's internal temperature drops below normal. It is caused by exposure to cold; is aggravated by wetness, wind, and exhaustion; and can be life-threatening.

To defend against hypothermia, stay dry. If hiking in wet weather, wear rain clothes that cover the head, neck, body, and legs and provide good protection against wind-driven rain. Most hypothermia cases develop in air temperatures between 30 and 50°F, but hypothermia can develop in warmer temperatures.

If your party is exposed to wind, cold, and wet, watch yourself and others for uncontrollable fits of shivering; vague, slow, slurred speech; memory lapses; incoherence; fumbling hands; frequent stumbling or a lurching gait; drowsiness; exhaustion; and inability to get up after a rest. When a member of your party has hypothermia, he or she may deny any problem. Even mild symptoms demand the following treatment:

- Get the victim out of the wind and rain.
- Strip off all wet clothes and get the victim into warm clothes.
- If the victim is mildly impaired, provide warm drinks.
- Get off the trail and seek medical attention as quickly as possible.

Heat-Related Illnesses

Hikers can avoid heat-related illness by avoiding activity in the heat of the day and staying hydrated. Selecting clothing that breathes, allowing perspiration to evaporate and cool the skin, and wearing a lightweight, brimmed hat will help. Applying sunscreen to all exposed parts of the body is always a good idea.

Watch for warning signs of heat-related illness, both in yourself and members of your party. These include nausea and/or vomiting; headache, light-headedness, and/or fainting; weakness, fatigue, and/or a lack of coordination; loss of concentration; and flushed skin.

Symptoms of heat exhaustion include all of the above, coupled with low blood pressure, heavy sweating, and a rapid pulse. If you or a member of your party exhibits these symptoms, seek shade, lie down and elevate the feet and legs, apply wet cloth to the head and neck (and other parts of the body, if you can), and drink cool liquids.

Heatstroke is life-threatening. Hikers who lose consciousness, vomit, have red, hot skin (moist or dry), a weak pulse, and shallow breathing are in danger of convulsions, coma, and death. Cool the victim by any means possible, as quickly as possible, and call for emergency medical aid.

Hydration

Hydration is important for hikers regardless of weather conditions. Hydrate before, during, and after your hike. Hydration bladders carried in backpacks are fabulous on the trail, as there is no need to stop and fish a water bottle out of your pack.

As far as quantity, there are no hard-and-fast rules. Drink as much as you can. Drink even when you are not thirsty. But at a minimum, plan on consuming 32 ounces of water for every two hours on the trail. That may mean carrying a filter or purification tablets so that you can refill water bottles or bladders from streams and lakes, even on day hikes (all backpackers should carry these).

Unless it's an emergency, do not drink untreated or unfiltered water from any water source.

Leave No Trace

Most of us know better than to litter—in or out of the backcountry. Be sure you leave nothing, regardless how small, along the trail or at a campsite. Pack everything out, including orange peels, flip tops, cigarette butts, and gum wrappers. Pick up any trash that others leave behind.

Follow the main trail. Avoid cutting switchbacks and walking on vegetation beside the trail. Don't pick up "souvenirs," such as rocks, antlers, or wildflowers. The next person wants to see them too, and collecting souvenirs violates park regulations.

Avoid making loud noises on the trail (unless you are in bear country) or in camp. Be courteous—remember, sound travels easily on the trail, especially across water.

Carry a lightweight trowel to bury human waste 6 to 8 inches deep and at least 200 feet from any water source. Pack out used toilet paper in a ziplock bag.

Go without a campfire if you can't find an established fire pit. Carry a stove for cooking and a flashlight, candle lantern, or headlamp for light. For emergencies, learn how to build a no-trace fire.

Camp in obviously used sites when they are available. Otherwise, camp and cook on durable surfaces such as bedrock, sand, gravel bars, or bare ground.

Leave no trace—and put your ear to the ground and listen carefully. Thousands of people coming behind you are thanking you for your courtesy and good sense.

The labyrinth on Lands End, pictured here in 2014, has been vandalized on occasion over the years, most recently in August 2015. Treat artifacts along the trail—recent and older—with respect so that the next hiker can enjoy them.

How to Use This Guide

How the Hikes Were Chosen

All of the hikes in this guide are day hikes and do not exceed 10 miles in length.

The boundaries of the San Francisco Bay Area are not hard and fast, but these hikes lie within its generally recognized borders. While most lie within a hour's drive of San Francisco (traffic permitting), there are a few worthy outliers.

All trailheads can be reached using passenger vehicles. Conditions on unpaved roads—there aren't many in this guide—vary with season, use, weather, and maintenance schedules; contact the land manager for the most current road status.

Tiger lilies pop against the ferns alongside a perennial waterfall on Mount Tamalpais.

Mileages

Trails were hiked using modern GPS technology, but exact mileages may differ from what appears on park maps. Distances listed on trail signs don't necessarily mesh with maps or GPS readings. I have recorded the mileages logged on my GPS unit for consistency's sake. Discrepancies seldom exceeded 0.5 mile and shouldn't affect a hiker's ability to gauge the difficulty or duration of a given hike.

Difficulty Ratings

The hikes are rated easy, moderate, or strenuous. In assigning a label, I took into account elevation gains and losses, hiking surfaces, and distances. Generally speaking, easy hikes are short and relatively flat. Moderate hikes involve greater distances and (perhaps) greater elevation changes. Strenuous hikes include steep ascents, long-distance loops, and routes that include challenging trail surfaces.

Keep in mind that every trail is only as difficult as you make it. If you keep a pace within your level of fitness, drink plenty of water, and stock up on good, high-energy foods, you can make any trail easy.

Route Finding

Trails in this guide are primarily located on public land and are generally well marked and maintained. None of the routes cross private property.

I've included GPS coordinates for trailheads. However, GPS units are notorious for taking travelers the long way—or the wrong way—to a given trailhead. Follow the written directions in this guide or on park websites, using the GPS coordinates as backup.

Maps

The USGS topographic maps that pertain to each route are listed in hike descriptions. If a trail map is available from another source, either from the land management agency or online, I've listed that resource. In the case of California State Parks, search for the park name on the agency website to go to the park homepage. Click on Brochures, then on Park Brochure. A pdf of the printed brochure for each state park in this guide includes a basic, but adequate, map.

Map Legend

Symbol	Label	Symbol	Label
80	Interstate Highway	⩜	Campground
101	US Highway	▲	Campsite
1	State Highway	⌒	Cave
	Local Road	†	Cemetery
= = = = = = =	Unpaved Road	—	Dam
——————	Paved Trail	⦙	Gate
- - - - - - - -	Trail	⋇	Lighthouse
▬▬▬▬▬▬	Featured Trail	⊥	Mine
‖‖‖‖‖‖	Boardwalk/Steps	Ⓟ	Parking
⊢—⊢—⊢—⊢	Railroad	⩟	Pass/Gap
•—•—•—•—	Pipeline/Utility Line	▲	Peak/Summit
⌇⌇⌇	Small River or Creek	⊞	Picnic Area
⌇ ⌇	Intermittent Stream	⬚	Ranger Station
⋰⋱	Sand	⬚	Restroom
⇁⇁	Marsh/Swamp	⬚	Scenic View/Viewpoint
⬭	Body of Water	⊶	Spring
⬚▲	State/County Park	⬛	Telephone
⬚▲	Miscellaneous Park	Ⓘ	Tower
✕	Airport	○	Town
═	Bench	①	Trailhead
⬓	Boat Ramp	⊢——⊣	Tunnel
⌣	Bridge	❓	Visitor/Information Center
■	Building/Point of Interest	⬚	Water

North Bay

Stinson Beach from the Dipsea Trail on Mount Tamalpais

1 | Stevenson Monument Trail

A short, shady study in switchbacks leads to a monument honoring writer Robert Louis Stevenson, who honeymooned on the lower slopes of Mount Saint Helena in 1880.

Start: Trailhead alongside CA 29
Distance: 1.4 miles out and back
Hiking time: About 1 hour
Difficulty: Moderate due to elevation gain
Trail surface: Dirt
Best season: Spring and fall
Other trail users: None (mountain bikers permitted on trail to summit of Mount Saint Helena)
Canine compatibility: Dogs not permitted
Land status: Robert Louis Stevenson State Park
Fees and permits: None
Schedule: Sunrise to sunset daily
Trailhead amenities: Small picnic area
Maps: USGS Detert Reservoir; map in park brochure, available for a fee at Bothe–Napa

Valley State Park or online at napavalleystateparks.org/robert-louis-stevenson-state-park
Special considerations: There have been auto break-ins at the trailhead parking area. Do not leave valuables in your vehicle. Mileage to the Stevenson Monument (one way) is listed as 1 mile on a trail sign and 0.8 mile on the trail map. The GPS mileage of 0.7 mile recorded on-site is used.
Trail contact: Bothe–Napa Valley State Park, 3801 St. Helena Hwy. North, Calistoga, CA 94515; (707) 942-4574; www.parks.ca.gov. Information is also available through the Napa Valley State Parks website at napavalleystateparks.org.

Finding the trailhead: From the junction of CA 29 and CA 128 at the stop sign in Calistoga, follow CA 29 north for about 8 miles to the trailhead at the summit. GPS: N38 39.143' / W122 35.992'

The Hike

A small stone monument topped with an open book commemorates Robert Louis Stevenson's visit to Mount Saint Helena. The weathered inscription on the open page, which can be difficult to break down in the filtered sunshine, reads:

"Doomed to know not winter only spring, a being
trod the flowery April blithely for awhile.
Took his fill of music, joy of thought and seeing,
came and stayed and went, nor ever ceased to smile."

In the late nineteenth century, before he hit the big time, Stevenson brought his new bride, Fanny, to an abandoned mining cabin on the flanks of the mountain, which was sacred to the Native Americans who once lived in the valley and site of a short-lived silver-mining operation. Both the cabin and Stevenson are long gone, but his connection to the region remains. The author of such classics as *Treasure Island*, *Kidnapped*, and *A Child's Garden of Verses* found inspiration on the massive peak at the head of the Napa Valley, and his sojourn in what was then wilderness became the inspiration for *The Silverado Squatters*.

The thick, tangled woodlands that garland the peak's lower reaches still evoke wilderness, though proximity to the nearby highway and its attendant road noise—and the temptations found among the thicket of wineries on the Napa Valley floor—necessitate a greater leap of imagination for the modern hiker than Stevenson had to make.

The trail is straightforward, climbing an easy series of switchbacks through mixed evergreen forest to a madrone- and fir-shaded clearing at the monument. Damage

Bothe-Napa Valley State Park

Robert Louis Stevenson has the bigger name, and the trail to the monument is on the tallest peak in the region, but nearby Bothe–Napa Valley State Park offers excellent hiking and interesting historic sites to explore as well. The most popular walks include the Redwood Trail, following sequoia-shaded Ritchey Creek, and the Coyote Peak Trail, a stiff climb to an overlook offering filtered views of the Napa Valley floor and the steep slopes of the Mayacamas Mountains. The creek and peak can be linked via a strenuous but scenic 5-mile lollipop loop that also incorporates the South Fork and Spring Trails, a portion of which follows an old skid road.

Other sites worth exploring include the visitor center, which was once the home of the Tucker family; family members are interred in the nearby Pioneer Cemetery. The Native American Garden and the former Paradise Park swimming pool, open seasonally, are also part of the park. The mile-long History Trail links the historic sites in Bothe–Napa Valley with Bale Grist Mill State Historic Park. Iterations of the gristmill date back to the 1840s, pre–gold rush; today the mill and granary are open for tours and educational programs.

The park is located just west of CA 29, about 4 miles south of Calistoga and 3 miles north of St. Helena (GPS: N38 33.117'/W122 31.135'). For more information, contact the park at (707) 942-4575 or visit napavalleystateparks.org. The park brochure is available at www.parks.ca.gov/pages/477/files/Bothe-NapaValleySP_Web2014.pdf.

An open book marks the spot where Robert Lewis Stevenson honeymooned on Mount Saint Helena.

wrought by careless hikers cutting the switchbacks is painfully obvious, with exposed red earth streaking the mountainside like tears down a dirty cheek. Road noise precludes a backcountry experience at the trail's outset, but by the time you reach the clearing, it has been swallowed by distance and the wind in the trees. After you've tarried a while, return to the trailhead via the same route.

Miles and Directions

0.0   Start from the parking lot. Climb a short flight of stairs, cross the picnic area, and mount a second flight of stairs past a trail sign.

0.7   End the switchbacking climb at the Stevenson Monument. Rest and relax, then retrace your steps.

1.4   Arrive back at the trailhead.

Options: From the monument, the Stevenson Memorial Trail leads to the fire road that climbs to summit of Mount Saint Helena. The views from the top, especially on a clear day, are sublime. The 10-mile round-trip to the summit mostly follows a dirt fire road and is easy to follow, but is steep and long. Hikers strong of leg and lung, and with plenty of time, will enjoy the trek.

Stevenson Monument Trail (Robert Louis Stevenson State Park)

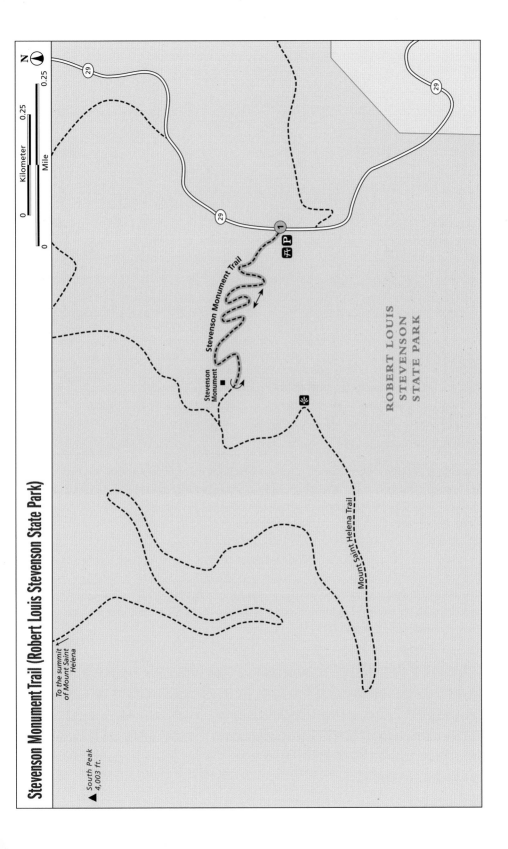

An overlook about a half-mile above the Stevenson Memorial offers views down into the Napa Valley.

If you are looking for a medium–difficulty option, ascend out of the Stevenson Monument hollow to the main fire road and climb 0.25 mile to a sweeping curve that offers a breathtaking view down the length of the Napa Valley. Views from here stretch south to Mount Diablo when the weather is clear. The trip out and back to the overlook totals 2.4 miles.

▶ It may not be obvious to casual visitors to California's Wine Country, but a rivalry exists between the neighboring Sonoma and Napa Valleys. The two valleys produce some of the world's most sought-after vintages, and each valley strives to produce the most award-winners. But when it comes to which valley produced the first recognized vintages, Sonoma takes the nod. Historian Arthur Dawson notes that William McPherson Hill produced the first Zinfandel in the mid-1800s from his Glen Ellen vineyard.

2 Wolf House, Beauty Ranch, and the Old Orchard

The village of Glen Ellen resonates with the legacy of writer Jack London. It's not just about his stories, however, as this long tour of his Beauty Ranch demonstrates.

Start: Signed trailhead below House with Happy Walls

Distance: 7.6 miles including three loops and a pair of out-and-back sections

Hiking time: About 4 hours

Difficulty: Strenuous due to distance and several significant climbs and descents

Trail surface: Pavement, dirt ranch road, dirt trail

Best season: Year-round

Other trail users: Mountain bikers and equestrians on ranch roads

Canine compatibility: Leashed dogs allowed in historic areas of park, including on trail to Wolf House. Dogs not permitted on backcountry trails or in historic structures.

Land status: Jack London State Historic Park

Fees and permits: Park entrance fee; additional fee to tour cottage

Schedule: Park open daily 9:30 a.m. to 5 p.m.; museum open daily 10 a.m. to 5 p.m.; cottage open daily noon to 4 p.m.; all facilities closed Christmas Day

Trailhead amenities: Restrooms, trash cans, water, picnic tables, information signboard with a park trail map

Maps: USGS Glen Ellen; maps posted at trailhead kiosks; maps and brochures available at House of Happy Walls and online at www.parks.ca.gov

Trail contact: Jack London State Historic Park, 2400 London Ranch Rd., Glen Ellen, CA 95442; (707) 938-5216; www.parks.ca.gov. Jack London Park Partners/Valley of the Moon Natural History Association have overseen operation of the park since 2012; www.jacklondonpark.com/index.html.

Finding the trailhead: From the stoplight at Arnold Drive and Sonoma Highway (CA 12), signed for Glen Ellen, take Arnold Drive west for 1 mile to its intersection with London Ranch Road (on the far side of the bridge). Turn right (west) onto London Ranch Road and go about 1.5 miles to its end at the entrance kiosk. The trailhead is in the lower parking lot to the left. GPS: N38 21.389' / W122 32.520'

The Hike

Jack London has been dead for a century, but in Glen Ellen, his spirit thrives. His name is everywhere: You can get a drink and a great burger at the London Lodge; London Ranch Road connects his property with "downtown"; you can drink wine distilled from grapes grown in the London vineyards; and, of course, you can spend a day exploring Jack London State Historic Park.

This tour of historical sites encompasses the ruins of the Wolf House, London's dream home; the remnants of his barn, winery, and Pig Palace; and the overgrown lake where Jack and his guests cooled off on hot summer afternoons. It also wanders back into the Old Orchard, which lies on land annexed to the park from the adjacent

Jack London's Wolf House was destroyed by fire before the author could take up residence. He died not long after it burned.

Sonoma Developmental Center, focus of one of London's lesser-known stories, "Told in the Drooling Ward." You can begin or end your hike with a tour of the House of Happy Walls, where London's beloved widow, Charmian, lived after her husband's passing.

London's ranch is set between the foot of Sonoma Mountain and quaint Glen Ellen, a little village with more than its share of fine restaurants and family wineries. London established the ranch at the turn of the twentieth century, building first a cottage that he shared with Charmian and then the stone-walled mansion that would succumb to fire before he could occupy it. Following London's death from kidney disease on November 22, 1916, Charmian, with the help of ranch superintendent Eliza Shepard and her family, continued to run the ranch, transforming it into a dude ranch. The family turned the House of Happy Walls, along with the 39-acre core of the Beauty Ranch, over to the state of California in 1960. The park's acreage has since grown, most recently with the annexation of the Old Orchard above the Sonoma Developmental Center.

▶ Sonoma Mountain is central to the Coast Miwok creation story.

The hike begins on the paved trail that leads from the parking lot to the House of Happy Walls, which houses the museum. From the museum, drop down a short trail to meet the paved roadway that leads to London's gravesite and the Wolf House. The gravesite is located in an oak-shaded glen: The author and his wife's cremains are interred under a moss-covered rock behind a picket fence. In a separate plot, the two children of homesteaders who came before him, David and Lillie Greenlaw, rest in peace.

Back on the trail to the Wolf House, a short hitch over a meadowy knoll drops into the redwood grove surrounding the ruins of the four-story architectural wonder. A trail circling the reinforced stone walls features information signboards that include architectural plans, and a viewing platform offers a second-story view down the length of the empty reflecting pool. Though built of materials meant to withstand both earthquake and fire, the house burned before the Londons could take up residence, and London died with it unfinished.

The second leg of the hike leads through historic ranch buildings, an operating vineyard, and up to London Lake. The route climbs through a eucalyptus-shaded picnic ground, then down past stone barns, the winery ruins, a cactus garden, and the London cottage, which is open for tours. Circle the vineyard to reach the footpath to the Pig Palace. Follow the ranch road/trail to the junction on the west side of the vineyard and climb to London Lake, corralled by a century-old half-moon dam. The lake has, over the years, filled with silt; there are plans to rehabilitate the site. In the meantime, it's a pleasing place for a picnic and supports a population of songbirds and ducks.

From the dam, continue up the Mountain Trail to the junction with the Upper Fallen Bridge Trail. The Upper Fallen Bridge Trail leads through the Woodcutters Meadow to the north fork of Asbury Creek; the path then descends steeply alongside the year-round stream. Redwood groves cluster around the watercourse, shading the route as it drops toward the Old Orchard.

A series of linked trails (the Apple Tree, the Apricot Tree, the Plum Tree, and the Pear Tree) lead in a mile-long loop around the orchard, which was once part of the Sonoma Developmental Center. The orchard is overgrown but the trees still bear fruit, and those closest to the trail can be harvested if hikers can beat the wildlife to the bounty. Views open across the orchard to the Mayacamas ridgeline on the east side of the Sonoma Valley.

The developed area at the southeast end of the trail loop is Camp Via, a Boy Scout camp. A brief section of the route follows the camp road; on the east side, before the pavement drops down into the developmental center proper, the Old Orchard loop breaks left, through a gate, and back into the overgrown trees. This route heads directly back through the orchard to the Fallen Bridge trails, but you can follow a short signed spur off the Plum Tree Trail that leads down to an ancient redwood known locally as the "grandmother tree."

Complete the orchard loop back at the junction with the Fallen Bridge trails. Cross the lower bridge to follow the New Fallen Bridge Trail, which curls alongside Asbury Creek and then up a secondary drainage as it heads back toward the Beauty Ranch. The New Fallen Bridge Trail ends on the Quarry Trail, a lovely path through redwoods with great views opening across the valley onto the Mayacamas Mountains. The Quarry Trail ends just above the dam on the Mountain Trail.

Back at London Lake, walk through the picnic sites to pick up the hikers-only Lake Trail at the north end of overgrown reservoir. The singletrack path descends through redwood groves to its junction with the main trail adjacent to the vineyard. From here, retrace your steps to the trailhead.

0.0 Start by following the paved path for about 400 feet to the House of Happy Walls and the signed trail to the Wolf House. Drop down the singletrack Wolf House Trail.

0.4 Meet the paved Wolf House Service Road at a bench and water fountain. Go left (east).

0.5 At the signed trail Y, go left on the singletrack path to Jack London's gravesite.

0.6 Arrive at the gravesite. Retrace your steps to the service road, and go left toward the Wolf House.

0.8 Arrive at the Wolf House. Circle the ruins, then retrace your steps to the junction with the trail to the House of Happy Walls.

1.2 At the Happy Walls trail junction, continue straight on the service road.

1.5 Arrive at the gated end of the service road. Cross the parking lot, then London Ranch Road, and climb through the upper parking lot to the trailhead for the signed Lake Trail.

1.6 Follow the gravel Lake Trail through the ranch, passing the barns, winery, cottage, silos, and Pig Palace. The road follows the fenced boundary of the vineyard.

2.2 At the junction with the hikers-only Lake Trail, stay straight on the service road. The Lake Trail is part of the return route.

2.5 Reach London Lake. Continue on the broad gravel track, tracing the dam, now on the Mountain Trail. At the far end of the dam, stay right on the broad Mountain Trail, passing signed junctions with the Vineyard Trail and the Quarry Trail, both on the left. The Quarry Trail is part of the return route.

2.7 Cross a seep and pass the junction with the Upper Lake Trail, staying left around the switchback on the Mountain Trail.

2.9 Break into the meadow at Mays Crossing, with a bench facing south. Pass the junction with the Old Fallen Bridge Trail on the left, staying right on the broad Mountain Trail.

3.1 At the junction, go left onto the Upper Fallen Bridge Trail to Asbury Creek.

3.4 Cross a bridge in a stately redwood grove.

3.7 Reach a second bridge as the steepness of the Asbury Creek drainage mellows. A left turn, across the bridge, leads to the junction with the New Fallen Bridge Trail. To reach the Old Orchard, stay right, follow the sign indicating "Sonoma Developmental Center Trails." Stay right at the next junction as well.

3.8 At the junction with the Apple Tree Trail in the orchard, go right, circling the orchard counterclockwise.

4.1 At the junction of the Apple Tree, Apricot Tree, and Orchard Trails, stay right on the Apricot Tree Trail.

4.4 At the junction with the dirt road signed for Camp Via, stay right on the Apricot Tree Trail. After about 400 yards, pass the junction with the Coon Trap Trail, staying on the Apricot Tree Trail toward Camp Via.

4.5 Drop to the paved road at Camp Via. Follow the road around the buildings.

4.6 Take the Plum Tree Trail, a dirt road that breaks left from the pavement and passes a gate. A trail map is posted on a signboard at the junction. At the trail fork about 200 feet beyond, stay left onto the Orchard Trail, which bends into the Camp Via Trail and cuts through the orchard. *Option:* Stay right, on the unsigned Plum Tree Trail. After about 0.2 mile, go right onto the trail to the ancient redwood. Drop about 0.1 mile to view the

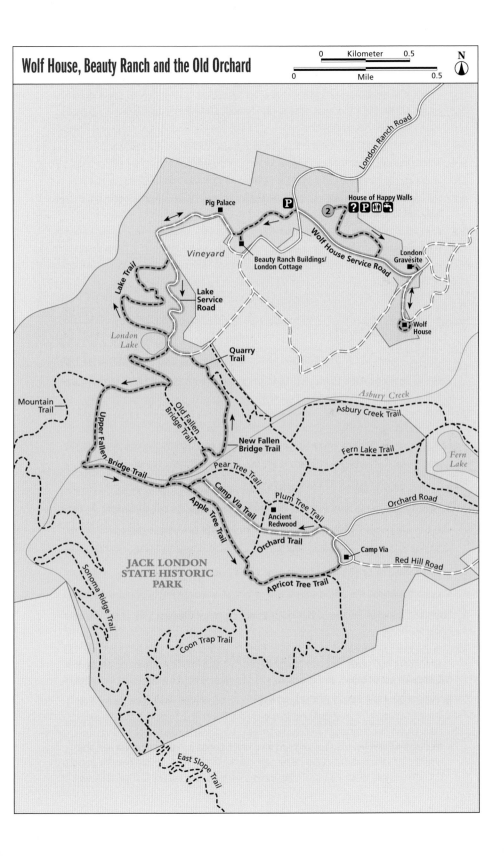

Wolf House, Beauty Ranch and the Old Orchard

0 Kilometer 0.5

0 Mile 0.5

N

London Ranch Road

Pig Palace

P

House of Happy Walls

2

Vineyard

Beauty Ranch Buildings/
London Cottage

Wolf House Service Road

London
Gravesite

Lake Trail

Lake
Service
Road

London
Lake

Quarry
Trail

Wolf
House

Mountain
Trail

Asbury Creek

Asbury Creek Trail

Old Fallen
Bridge Trail

Upper Fallen

New Fallen
Bridge Trail

Fern Lake Trail

Fern
Lake

Bridge Trail

Pear Tree Trail

Camp Via Trail

Apple Tree Trail

Plum Tree Trail

Ancient
Redwood

Orchard Road

Orchard Trail

Camp Via

JACK LONDON
STATE HISTORIC
PARK

Apricot Tree Trail

Red Hill Road

Sonoma Ridge Trail

Coon Trap Trail

East Slope Trail

stunning tree, then return as you came, picking up the Plum Tree Trail and heading right onto the Pear Tree Trail to complete the orchard loop. Hiking out and back to the ancient redwood will add about 0.4 mile round-trip.

5.2 Reach the Pear Tree Trail. Turn left and climb about 100 yards to an unsigned trail that heads right into the woods.

5.3 At the junction with the Upper Fallen Bridge Trail, go right.

5.4 At the junction, cross the bridge onto the New Fallen Bridge Trail.

5.6 At the junction with the Old Fallen Bridge Trail, stay right on the New Fallen Bridge Trail.

5.9 The New Fallen Bridge Trail ends at a junction with the signed Quarry Trail and the Vineyard Trail. Stay left on the Quarry Trail.

6.2 The Quarry Trail ends on the Mountain Trail just above the dam. Turn right and descend to London Lake.

The Drooling Ward

To quote a member of the coalition working to preserve some semblance of the Sonoma Developmental Center (SDC) in the wake of a decision by the state of California that the facility must close by 2018, the "history of the SDC is the history of the people who live there." The origins of the developmental center date back to the late nineteenth century, when the mothers of two disabled children lobbied for the establishment of an institution where their handicapped offspring could be safe and nurtured. Initially known as the California Home for the Care and Training of Feeble-Minded Children, the idea was that the center would also be self-sustaining. To that end, the SDC property has its own water system (with two scenic reservoirs skirted by hiking trails), its own power grid and sewer system, and an old orchard that has been annexed to neighboring Jack London State Historic Park. Reaching midway up Sonoma Mountain, the SDC property is also part of a recognized wildlife corridor that stretches from the Pacific to the Mayacamas range on the east side of the Sonoma Valley.

The coalition, composed of conservation and open space groups, the SDC's parent hospital association, and the county of Sonoma, seeks to involve the community in determining the future of the land and facilities, which have been, according to one local historian, an "architect of Glen Ellen." For more information, visit www .transformsdc.com.

Ferns crowd the edge of a stairway leading up to viewing platforms at Jack London's Wolf House.

6.3 Follow the eastern shoreline of London Lake past the bathhouse; the trail narrows to singletrack.

6.5 Turn right onto the signed Lake Spur.

6.6 At the junction with the signed Lake Trail, go left, descending through redwoods toward the ranch.

6.9 Drop onto the broad trail/road above the vineyard. Turn left, and retrace your steps to the parking area.

7.6 Arrive back at the trailhead.

Options: The Mountain Trail, which leads to the summit ridge of Sonoma Mountain, is well worth the 8-mile round-trip trek for experienced hikers. Several additional trails were linked to the park in 2014 and 2015, including the North Sonoma Mountain Trail, which heads north along the slopes to Jacobs Ranch, and the East Slope Trail, which heads southeast near the ridgetop. Both are part of the Bay Area Ridge Trail. Consult a trail map for additional options.

3 Sonoma Overlook Trail

Trails on the hillsides that form downtown Sonoma's backdrop loop across former pastureland, past an old quarry, to a overlook that, on a clear day, encompasses major Bay Area landmarks, and through a historic cemetery.

Start: Trailhead adjacent to entrance to Mountain Cemetery
Distance: 4.5 miles (may vary depending on explorations within Mountain Cemetery)
Hiking time: About 2 hours
Difficulty: Moderate due to distance and some inclines
Trail surface: Mostly singletrack/packed dirt; pavement in Mountain Cemetery
Best season: Year-round
Other trail users: None
Canine compatibility: No dogs allowed

Land status: Sonoma County Open Space
Fees and permits: None
Schedule: Sunrise to sunset daily
Trailhead amenities: Information signboards, trash cans, picnic site. Stone benches along the summit loop can be used for picnicking.
Maps: USGS Sonoma; map in interpretive brochure available at trailhead kiosk
Trail contact: Sonoma Overlook Trail/Sonoma Ecology Center, PO Box 533, Sonoma, CA 95476; www.sonomaecologycenter.org

Finding the trailhead: From the junction of Broadway and Napa Street (CA 12) in downtown Sonoma at the plaza, go west 1 block to First Street West. Turn right (north) on First Street West and go 0.5 mile to the Mountain Cemetery and signed trailhead on the right. GPS: N38 17.979' / W122 27.430'

The Hike

Ascending a hillside behind Sonoma's historic plaza, the Sonoma Overlook Trail leads to some of the most breathtaking views in the Sonoma Valley. On a clear day, from thoughtfully placed benches along the summit loop, you can gaze south across the Carneros wine region to San Pablo Bay, with Mount Diablo and Mount Tamalpais anchoring the southeast and southwest horizons, respectively. Sonoma Mountain, an ancient volcano now rounded and fruitful, sprawls directly to the west.

The overlook trail and the Montini ranch trails also showcase Sonoma's natural and human history, from vivid springtime wildflower displays to the sloping graveyard where some of the region's founding families rest in the shade of ancient oaks and bay laurels. The Montini ranch lands, which until 2014 were frequented only by cattle and those who tended them, are a natural extension of the viewscape and also offer access to an old quarry.

The overlook trail begins at the entrance to the Mountain Cemetery. The kiosk at the trailhead provides extensive information about the flora and fauna you'll encounter along the route and a synopsis of Sonoma Valley history. Follow the gently climbing singletrack through riparian habitat to a creek crossing. Keep an eye out for

Rock walls line a portion of the trail on the Montini Ranch addition to the Sonoma Overlook Trail.

discreet placards that identify the native plants alongside the pathway. Beyond the creek, a series of easy switchbacks and long traverses lead up onto Schocken Hill, passing stone memorial benches along the way.

The signed trail to the Montini addition breaks left at the 0.5-mile mark; take this (the Rattlesnake Gulch Trail—and yes, you might see or hear a rattler on this hike in season) to paved First Street West. Cross the roadway to where the trail resumes, with a sign and map. Follow the Valley of the Moon Trail to the Two Goat Point Trail, enjoying views from Mount Diablo to Treasure Island as the path traverses through patches of open meadowland. The wide, well-graded trail then descends to the open space boundary, marked by a fence. A former ranch road, not labeled on the map but obvious on the ground, drops toward large green water tanks; take this unlabeled road down to the junction with the trail that connects to neighborhood access from Fourth Street West. Turn left on the trail above the tanks, looping back toward the Sonoma Overlook Trail.

Just beyond a rustic stone wall, the path crosses a streamlet, and the "red quarry" opens on the left. This alcove, the remnants of one of the quarries where basalt was harvested for use in area construction projects, including some of the stone buildings in the Mountain Cemetery, is dotted with rock cairns carefully constructed by hikers who've come before; add a stone if you like. Depending on the season and the

Historic Sonoma

The fertile and inviting home of the Wappo and Pomo, who were indigenous to the region, would prove equally enticing to Spanish settlers who arrived in the Sonoma Valley in the early 1800s. Mission San Francisco Solano, also known as the Sonoma Mission, was founded in the valley in 1823, the northernmost on the El Camino Real and the last in California's historic mission chain. General Mariano Vallejo, who oversaw the building of the early Sonoma pueblo—its central plaza remains the community focal point—commanded the troops who guarded the Frontera del Norte, Mexico's northern frontier. Other historic sites dating to the Mexican era include the Sonoma Barracks; the neighboring Toscano Hotel; the Blue Wing Inn, located opposite the chapel of Mission San Francisco Solano; and Lachryma Montis (Tears of the Mountain), Vallejo's stunning Gothic home. Downtown Sonoma, where the short-lived Bear Flag Republic flared and fizzled, encompasses a number of other historic buildings, including the Sebastiani Winery and Sebastiani Theater. Many of these sites are part of Sonoma State Historic Park, which is headquartered at 363 Third St. West in downtown Sonoma. For more information, call (707) 938-9560 or visit the website at www.parks.ca.gov/?page_id=479.

Hikers have constructed rock cairns in an old quarry on the Montini Ranch addition to the Sonoma Overlook Trail.

amount of rainfall, a short waterfall may tumble into the quarry. Resume the route by continuing on the main trail, climbing easily back to the junction with First Street West. Follow the Rattlesnake Gulch link back to the Sonoma Overlook Trail.

Climbing again on the Sonoma Overlook Trail, the path to the Toyon trailhead in the Mountain Cemetery breaks right. Ignore it on the ascent, staying left and uphill; you'll follow the Toyon Trail into the Mountain Cemetery on the return leg.

A final rocky stretch leads to the junction with the Upper Meadow Loop. You can hike the 0.3-mile loop in either direction, but it's described here clockwise, climbing past stone benches dedicated to lovers of Sonoma's wildlands. Lichen-stained rocks jut from the grasses, which are vibrant with wildflowers in spring—lupine, poppy, blue-eyed grass, sticky monkey flower, vetch, fiddleneck, clover, and more. Coyote brush crowds the trail at the top of the loop. As the loop begins its descent, an interpretive sign identifies the peaks spread across the horizon, from Rocky Ridge to Mount Tamalpais.

Close the loop (or take the signed "steep unmaintained trail" back to the overlook trail proper), and retrace your steps to the Toyon junction. Go left on the Toyon Trail to the Mountain Cemetery boundary. Pass the graves of the Rose family as you reach paved Toyon Road, then follow quiet cemetery lanes down to the entrance gates and the trailhead. A brochure for a walking tour of the cemetery, produced by the Sonoma Ecology Center, may be available in the box where the trail meets the road.

The historic cemetery, established in 1841, is engrossing. Some of the gravestones and monuments bear names that are familiar: General Mariano Vallejo is buried here, along with Henry Ernest Boyes, founder of Boyes Hot Springs; George Fetter, founder of Fetters Hot Springs; Franklin Sears, whose family ranch occupied Sears Point (site of the Sonoma Raceway); and William Montini Sr., whose family ranch is now open space. Others are less familiar: Italian immigrants who became ranchers, quarrymen, and winemakers; a single Japanese man whose family members were sent to internment camps during World War II; a contractor who worked on the Sonoma City Hall; a member of the PG&E Gas Construction Gang; cooks; ranch hands; children; a naturalist and mountaineer who was friends with Jack and Charmian London; a Revolutionary War veteran; and others whose stories can only be inferred by the names, dates, and artwork on their headstones.

Miles and Directions

0.0 Start by climbing the singletrack trail behind the information kiosk.

0.2 Cross the streamlet and begin the easy, switchbacking ascent.

0.3 Catch a preview of the summit views and pass a stone memorial bench dedicated to Gypsy Bob.

0.5 At the junction, go left on the signed trail into the Montini addition (the Rattlesnake Gulch Trail).

0.9 Cross First Street West, picking up the signed Valley of the Moon Trail.

1.0 At the junction, go right, continuing on the Valley of the Moon Trail toward the Two Goat Point Trail.

1.3 Cross a seasonal stream that is dry in late season.

1.4 Drop to the open space boundary at the fence line. Follow the former ranch road (unsigned) downhill to the left, dropping toward the water tanks.

1.7 At the junction with the neighborhood access trail, go left on the Holstein Hill Trail, looping back toward downtown Sonoma.

1.9 At the junction near the stone wall, stay left on the Spotted Fawn Trail (unsigned).

2.1 Cross a streamlet that runs dry in late season, and then reach the "red quarry." Explore the quarry, then return to the main trail and continue to the left.

2.2 Close the loop. Cross First Street West, and backtrack along the Rattlesnake Gulch Trail.

2.5 Arrive back at the Sonoma Overlook Trail. Turn left to continue uphill on the overlook trail.

2.9 Pass the junction with the Toyon Trail, staying left (straight) on the ascending path.

3.2 Pass a trail that climbs steeply to the right, continuing to the junction with the Upper Meadow Loop Trail. Go left (clockwise), passing a series of stone viewing benches and an interpretive sign.

3.6 Close the loop, either returning to the junction with the overlook trail or taking the path marked "steep unmaintained trail." Turn left on the overlook route, and retrace your steps to the Toyon Trail junction.

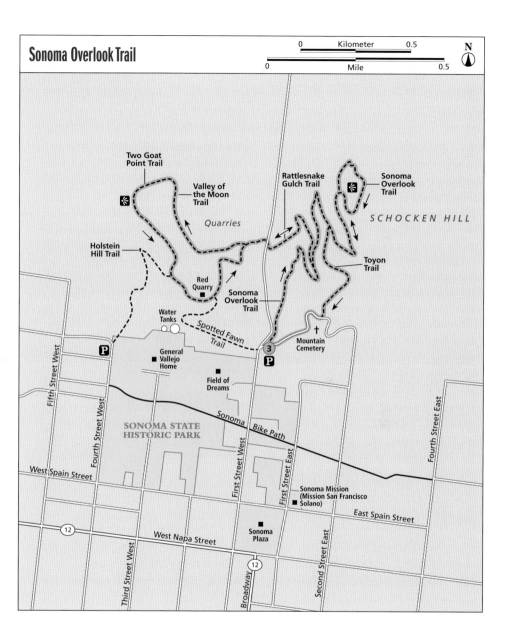

0   Kilometer   0.5

0   Mile   0.5

N

Two Goat Point Trail

Valley of the Moon Trail

Rattlesnake Gulch Trail

Sonoma Overlook Trail

Quarries

SCHOCKEN HILL

Holstein Hill Trail

Toyon Trail

Red Quarry

Sonoma Overlook Trail

Water Tanks

Spotted Fawn Trail

Mountain Cemetery

Fifth Street West

P

General Vallejo Home

3

P

Field of Dreams

Fourth Street West

Fourth Street East

SONOMA STATE HISTORIC PARK

Sonoma Bike Path

First Street West

First Street East

West Spain Street

Sonoma Mission (Mission San Francisco Solano)

East Spain Street

12

West Napa Street

Sonoma Plaza

12

Third Street West

Broadway

Second Street East

3.9 Go left on the Toyon Trail toward the Mountain Cemetery.

4.0 Reach the Mountain Cemetery boundary. Turn right on Toyon Road and follow cemetery roads down to the base of the hill.

4.5 Pass the cemetery gates and arrive back at the trailhead.

4 Shoreline Trail to China Camp

A pocket of local Chinese-American history is showcased at the end of this long, scenic ramble.

Start: Signed Shoreline trailhead in campground parking lot
Distance: 8.8 miles out and back
Hiking time: About 5 hours
Difficulty: Moderate due to length
Trail surface: Dirt/gravel, boardwalk, short sections of pavement
Best season: Year-round
Other trail users: Mountain bikers, equestrians
Canine compatibility: No dogs on trails; leashed dogs permitted in developed areas
Land status: China Camp State Park
Fees and permits: Entrance fee
Schedule: Trails open sunrise to sunset daily; campground available 24 hours daily

Trailhead amenities: Restrooms, trash cans, water, information signboards, camping. Picnic facilities, restrooms, information, a museum, swimming, and boating facilities are available at China Camp Village. The Quan Bros. snack shack is open on weekends.
Maps: USGS Petaluma Point; China Camp map available in park brochure and online
Special considerations: Please do not remove or disturb cultural or historic features within the park.
Trail contact: China Camp State Park, 101 Peacock Gap Trail, San Rafael, CA 94901; (415) 456-0766; www.parks.ca.gov/chinacamp

Finding the trailhead: From US 101 in San Rafael, take the North San Pedro Road exit. Head east on North San Pedro Road for 2.8 miles, passing the park boundary, to the access road for Back Ranch Meadows campground. Pay the fee, then proceed down the campground access road for 0.3 mile to the campground parking area. The trailhead is on the bay side of the parking lot. GPS: N38 00.398' / W122 29.676'

The Hike

Human habitation at China Camp, tucked in a shallow cove on San Pablo Bay, has been continuous since the days when the Coast Miwok hunted, fished, and gathered at the spot. The setting is superlative, with views opening across the bay (on clear days) to Vallejo in the east, the Oakland hills and Mount Diablo to the south, and north toward Sonoma and the mouth of the Petaluma River. Not far to the south, through the strait between Point San Pedro and Point San Pablo, the bay opens into San Francisco Bay proper.

The shorelines of Point San Pedro, as well as the oak woodlands to the west, provided the Coast Miwok with both acorns, a staple food, and wildlife to hunt and

▶ The salt marshes of China Camp serve as a living laboratory for the National Estuarine Research Reserve System. This is also habitat for the endangered salt marsh harvest mouse.

An interpretive trail leads around Turtle Back Hill.

fish. The marine creatures that thrive in the salt marshes—clams, worms, birds, and grass shrimp—would later sustain the Chinese immigrants who established a fishing village here.

Between the time of the Miwok and the arrival of the Chinese, the state park was part of a rancho called San Pedro, Santa Margarita y Las Gallinas. Portions of the rancho passed to the Murphy family and then on to McNear brothers John and George, who ran dairy cows on the property through the early part of the twentieth century. During the McNears' tenure, the cove now known as China Camp was sublet to Chinese fishermen, men who were no longer able to make a living in Sierran gold mines or on construction of the transcontinental railroad. Fishing camps such as this, one of several around San Francisco Bay, allowed the Chinese to catch, dry, and export shrimp to China.

▶ The Friends of China Camp (FOCC), a nonprofit organization, has helped provide financial and operational support for the park since 2012, when a funding scandal resulted in threats of closure of a number of California state parks. The FOCC website offers plenty of information on the park, including a podcast describing its history featuring longtime China Camp resident Frank Quan. For more information, visit www.friendsofchinacamp.org.

A former Chinese shrimping camp is now a popular destination for hikers, mountain bikers, and beachgoers.

At its height, more than 500 people lived and worked at China Camp. The camp went into decline in the late 1800s for a number of reasons, most significantly because of the Chinese Exclusion Act of 1882 and other discriminatory legislation and prohibitions. But the Chinese presence at the camp has endured: Frank Quan, grandson of Quan Hung Quock, who opened a general store in the cove around the turn of the twentieth century, still runs a family business in the park.

Preservation of China Camp came on the heels of threats of development in the 1960s and 1970s. Property owners surrounding the future park fought plans for industrial, commercial, and residential construction, and eventually the property was purchased from the developers and transferred to the state parks department in 1977.

This hike begins with an exploration of the tidal marshlands that stretch between the mainland and the deep waters of San Pablo Bay. At low tide, the shallow, sponge-like marshes are exposed, the rusty colors and gloppy mud belying the richness of the habitat. Two islands—sometimes attached to the mainland by land bridges—rise not far offshore. The interpretive and accessible Turtle Back Trail, reached via the Shoreline Trail from Back Ranch Meadows campground, circles Turtle Back Hill, offering views of Jakes Island.

The Shoreline Trail is also accessible, linking Turtle Back Hill with the Miwok Meadows Day Use Area via a gravel and stonework path through grasslands. Beyond

Shoreline Trail to China Camp (China Camp State Park)

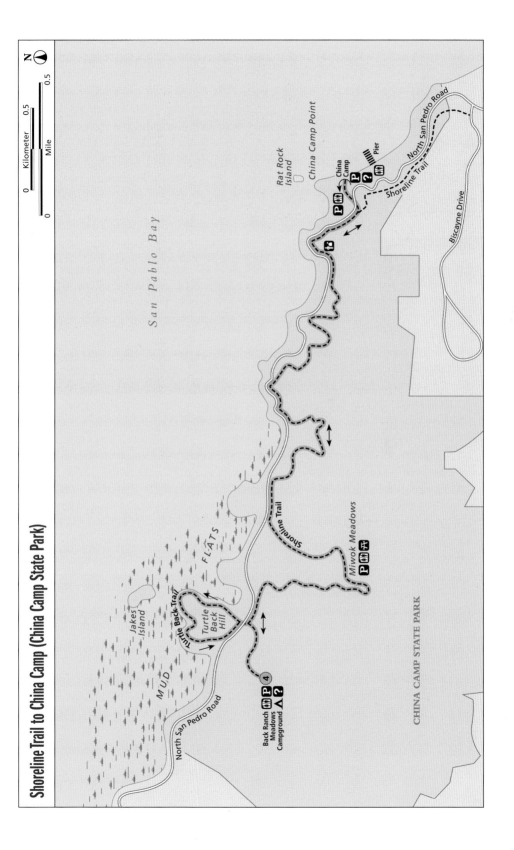

Miwok Meadows, the Shoreline Trail is nicely maintained and graded, wide enough for hikers to walk and talk. The park is extremely popular with mountain bikers, so hikers can expect to share the trail with them. Hiking midday on weekdays is best, as the cyclists tend to clot the routes on weekends and on long evenings after work.

After alternately curling through hollows shaded by oak and bay laurel and then cruising alongside the shoreline, the Shoreline Trail drops onto China Camp Point. A quick descent down the paved access road lands in China Camp Village, where you can enjoy a variety of activities, including swimming, boating, and exploring the historic sites and museum. When the day is done, retrace your steps on the Shoreline Trail to the trailhead.

Miles and Directions

0.0 Start on the signed Shoreline access trail in the Back Ranch Meadows campground parking lot. The access trail reaches the accessible trail in about 400 feet. At the junction, go left on the accessible Shoreline Trail.

0.3 Reach North San Pedro Road. Cross the road to the signed Turtle Back Trail. Go right to circle Turtle Back Hill counterclockwise.

0.6 The trail drops onto a boardwalk skimming the marsh between Turtle Back Hill and Jakes Island.

1.0 Close the loop, cross the roadway, and go left on the signed Shoreline Trail toward Miwok Meadows.

1.5 Pass the junction with the Bullet Hill Trail, staying right (straight) on the Shoreline Trail.

1.7 Cross a bridge as the trail circles through a shady dell.

1.9 Arrive at the Miwok Meadows Day Use Area. Follow the paved park road east toward the bay shore.

2.3 Pick up the Shoreline Trail at the San Francisco Bay Trail signboard. Go right on the obvious path headed south.

2.5 Climb gently to a bridge crossing a seasonal stream.

2.9 Cross a second bridge.

4.0 Reach the junction with the Oak Ridge Trail. Go left and downhill on the Shoreline Trail.

4.1 Arrive at the ranger station. Cross the road and climb switchbacks, continuing on the Shoreline Trail toward China Camp Village.

4.5 At the trail junction, stay left on the signed Village Trail toward China Camp Village. The Shoreline Trail continues to the right. Blackberries, which ripen in August, form a wall alongside the Village Trail as it descends.

4.6 Cross the park road and stay right on the Village Trail. Stay right again at the Y, continuing to the restrooms and parking lot at China Camp Point. Follow the paved park road down to China Camp Village.

4.9 Arrive at China Camp Village. Explore, then return as you came, excluding the Turtle Back Hill loop.

8.8 Arrive back at the trailhead.

5 Earthquake and Kule Loklo Trails

Explore the volatile geology that underlies the California coastline and learn about the native people who once called the Bear Valley home on two short trails that begin near the Point Reyes National Seashore's Bear Valley Visitor Center.

Start: Large gravel parking lot of Bear Valley Visitor Center
Distance: 0.7 mile for Earthquake Trail loop; 1.0 mile out and back to Kule Loklo; 1.9 miles for both
Hiking time: About 30 minutes for each; about 1 hour for both
Difficulty: Easy
Trail surface: Earthquake Trail is asphalt and accessible; Kule Loklo Trail is dirt.
Best season: Year-round
Other trail users: None

Canine compatibility: No dogs allowed
Land status: Point Reyes National Seashore
Fees and permits: None
Schedule: Sunrise to sunset daily
Trailhead amenities: Picnic facilities, restrooms, water, information/visitor center
Maps: USGS Inverness; Point Reyes National Seashore map available in visitor center and online
Trail contact: Point Reyes National Seashore, 1 Bear Valley Rd., Point Reyes Station, CA 94956; (415) 464-5100, ext. 2; www.nps.gov/pore

Finding the trailhead: From the junction of CA 1 and Sir Francis Drake Boulevard in Olema, go right (north) about 0.1 mile to Bear Valley Road, signed for the Point Reyes National Seashore. Turn right onto Bear Valley Road, and go about 0.4 mile to the signed park entrance. Follow the entrance road to the parking lots at the Bear Valley Visitor Center and trailhead. The Earthquake trailhead is wedged between the restrooms and the picnic area at the southeast end of the gravel parking lot and is marked by a large informational sign. GPS: N38 02.397' / W122 47.980'

The Hike

On the morning of April 18, 1906, the San Andreas Fault snapped, unleashing an earthquake that would become legendary. The infamous San Francisco temblor, and the fire that followed, destroyed much of the City by the Bay—more than 500 city blocks were leveled, and thousands of people were killed.

But the damage wasn't limited to San Francisco; communities throughout Northern California were devastated. Santa Rosa, located about 50 miles north of San Francisco, was demolished. Graphic evidence of how the violent rupture altered the landscape—and the unnerving opportunity to actually stand on the fault line—lies along the Earthquake Trail in Point Reyes National Seashore. Interpretive signs along the easy, paved path illustrate the quake's effects on the Olema Valley, the fault zone within Point Reyes, as well as the geology that will one day transport the peninsula to Alaska. Perfect for families, the hike is provocative no matter your age.

The trail begins by passing through an arm of the meadow that surrounds the visitor center. After about 50 yards the trail forks; stay left (east), following the arrows

The Earthquake Trail approaches the cover of oak woodland along the creek.

on the pavement. The grasses of the meadow harbor the vivid California poppy, among other wildflowers, in spring and summer.

Beyond the meadow the trail dips into a fragrant, birdsong-filled forest of bay and oak, with blackberry brambles edging the pavement. Drop to the bridge that spans Bear Valley Creek, a tributary of Olema Creek, at about 0.2 mile, then the trail swings south, curling along the ecotone between the creek-side riparian habitat and the grassland on the hillside. The blue posts in a line on the hillside demark the fault, which moved Point Reyes 20 feet northward in 1906. Ordinarily the fault, which marks the boundary between the Pacific and North American tectonic plates, shifts about 2 inches in a year.

The next interpretive markers are at a rustic ranch fence line that was offset in the quake; a short dirt footpath leads up a set of stairs to yet another interpretive sign at the fence on the fault.

Several more interpretive signs describe earthquake dynamics as the trail reenters the meadow. The broad, multi-limbed base of a great bay laurel is a great place for the kids to play before the path arcs north toward the trail intersection near the trailhead. Close the loop and head back toward the visitor center to pick up the trail to some-place entirely different. . . .

Earthquake and Kule Loklo Trails (Point Reyes National Seashore)

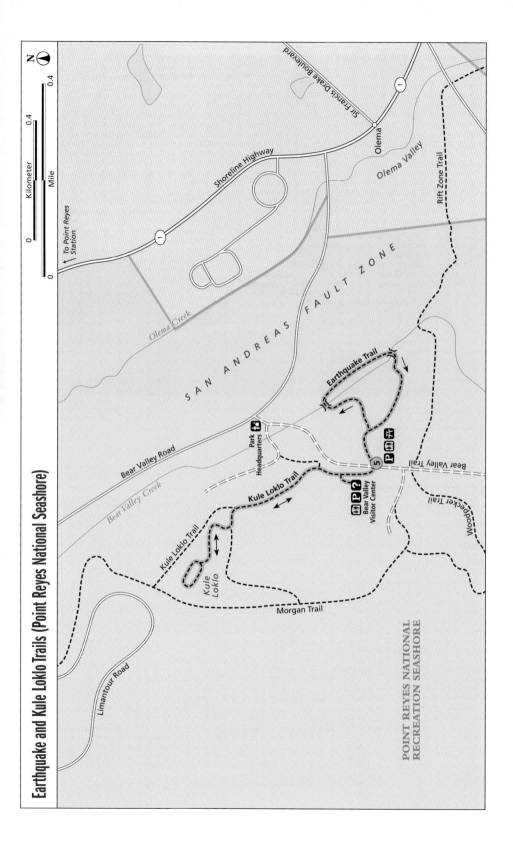

A stand woven of twigs and twine forms a platform for acorns in a reconstructed bark-walled granary in Kule Loklo.

For decades, in the heat of summer, the Coast Miwok and their neighbors have gathered in the spreading shade of twisted oaks at Kule Loklo to celebrate the culture that their people cultivated for 8,000 years in the North Bay. The event is called the Big Time, and the celebrants chant and stomp the ground in ritual dances, as well as share skills handed down for generations with visitors and each other, from flint-knapping (making stone tools) to basket-weaving (the Miwok used baskets for food preparation and cooking, among other things), to making clam-shell beads (which were a form of currency used in trade).

▶ More than 290 miles of the northernmost stretch of the San Andreas Fault shifted in the 1906 San Francisco earthquake. By contrast, the length of the rupture in the Loma Prieta quake, which occurred in 1989 and was the most significant temblor to hit the area since 1906, was about 25 miles.

When Kule Loklo doesn't ring with the chants of celebrants or interpreters, it can be a quiet place, the stillness evocative of the tragedy that overtook those who once lived in villages like it. Visitors may find themselves alone among the structures that were central to village life for the Coast Miwok: *kotchas* (huts made of tule or redwood bark), granaries where acorns were stored, a sweat lodge. It's a living village, not a museum, so all but the roundhouse are open for exploration.

The start of the trail to Kule Loklo, which means "Bear Valley" in Coast Miwok, is marked with an interpretive sign. Climb the broad track northward into the shade of oaks and bay laurels, with a sun-drenched fenced pasture to your left (west). A great moss-covered tree limb arcs over the path; all but children must duck to pass.

About halfway to the village, the trail curves west and parallels a bank of eucalyptus. These are nonnative trees, planted on ranches in West Marin as windbreaks. At the next trail sign, head right (north), through the wall of peeling trunks. The trail arcs back to the west, and the clearing that holds the village comes into view.

Once you've explored and/or enjoyed a picnic beneath the bough-draped shelters or oaks dripping with lacy lichens, head back as you came.

Miles and Directions

0.0 Begin on the paved Earthquake Trail, staying left at the Y to follow the loop in a clockwise direction (as per the arrows).

0.2 Cross the bridge over the little creek.

0.3 Take the spur trail up to the dislocated fence line.

0.7 Close the loop and return to the gravel parking lot and the Earthquake trailhead. Cross the lot and the paved park road, pass the entrance to the Bear Valley Visitor Center, and follow the sidewalk down to the end of the smaller paved lot, where a sign marks the beginning of the trail to Kule Loklo.

0.9 Head left on the signed trail to Kule Loklo.

1.2 Go right on the signed trail through the bank of eucalyptus.

1.4 Reach Kule Loklo. Explore, then retrace your steps to the trailhead.

1.9 Arrive back at the trailhead.

6 Chimney Rock and Drakes Bay

The trail onto the headland at Chimney Rock is renowned for its springtime wild-flower bloom, but it also offers bird's-eye views of the white cliffs backing Drakes Bay, where the fabled explorer Sir Francis Drake is said to have landed in 1579. Follow a second path to check out a historic lighthouse station, and another short path that leads to a viewpoint overlooking a beach where elephant seals sun.

Start: Parking lot at end of Chimney Rock Road
Distance: 1.8 miles out and back to Chimney Rock; 2.2 miles out and back with side trip to historic lifeboat station; 2.7 miles if you include Elephant Seal Overlook Trail
Hiking time: About 2 hours
Difficulty: Easy
Trail surface: Dirt, gravel, pavement
Best season: Year-round
Other trail users: None
Canine compatibility: No dogs allowed
Land status: Point Reyes National Seashore
Fees and permits: None
Schedule: Sunrise to sunset, though trails are accessible 24 hours a day, every day.

Trailhead amenities: Restrooms, picnic sites, shuttle stop
Maps: USGS Drakes Bay OE S; Point Reyes National Seashore map available in visitor center and online
Special considerations: The trail is exposed in brief sections and passes near unstable cliffs; remain on the designated route. Avoid the unauthorized trails on the Chimney Rock headland, which lead to bluffs that are inherently unstable. The park cautions that it "is very dangerous to climb or walk along the edge of cliffs."
Trail contact: Point Reyes National Seashore, 1 Bear Valley Rd., Point Reyes Station, CA 94956; (415) 464-5100, ext. 2; www.nps.gov/pore

Finding the trailhead: From downtown Point Reyes Station, take CA 1 (Shoreline Highway) south to the junction with Sir Francis Drake Boulevard. Turn right onto Sir Francis Drake Boulevard, signed for Inverness. Follow Sir Francis Drake Boulevard for 18.7 miles to the Chimney Rock turnoff, passing through Inverness Park and Inverness before heading west through the rolling pasturelands of the point. Alternatively, from the Bear Valley Visitor Center just west of CA 1 in Olema, follow the access road to Bear Valley Road. Turn left (north), and follow Bear Valley Road for 1.7 miles to its intersection with Sir Francis Drake Boulevard. Turn left (north) on the highway, and follow it for 17.7 miles to the Chimney Rock turnoff. Turn left (east) on the Chimney Rock access road, and go 0.9 mile to the trailhead and parking area. If the lot is full, park carefully alongside the access road, allowing room for traffic. GPS: N37 59.707' / W122 58.775'

The Hike

In spring, the trail to Chimney Rock passes through the premier wildflower display on the Point Reyes peninsula. The palette is dazzling: flowers of all colors—yellow and orange poppies, red paintbrush, blue and purple lupine and violets—all set against verdant waist-high grasses and the bright blues of sea and sky.

The trail to Chimney Rock looks back toward the white cliffs rising above Drakes Bay.

But hiking around Chimney Rock is delightful even when the flowers aren't peaking. The trail winds through coastal scrub to the brink of the peninsula, where a bench overlooks the white cliffs and dazzling waters of Drakes Bay, the sweep of the coast south past the Golden Gate to Lands End, and the shimmering Pacific. The bay itself, landing site of Sir Francis Drake during his circumnavigation of the globe in the late sixteenth century, and the restored lifeboat station tucked in a quiet cove not far from the wide Pacific are the historic fulcrums of this three-pronged route.

The irony, of course, is that the Coast Miwok lived in Point Reyes for thousands of years before it was "discovered." But it wasn't until Francis Drake, then merely a captain, brought the *Golden Hind* into Drakes Bay that Point Reyes finally made the map. Drake would spend more than a month in what he dubbed "Nova Albion" in 1579, repairing his leaking vessel in the calm waters of Drakes Estero. That Drake actually landed in Drakes Bay was long the subject of controversy, but that was "officially" put to rest when the bay was declared a National Historic Landmark by the US Department of the Interior in 2012.

The hike begins in the southwest corner of the parking lot, with the white cliffs to your back. The trail climbs gently through the scrub, buffered from ocean breezes by the slope of the bluff on the right. Pass above the lifeboat station, then round a bend

Drakes Bay and the Explorers

Sir Francis Drake's "discovery" of Nova Albion (California) occurred during the English privateer's circumnavigation of the globe between 1577 and 1580. By the time Drake landed in the sheltered bay that now bears his name, where he would spend a month repairing the leaking *Golden Hind*, he'd already sailed around Cape Horn, establishing the Drake Passage, and raided Pacific Coast ports in South America and Mexico. His ship laden with millions of dollars in booty that he intended to bring to his sovereign, Queen Elizabeth I, Drake traveled north along the California coastline seeking the Northwest Passage—the undiscovered easy way home. It was during this fruitless search that he took refuge inside the arc of Point Reyes and claimed the land beyond the white cliffs for queen and country.

For the indigenous Coast Miwok, despite Drake's "conquest," the encounter with the English was short and peaceful. They'd have no further contact with Europeans until the Spanish truly colonized the region—a conquest much longer and devastating.

into a saddle at about the quarter-mile mark. A break in the bluff allows the brightness of the sun reflecting off the ocean to flood the trail, and steep cliffs drop toward the sea. Avoid the social trails that lead to the cliff's edge, for safety's sake and to reduce erosion. The main trail stays below the edge, well within the safety zone, but offers ample views.

▶ According to park literature, approximately 1,200 northern elephant seals winter on beaches at the Point Reyes National Seashore, with as many as 100 animals gathering below the Elephant Seal Overlook.

A short, steep pitch climbs away from the saddle; the trail tops out on the bluff at about 0.5 mile. Signed "unauthorized" trails again break away from the obvious main route; stick to the formal path headed straight south, allowing the native flora to reclaim the informal lines. The trail flattens, then dips through another small saddle as it approaches the point, where the broad bay on the left (northeast) meets the ocean spreading endlessly on the right (south). Climb to the fence at the brink of the headlands at 0.9 mile.

A pair of sun-bleached benches near the fence line offer respite for the weary or the contemplative. The vistas, of course, are wonderful. Chimney Rock, the largest of a small cluster of sea stacks just off the tip of the point, is battered by the surf, but that doesn't seem to bother the seabirds that gather on its craggy summit. Turn around to take in the breadth of Drakes Bay, its sprawling beach, and the pale bluffs behind.

Once his vessel was repaired, Drake completed his epic voyage, sailing across the Pacific and Indian Oceans, around the Cape of Good Hope, then up the east coast of Africa back to England. Knighted by Queen Elizabeth in 1581, he found continuing success as a politician, adventurer, and military man until he was felled by fever off the coast of Panama in 1596.

Other Europeans "discovered" Point Reyes after Drake, among them Sebastián Rodriguez Cermeño, a Portuguese ship captain and trader charged by Spanish authorities with the task of claiming lands for the Spanish empire. Cermeño's ship, the *San Agustin*, foundered in Drakes Bay in 1595, and its cargo, including Chinese pottery, has washed onto nearby beaches into modern times. Cermeño happened to be ashore when the ship sank; he and his crew used a small launch to sail back to Spanish ports in Mexico.

Later came Don Sebastián Vizcaíno, a Spaniard who visited Drakes Bay during his explorations of the coast in 1603. Sailing past the rocky headlands on a Catholic holiday known as the Feast of the Three Kings, he dubbed the landform La Punta de los Tres Reyes, the Point of the Three Kings, a name that has been abbreviated to Point Reyes. The king of points. It fits.

When you're ready, return as you came to the base of the one steep hill on the trail. An overgrown path that you may not have noticed on your way out to the point breaks to the right, angling gently downhill to meet the paved road above the lifeboat station. Turn right on the roadway and head down to the restored building.

Historic records of efforts to rescue mariners whose ships ran afoul of the rocks, beaches, and turbulent water off Point Reyes date back to the mid-1800s, long before either the Point Reyes Lighthouse or the lifeboat station on Drakes Bay was built. According to a history produced by the National Park Service, local ranchers came to the aid of the crew of the *Ayacucho* when the ship foundered at Limantour Beach in 1841 (the beach now bears the surname of the *Ayacucho*'s captain). For many years, the ranchers at Point Reyes were the only hope seamen had of rescue if their vessels ran aground.

It was hoped that construction of the Point Reyes Lighthouse would put an end to the legacy of shipwrecks at the point, but they continued—more than forty in the sixty years after the light was built. So, in 1889, the US Life-Saving Service built a lifeboat station on the Great Beach adjacent to the light, and the tradition of heroic lifesaving efforts at Point Reyes was formalized.

But working as a surfman on the Great Beach proved a dangerous, difficult job, with four men losing their lives in the early years of the lifeboat station's operation. Those difficulties eventually resulted in abandonment of that station and construction of a second, more modern station at Drakes Bay. The new facilities, which overlook the bay today, included a boathouse with a marine railway on its first story and quarters for the men on its second story. The accommodations and railway enabled men to quickly launch their 36-foot motor lifeboats; they saved more than forty-five ships in the lifeboat station's first ten years.

The Point Reyes Lifeboat Station fell into disuse following the construction of the US Coast Guard Station at Bodega Bay, north of Point Reyes, in 1963. By 1968 the station was closed. In 1969 it became part of the Point Reyes National Seashore, and it was designated a National Historic Landmark in 1990. Though closed to the public except for special events, you can peek in through the windows of the neat white-and-green building, walk around the grounds (there are picnic tables and portable toilets here), and check out the railway that leads down into the dark waters of the bay.

From the lifeboat station, climb the paved roadway past the charming two-story house that once was the residence of the station's officer-in-charge and now is a park residence. The access road meets another paved road just below the parking lot; turn right to make one last stop on a tour of the point.

The park's Elephant Seal Overlook is located on a hillside overlooking the westernmost stretch of Drakes Beach and offers great views of a colony of elephant seals that returns to the beach annually to breed, then birth and raise pups. Impressively

The marine railway at the Point Reyes Lifeboat Station allowed surfmen to launch rescue vessels.

Chimney Rock and Drakes Bay (Point Reyes National Seashore)

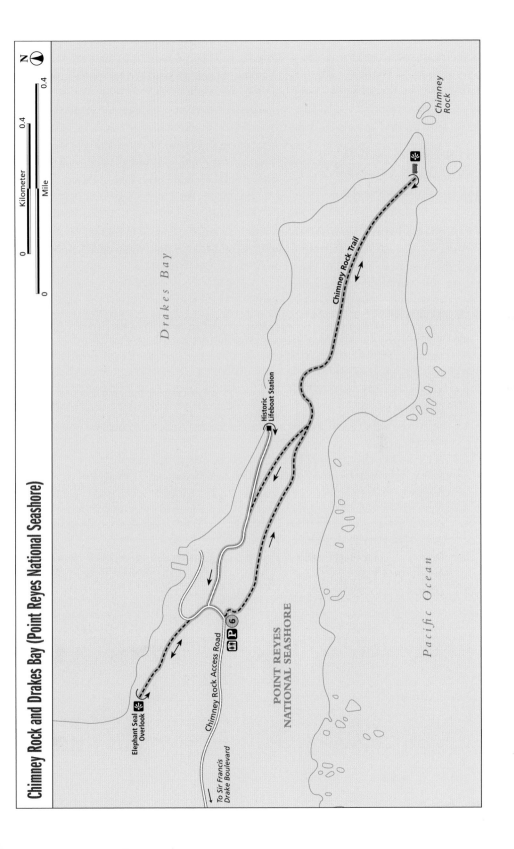

bulky (full-grown males may weigh as much as 5,000 pounds), they are even more curious to hear. Clunking, thumping, snorting, bleating, chortling, hiccupping, bellowing—they sound like plumbing gone horribly wrong.

▶ When the Pacific gray whales are migrating, from January to April, the Chimney Rock overlook is a popular whale-watching spot.

To reach the overlook, go about 100 yards down the pavement from the junction below the parking lot to where the gravel Elephant Seal Overlook Trail breaks to the left (northwest). The trail traverses the scrubby hillside overlooking Drakes Bay to the fenced viewpoint. Do not approach the seals: Despite their imposing size, elephant seals can be frightened if a human comes too close, with reactions ranging from backing away to moving so quickly that they crush a pup or separate a pup from its mother. Elephant seals also have been known to charge and bite people. After checking out the scene, retrace your steps to the parking area.

Miles and Directions

0.0 Start by ascending the trail that traverses across the bluff, passing above the lifeboat station.

0.5 Reach the top of the bluff.

0.9 Arrive at the bench overlooking Chimney Rock. Retrace your steps to the steep hill above the lifeboat station.

1.5 At the base of the hill, take the narrow, unmarked trail that breaks right toward the lifeboat station.

1.7 At the junction with the paved lifeboat station access road, go right (downhill) to the station. When ready, follow the paved road uphill, past the trail junction and the park residence.

2.2 At the junction with the road that leads uphill to the parking area on the left, go right and downhill to the signed Elephant Seal Overlook Trail, which breaks left where the pavement switchbacks down toward a gate. Go left onto the gravel trail to the overlook.

2.4 Reach the Elephant Seal Overlook. Retrace your steps, staying right on the paved roadway to the parking area.

2.7 Arrive back at the trailhead.

7 Point Reyes Lighthouse

A short trail leads to 308 stairs that drop to the Point Reyes Lighthouse and its auxiliary buildings, which are anchored onto a pillar of rock at the westernmost tip of the peninsula.

Start: Paved parking area at end of Sir Francis Drake Boulevard
Distance: 1.9 miles including side trips to overlooks
Hiking time: 1–2 hours
Difficulty: Strenuous due to staircase
Trail surface: Pavement, dirt, steep stairway
Best season: Year-round. Whale-watching is best in Jan, with a second prime viewing time in Mar/early Apr.
Other trail users: None
Canine compatibility: No dogs allowed
Land status: Point Reyes National Seashore
Fees and permits: None
Schedule: Lighthouse stairs and visitor center exhibits open 10 a.m. to 4:30 p.m. Thurs through Mon, weather and staffing permitting; closed Tues and Wed
Trailhead amenities: Restrooms, shuttle stop; more restrooms are next to the garage near the Lighthouse Visitor Center. Renovation and expansion of the center were under way in mid-2015; when completed, the center will feature north-facing windows that will allow comfortable whale-watching in frigid weather.

Maps: USGS Drakes Bay OE S; Point Reyes National Seashore map available in visitor center and online
Special considerations: Avoid the unauthorized trails on the headland, which may lead to bluffs that are inherently unstable. The park cautions that it "is very dangerous to climb or walk along the edge of cliffs."

The area around the Point Reyes Lighthouse is extremely popular. The parking lot is full on most weekend days and during the weeks when the whale migration is in full swing. The park service closes Sir Francis Drake Boulevard at Drakes Beach on weekends and holidays from about New Year's Day to Easter, and provides a shuttle service from the Ken Patrick Visitor Center to the lighthouse parking lot. Tickets for the shuttle are available at the Ken Patrick Visitor Center. For more information on shuttle schedules and road closures, call (415) 464-5100 (ext. 2, then ext. 3, then ext. 1).
Trail contact: Point Reyes National Seashore, 1 Bear Valley Rd., Point Reyes Station, CA 94956; (415) 464-5100, ext. 2; www.nps.gov/pore

Finding the trailhead: From downtown Point Reyes Station, take CA 1 (Shoreline Highway) south to the junction with Sir Francis Drake Boulevard. Turn right (north) onto Sir Francis Drake Boulevard, signed for Inverness. Pass over the Inverness Ridge, then through rolling pasturelands, traveling a total of 20 miles to the lighthouse parking lot. Alternatively, from the Bear Valley Visitor Center just west of CA 1 in Olema, follow the access road to its intersection with Bear Valley Road. Turn left (north) on Bear Valley Road, and drive 1.7 miles to its intersection with Sir Francis Drake Boulevard. Turn left (north), and travel 19 miles to the lighthouse parking lot. If you can't find a spot in the lot, park alongside Sir Francis Drake Boulevard, taking care that your vehicle is well off the roadway. GPS: N37 59.873' / W123 00.724'

Viewed on a map, land's end at Point Reyes resembles a hammerhead shark's head, sweeping east to west from the mouth of Drakes Bay into the Pacific. The point itself is on the west side of the hammerhead's face, a narrow ridge jutting into the Pacific. At its very end, 440 feet above the sea, the stubby, whitewashed tower of the Point Reyes Lighthouse is a stunning exclamation point on a stunning landform.

Shipwrecks were an appallingly frequent occurrence in the early days of navigation along the rugged coast of Northern California. Records of maritime carnage around Point Reyes begin in 1595, with the foundering of the *San Agustin* in Drakes Bay, and continue up until, and even after, the lighthouse was built in the late nineteenth century. Hidden rocks, turbulent currents, and infamously thick fogs, not to mention the fact that the point juts more than 10 miles west of the adjacent coastline, all contributed to an accumulation of wrecks—fifty-six between 1841 and 1934 alone, according to park service documents.

Congress, prodded by ship owners struggling to preserve cargo during the glory days of California's gold rush, approved construction of the lighthouse in the 1850s. But various delays—problems acquiring the property, difficulties in building on the site—meant the lighthouse didn't begin operation until 1870. Its distinctive signal, flashed out to sea by a beautifully faceted Fresnel lens, enabled sailors to both identify their positions and steer clear of the dangerous waters off the point. A foghorn augmented the warning capabilities of the lighthouse.

Keepers of the Light

The Point Reyes Lighthouse was manned by dedicated keepers who endured ferocious weather, repetitive tasks, and loneliness. The light was tended by a team of four, who worked in six-hour shifts day in and day out, cleaning the lens, maintaining the exterior of the iron structure, and trimming the wicks of the lanterns so that the light functioned optimally. The work ethic of these keepers—and the sturdiness of the lighthouse—was graphically illustrated after the 1906 earthquake: According to park literature, the lighthouse moved north an astonishing 18 feet, but the light itself, though shaken off its tracks, was back online in 13 minutes. This is not to say the light keepers were uniformly dedicated: A logbook entry recounts one keeper who went AWOL, taking the government horse without permission and returning that night too drunk for duty.

A long, long flight of stairs leads down to the lighthouse on the tip of Point Reyes.

The lighthouse operated for more than a century before it was shut down in 1975. These days, an automated light and foghorn, located in a building below the historic lighthouse, warn vessels away from the jagged coast. But the old Fresnel light still works, the "last functioning intact light of its kind on the West Coast."

The lighthouse is reached via a short trail/access road that begins at the main parking area at the end of Sir Francis Drake Boulevard. The route described is book-ended with short side trails to viewpoints, the first showcasing the steep cliffs to the south of the point itself. Climb to the overlook via a brief dirt path, check out the escarpment, and then return as you came to pick up the main route.

To reach the light from the roundabout at the end of the road, walk around the gate and follow the pavement west, passing through an open landscape of coastal scrub that allows great views west and north, along the Great Beach, when the fog is out.

Pass a windbreak of cypress that has been sculpted into an arch over the road-way at about the halfway point. Beyond lies park housing, the driveway sporting a weather-beaten painting of a whale. Next up: the tiny Point Reyes Lighthouse Visitor Center, which is stationed in the lee of a large rock outcrop.

Though small, the lighthouse visitor center is far from spare. Not much larger than a small cottage, it is packed with interpretive displays covering whales, birds, seals,

Point Reyes Lighthouse (Point Reyes National Seashore)

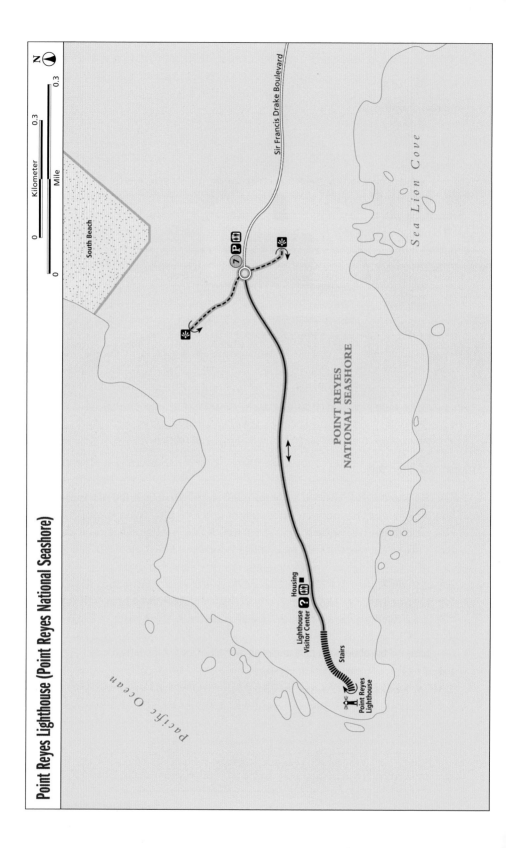

> The Fresnel light is composed of 1,032 glass prisms that refract and focus the lamp lit within. The five-second flash could be seen 24 nautical miles distant.

the lighthouse, the lifeboat station, and more, with just enough space left over for a gift shop and a desk for the ranger that staffs the center.

The visitor center is at the top of the long flight of stairs that leads to the lighthouse itself. Circle around the left (south) side of the rock outcrop, past the skull of a whale on the right and the rounded tops of the light's concrete cisterns on the left, to a platform overlooking the lighthouse and the sea beyond. A popular whale-watching vantage point, benches on the platform provide respite for those tired of standing by the railing during long vigils.

The steep concrete staircase—308 steps, most numbered so you can mark your progress on the long climb up—descends to the lighthouse and attendant structures, which are anchored onto a pillar of rock at the very tip of the peninsula. You may find a ranger in the lighthouse lens room, offering interpretation of the light and its history; you can also walk around the lighthouse on a narrow gangway. To check out foghorns and other historic equipment, as well as entries from a lighthouse keeper's logbook, visit the wood-paneled building just above the light.

Climb back the way you came, taking advantage of the small viewing platforms if you need to catch your breath. Continue past the visitor center, retracing your steps to the gate at the trailhead. Pick up the trail on the left, near the shuttle stop shelter, and follow the narrow dirt track down to another viewpoint. This is a whale-watching overlook, but even when the gray whales aren't running it offers stunning vistas northward along the Great Beach. Return as you came.

Miles and Directions

0.0 Start by taking the unmarked but obvious trail that leads left (south) from the parking area.

0.1 Reach the cove and cliff overlook, with a low fence. Return as you came.

0.2 Back at the trailhead, go right (west) and pass the gate, walking up the paved access road.

0.5 Pass the bower of cypress and the park housing complex.

0.6 Pass the lighthouse visitor center and begin down the long staircase to the lighthouse.

0.8 Arrive at the lighthouse. Tour the buildings, then retrace your steps.

1.7 Back at the gate near the trailhead parking area and shuttle stop, go left onto the unsigned but obvious dirt path toward an overlook of the Great Beach.

1.8 Reach the overlook. Return as you came.

1.9 Arrive back at the trailhead.

8 Olompali Loop Trail

One of the most overlooked parks in San Francisco's North Bay harbors unexpected historic and trail treasures.

Start: Parking lot trailhead leading into ranch site
Distance: 3.8-mile lollipop
Hiking time: About 3 hours
Difficulty: Moderate
Trail surface: Dirt, gravel
Best season: Year-round
Other trail users: Equestrians
Canine compatibility: No dogs allowed
Land status: Olompali State Historic Park
Fees and permits: Entrance fee

Schedule: Park open 9 a.m. to 5 p.m. Wed through Sun; closed Mon and Tues
Trailhead amenities: Water, information, and picnic facilities available in developed section of park
Maps: USGS Novato
Trail contact: Olompali State Historic Park, PO Box 1016, Novato, CA 94948; (415) 892-3383; www.parks.ca.gov/olompali. The Olompali People (nonprofit volunteer support organization); (707) 762-9715; www.olompali.org.

Finding the trailhead: From US 101 in Novato, take the Atherton Avenue exit. Follow the frontage road (Redwood Boulevard) on the west side of the highway north for 2.1 miles to the signed entrance to Olompali State Historic Park. GPS: N38 09.092' / W122 34.297'

The Hike

The depth of history contained in this humble little park, wedged between sprawling Mount Burdell and a busy stretch of freeway, is astounding. The land was, for thousands of years, occupied by a tribelet of the Coast Miwok known as the Olompali, which flourished on a land flush with resources including acorns and other edible and medicinal flora, wild game, and seafood from the Petaluma River delta and nearby San Pablo Bay. Archaeological studies of the site have revealed not only the depth and breadth of the Olompali footprint but also artifacts that link to the European age of exploration, including a silver coin from the late sixteenth century, when English privateer Francis Drake made landfall on the coastline west of the village.

Following this fleeting European contact, the Olompali culture continued relatively undisturbed until the arrival of Spanish colonialists in the early nineteenth century. Missions were established north and south of the Olompali village, in Sonoma and San Rafael, and the Olompali suffered the fate of many California natives, the population "Christianized," deprived of the land that sustained them, and decimated by disease.

The village was incorporated into a rancho under the auspices of General Mariano Vallejo, governor of the Mexican province of Alta California, and granted to an Olompali *hoipu*, or headman, named Camilo Ynitia. A hike through Olompali begins

The old Burdell barns and the massive, sun-silvered stump of a eucalyptus mark the start and finish of a loop through Olompali State Historic Park.

by passing the preserved remains of Ynitia's adobe. The adobe later became part of the mansion of the ranching family that acquired the land in 1863, when then-owner James Black gave it to his daughter, Mary, upon her marriage to San Francisco dentist Galen Burdell.

The buildings in the developed area of the park, including the frame house that holds the visitor center, were built by the Burdells. Mary Burdell's Victorian garden, "one of the only surviving examples of the gardens of the 1870 period in the Bay Area and California," is being restored by the park's volunteer organization. Paved and dirt paths wander through these buildings—the barns, the shops, the residences—then the main loop trail hitches westward and onto the skirts of Mount Burdell.

But before the route enters the wilder reaches of the park, it passes a reconstructed Coast Miwok village consisting of several structures including a granary and a *kotcha*, or bark shelter. A gravel path leads through a native plant garden, with signs explaining how the plants were used by the Olompali and other California natives as medicine, food, or tools. Coffeeberry for laxative, the ash of honeysuckle for tattooing, boughs from the manzanita for arrows, soaproot for brushes and to stun fish in the stream—it's a fascinating foray into the abundance the Olompali found here.

A dam and brick cistern on Olompali Creek helped supply water for the ranching operations of the Burdell family.

From the village, the loop part of the trail climbs alongside Olompali Creek, past a small reservoir, and into the wooded folds at the base of Mount Burdell. The climb is straightforward and well shaded, a good option even on a hot summer day. At the junction with the trail that leads to the exposed top of Mount Burdell—not a good option on a hot summer day—the loop bends back toward the ranch, descending via switchbacks and traverses, with openings in the oak canopy allowing views eastward across the Petaluma River wetlands toward San Pablo Bay and the inland ridges of the Coast Range.

The trail reconnects with the paths through the ranch buildings behind the Burdells' dairy barn. Backtrack to the path that leads up to the visitor center, where interpretive signs describe the more recent history of Olompali, including its brief occupation by the Grateful Dead, who entertained rock luminaries Janis Joplin and Grace Slick, among others, at the site. Olompali was also owned by the University of San Francisco and used as a Jesuit retreat, and was a "hippie" commune in the 1960s. The heptagonal concrete platform adjacent to the visitor center, near trail's end, was used by the commune, known as "The Chosen People," to make "mushroom bread" that was sold in San Francisco's Haight-Ashbury district, epicenter of the hippie movement. What is mushroom bread? The sign describes how dough was placed in cans on the hot stone, which then rose over the tops of the cans to resemble mushrooms. Right.

Olompali Loop Trail (Olompali State Historic Park)

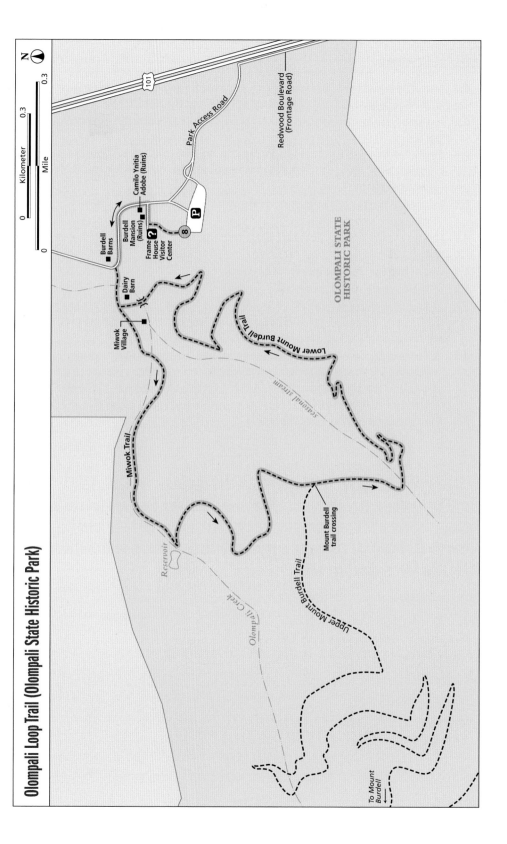

N

Kilometer
0   0.3

Mile
0   0.3

101

Park Access Road

Redwood Boulevard
(Frontage Road)

Burdell Barns

Dairy Barn

Camilo Ynitia Adobe (Ruins)

Burdell Mansion (Ruins)

Frame House Visitor Center

P

8

Miwok Village

Miwok Trail

Lower Mount Burdell Trail

seasonal stream

OLOMPALI STATE
HISTORIC PARK

Reservoir

Olompali Creek

Mount Burdell trail crossing

Upper Mount Burdell Trail

To Mount Burdell

Miles and Directions

0.0   Start at the signed trailhead leading into the Burdell Ranch grounds. Explore the grounds, following signs pointing to the Miwok Village and the Mount Burdell Loop Trail.

0.2   Turn sharply left, heading uphill past the old barns. Continue to the junction with the Village Trail.

0.5   Arrive at the reconstructed Coast Miwok Village. The site is outfitted with picnic facilities, interpretive signs, trash cans, and a rustic amphitheater. Follow the gravel trail through the native plants garden.

0.7   Resume the loop by continuing uphill on the loop trail/dirt roadway, climbing into a shaded hollow thick with ferns.

0.9   Pass the small reservoir on Olompali Creek. A brick cistern/well is next to the ramshackle dam.

1.1   Pass a "loop trail" sign at a bend in the broad trail.

1.2   At the switchback, stay left on the trail. A use trail drops right to the creek.

1.8   Arrive at the junction with the Mount Burdell Trail. A sign indicates the top of Mount Burdell is 3.3 miles to the right. Continue left/downhill on the loop trail. Long traverses between switchbacks on the descent offer views across the Petaluma River delta.

3.3   Reach the bridge behind the dairy barn, closing the loop. Turn right, heading back into the ranch exhibits. Explore at will, following paths lined with interpretive signs past the ranch buildings, the structure protecting the Ynitia adobe, the old Burdell mansion, the garden, and up toward the visitor center.

3.8   Arrive back at the parking lot and trailhead.

▶ The only battle of California's Bear Flag Revolt took place on what was then Camilo Ynitia's rancho. The revolt began in nearby Sonoma in the summer of 1846, when American settlers declared California, then part of Mexico, an independent state. One Mexican officer lost his life in the Battle of Olompali. The Republic of California was abandoned following annexation of the territory into the United States; it lasted about three weeks.

9 Matt Davis and Steep Ravine Loop

Climb from the seaside village of Stinson Beach to Pantoll, about midway up Mount Tamalpais, then descend back to the sea via the magical redwood forest within the Steep Ravine.

Start: At formal Stinson Beach parking lots
Distance: 8.2-mile loop
Hiking time: 5-6 hours
Difficulty: Strenuous
Trail surface: Mostly dirt singletrack, some pavement, stairs, and a ladder
Best season: Spring, summer, and fall
Other trail users: Trail runners
Canine compatibility: Dogs not permitted
Land status: Mount Tamalpais State Park
Fees and permits: None
Schedule: Sunrise to sunset daily
Trailhead amenities: None at trailhead proper. However, all amenities, including restrooms, water, and picnic sites, are available just down the street at Stinson Beach. Water, restrooms,
and information are also available at apex of hike at Pantoll Ranger Station. Camping is available at Pantoll and elsewhere in Mount Tamalpais State Park.
Maps: USGS Bolinas and San Rafael; map in park brochure available online at www.parks .ca.gov; online at www.onetam.org/map-and-trails and www.friendsofmttam.org
Trail contact: Mount Tamalpais State Park, 801 Panoramic Hwy., Mill Valley, CA 94941; (415) 388-2070; www.parks.ca.gov/mttamalpais. OneTam/Tamalpais Lands Collaborative; (415) 561-3000; www.onetam.org. Friends of Mt. Tam, PO Box 7064, Corte Madera, CA 94976; (415) 258-2410; www.friendsofmttam.org.

Finding the trailhead: The trailhead is located on Belvedere Avenue behind the Stinson Beach Community Center. From CA 1 at the stop sign in downtown Stinson Beach, turn up onto Calle Del Mar. Go 1 long block, then turn right onto Buena Vista, which is a one-way street. Buena Vista becomes Belvedere at a sharp bend; the Matt Davis trailhead is on the left side of the road. Street parking is extremely limited at the trailhead proper and no parking is allowed at the community center. Please park in the formal lots for Stinson Beach. GPS: N37 53.979' / W122 38.245'

The Hike

The accolades are well deserved, and I add my voice to the choir: This hike on the western skirts of Mount Tamalpais is one of the best in the Bay Area. Yes, there's a lot of climbing; yes, there are stairs and a ladder; yes, the parking is difficult; yes, road noise impinges on the wildland experience at times. But . . .

From beginning to end, the trail traverses spectacular terrain. It starts in a fairy oak woodland, weaving uphill via switchbacks through dappled light. Enter the chaparral, where breaks in the canopy afford peekaboo glimpses of the white-sand arc of Stinson Beach. Higher up on the mountain, in the sunny grasslands, springtime gardens of lupine and poppy quilt the green slopes. From the high point at Pantoll, the route drops into the Steep Ravine, where columns of redwoods reach from cascading Webb

Looking back down the Matt Davis Trail toward the Pacific

Creek toward the sun. The final stretch rolls along the Dipsea Trail amid fragrant coastal scrub, with views stretching out along Stinson, past the Bolinas Lagoon, and beyond Duxbury Point to the sea.

The trail begins and ends in the small town of Stinson Beach. Though there's no denying the fog, this is a place of sun and surf, long a premier recreational destination for San Franciscans and Marinites. It didn't start that way: In its early days as a settlement, Stinson was part of a Mexican land grant known as Rancho Las Baulinas. Prior to construction of a dirt road in the late nineteenth century, travelers to "Willow

Of Cows and Conservation

Historic Point Reyes Station, at the north end of the Olema Valley where the San Andreas Fault dives into Tomales Bay, has long been the ranching heart of West Marin.

The grasslands that flourish on the Point Reyes peninsula, as well as on the rolling hills east of Tomales Bay and in the Nicasio and San Geronimo Valleys, have supported dairy ranches since the mid-1800s. The premium milk and butter produced in the region has nourished San Franciscans for more than 150 years, from the gold rush to the high-tech revolution. These days, cheese, yogurt, cream, and other products from Point Reyes dairy farms are used in a slew of high-end Bay Area restaurants.

The Spaniards first brought cattle to Alta California. When the Mexicans gained control of the future Golden State, they divvied up the land into ranchos and continued the bovine bonanza, thus initiating a ranching tradition that would enable Americans and other emigrants to transform Point Reyes into an empire of dairies. These dairies thrived until threat of development loomed in the 1960s and 1970s. The partnership created to parry those threats—an alliance of the Marin Agricultural Land Trust, the National Park Service, the ranchers, and others—has resulted in a peaceable and productive mesh of "utilization, preservation, and conservation" on the historic ranchlands.

The Lagunitas Creek Extension Trail, which winds through the former Giacomini dairy and ranch, is a nice, easy ramble to add to the beginning or end of an exploration of the shops, markets, and restaurants/bakeries along CA 1 as it runs through Point Reyes Station. One short loop on a good gravel path circles through the recovering marshlands surrounding the old Giacomini barn. Another trail (none are signed) leads straight into the wetlands and back, the thick, towering foliage on either side of the track bearing witness to the success of the ongoing Giacomini Wetlands Restoration Project. More than 550 acres of land that had been drained via levees to cultivate forage for cattle is in the process of being returned to its natural state. A third "loop" explores the riparian zones along the outlet of Lagunitas Creek. Combine the routes for a total of about 2 miles.

The trailhead is located on C Street at its junction with Third Street in Point Reyes Station. GPS: N38 04.032' / W122 48.468'

Camp" arrived by sea or by foot via the Dipsea Trail. Visitors could also reach the camp from the Mount Tamalpais and Muir Woods Railway via stagecoach from West Point Inn. The town became Stinson Beach once postal service commenced in 1916, taking the name of one of its most prominent landholders. Once access became easier, the town's scenic setting and sandy beach sparked an ongoing growth in popularity, both as a residential area and a tourist destination.

▶ In her history titled *Bolinas: A Narrative of the Days of the Dons*, Marin Waterhouse Pepper writes that the word *baulinas* is of native origin, meaning "whale's playground."

Neighboring Bolinas, at the far end of the miles-long stretch of sand and separated by the outlet of the Bolinas Lagoon, has a more exclusive and bohemian feel. This is perhaps best captured in the fact that, for years and years, locals removed any signage that directed day-trippers on CA 1 to the town. Its agrarian roots remain intact: Also part of the Mexican Baulinas rancho, these days farmers in Bolinas raise sought-after organic and sustainably raised produce. An epicenter for counterculture, the town has also long been a magnet for the creative—visual artists, writers, musicians, and other independent thinkers. Make note: Its beach, tiny by comparison to Stinson, was once famously nudist; these days nudity is outlawed, but Bolinas is historically outlaw, so . . .

Hiking the Matt Davis–Steep Ravine Loop is straightforward. Though you can travel in either direction, the route is described here beginning on Matt Davis and concluding with the Steep Ravine and Dipsea Trails. Some folks also start and end at Pantoll; the parking is arguably easier here, but, particularly if you end on the Steep Ravine, finishing an 8-mile hike with a stiff climb is not ideal.

The trail begins by climbing the steady but easy switchbacks of the Matt Davis Trail, named for a trail builder whose genius is obvious. The route winds first through oak woodlands, then climbs short staircases that lead around a prominent rock outcrop known as Table Rock, with Table Rock Creek cascading alongside.

The route ascends through a band of evergreens dominated by Douglas firs before emerging onto steep, grassy slopes. Long traverses lead through the grass, arcing through shady ravines where seasonal streams water fern gardens and bowers of oak and laurel. Pass the junction with the Coastal Trail, which climbs onto the Bolinas Ridge, as well as a couple of side trails to viewpoints.

Road noise from the winding Panoramic Highway encroaches as you near the Pantoll Ranger Station. The Matt Davis Trail crosses the highway at Pantoll, which is outfitted with a ranger station, parking lots, restrooms, and a small campground. Pantoll is also the hub for a number of trails on the mountain, including the Steep Ravine.

Head down through the parking lot to the signed Steep Ravine trailhead. The path dives via switchbacks and short staircases toward the bottom of the Webb Creek gully. While the sharpness of descent mellows in the cradle of the ravine, the wonder escalates. The redwood forest that thrives here, nurtured by heavy fog and the creek, which flows year-round, is top-of-the-list beautiful. Each in its season, an understory of fern, redwood sorrel, trillium, poison oak, thimbleberry, and other moisture- and shade-loving plants blooms along the creek bed and creeps up the walls of the gully. Highlights include a pinch in the trail as it passes between two massive coast redwoods and the ladder that drops alongside a 10-foot waterfall.

▶ Smiley's Schooner Saloon, which calls itself "The Oldest Saloon West of the Mississippi," was established in 1851.

Cross a succession of bridges before the junction with the Dipsea Trail. Here the descent is broken, in devious Dipsea style, by a couple of short, steep climbs. But on the long final approach to Stinson Beach, the Dipsea traverses through fragrant coastal scrub and affords sprawling views of the long arc of Stinson Beach.

The route ends by crossing the Panoramic Highway and then dropping alongside CA 1 on the north boundary of town; it's a quick walk past the fire station and up Belvedere to the trailhead.

Miles and Directions

0.0 From parking at Stinson Beach, walk up Belvedere Avenue to the signed trailhead. Start by crossing the bridge and entering the oak woodland at the base of the Matt Davis Trail.

0.2 At the unsigned trail junction, stay left, dropping across a bridge spanning a seasonal stream.

0.3 Pass a trail and park boundary sign.

0.5 Views open as you pass through scrub.

0.7 Cross a third bridge and climb the sets of stairs switchbacking around Table Rock.

1.5 Switchbacks lead into a forest dominated by Douglas fir.

2.3 Pass from the forest into the grassland.

2.7 At the trail junction, stay right on the Matt Davis Trail. The Coastal Trail to the left climbs onto the Bolinas Ridge.

3.0 At the junction with unmarked side trails, stay on the obvious Matt Davis Trail (signed 1.4 miles to Pantoll).

4.4 Arrive at Pantoll. Carefully cross the Panoramic Highway to the parking lots for the ranger station; there are restrooms, water fountains, picnic tables, and campsites here. Go right, to the lower corner of the lot, to a signed crossroads of trail. The Steep Ravine Trail descends to the right.

5.0 At the base of the switchbacks, the trail parallels Webb Creek and continues to descend through the redwood forest.

5.1 Cross the first of a number of bridges in the Steep Ravine.

5.6 Descend the ladder alongside the waterfall.

6.0 Cross the first in a quick succession of bridges crisscrossing the creek bottom.

6.7 Reach the junction with the Dipsea Trail. Stay right on the Dipsea, passing a pond and a dam as you climb away from the creek.

6.8 At the junction, stay straight on the Dipsea Trail.

Matt Davis and Steep Ravine Loop (Mount Tamalpais State Park)

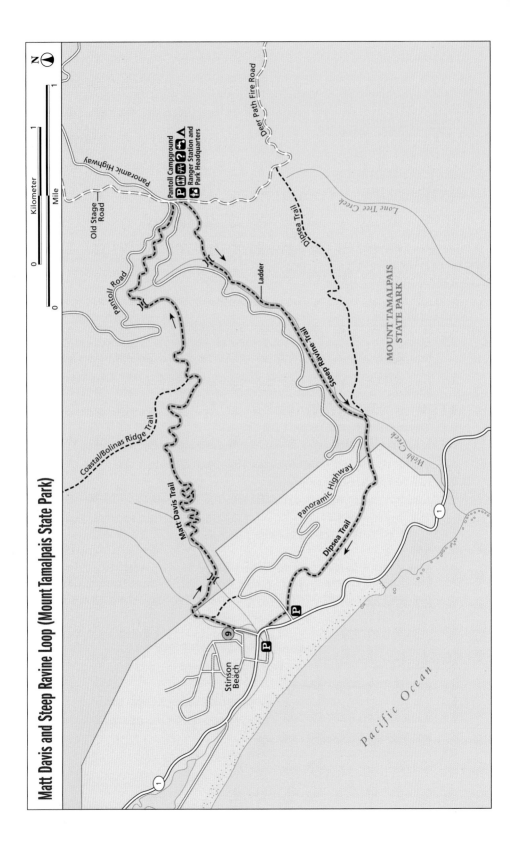

The Dipsea Trail drops a final, spectacular mile to Stinson Beach.

6.9 At the junction, stay left on the signed Dipsea Trail, which begins its long, view-full traverse into Stinson Beach.

8.0 Cross the Panoramic Highway, picking up a signed extension of the Matt Davis Trail on the other side.

8.1 The dirt track ends at CA 1. Turn right and follow the pavement downhill to the fire station and a right turn onto Belvedere.

8.2 Arrive back at the trailhead, then follow Belvedere back to parking lot at Stinson Beach.

Option: If you are visiting Stinson Beach or Bolinas at low tide, drive out across the Bolinas mesa to the coastline at Duxbury Reef and Agate Beach. A short trail leads down to the reef's extensive tide pools and then climbs onto the bluff overlooking Bolinas Bay as it opens onto the Pacific. It's more an exploration than a proper hike, though the bluff-top section does involve climbing a staircase to reach easy hiking on a narrow bluff-top pathway. When you've finished checking out the tide pools, which are part of Duxbury Reef State Marine Conservation Area, a short drive takes you down into eclectic "downtown" Bolinas, with access to Bolinas Beach.

To reach the reef from CA 1 in Olema (the junction of Sir Francis Drake Boulevard and CA 1), turn left onto CA 1 and drive 9 miles south, toward Bolinas and Stinson Beach. Where the road forks at the Bolinas Lagoon, stay right on the unsigned Olema-Bolinas Road into Bolinas. Travel 1.3 miles to the stop sign at Horseshoe Hill Road; stay left (southbound) on the Olema-Bolinas Road. At the junction with Mesa Road, turn right. Go 0.5 mile on Mesa Road to Overlook Drive and turn left. Follow Overlook Drive, passing through the mesa-top neighborhood, for 0.4 mile to Elm Road and turn right. Follow Elm Road for 0.8 mile to its end, going left into the parking area for Agate Beach County Park and Duxbury Reef. GPS: N37 53.799' / W122 42.515'

10 Gravity Car and Old Railroad Grade Loop

A hike on the old rail bed of "The Crookedest Railroad in the World" features panoramic views of the Bay Area from the slopes of Mount Tamalpais.

Start: Trailhead near Mountain Home and Throckmorton Fire Station
Distance: 5.6-mile loop
Hiking time: About 4 hours
Difficulty: Moderate due to length and grade
Trail surface: Dirt, ballast
Best season: Spring and fall. The trail can be used year-round but may be muddy when it rains. Stretches of the grade are exposed to the sun, so it can be hot in summer. Also, the mountain may be swathed in frigid fog, even in summer, so be prepared for changing weather conditions.
Other trail users: Mountain bikers, trail runners
Canine compatibility: Leashed dogs permitted
Land status: Marin Municipal Water District
Fees and permits: None
Schedule: Trails accessible 24 hours a day, 7 days a week, year-round; visitor center on East Peak open weekends 11 a.m. to 4 p.m.; Gravity Car Barn, with its replica gravity car and exhibits, open weekends 11 a.m. to 4 p.m. and staffed by docents
Trailhead amenities: None. Parking is limited and fills quickly on weekends. If you can't find parking in the trailhead lots, park carefully out of traffic lanes along the Panoramic Highway.
Maps: USGS San Rafael; map in park brochure available online at www.parks.ca.gov; online at www.onetam.org/map-and-trails and www.friendsofmttam.org
Trail contact: Mount Tamalpais State Park, 801 Panoramic Hwy., Mill Valley, CA 94941; (415) 388-2070; www.parks.ca.gov/mttamalpais. OneTam/Tamalpais Lands Collaborative; (415) 561-3000; www.onetam.org. Friends of Mt. Tam, PO Box 7064, Corte Madera, CA 94976; (415) 258-2410; www.friendsofmttam.org.

Finding the trailhead: From US 101 in Mill Valley, take the CA 1/Stinson Beach exit. Head west on CA 1, winding about 2.5 miles up through hillside neighborhoods to the intersection with the Panoramic Highway. Turn right (north) on the Panoramic Highway, and climb about 2.6 miles, past the turnoff for Muir Woods National Monument, to the Mountain Home Inn. There is parking in the lot across the street from the inn, in the small lots at the trailhead, and alongside the Panoramic Highway. GPS: N37 54.653' / W122 34.626'

The Hike

On clear days, views from the upper slopes of Mount Tamalpais, Marin County's Sleeping Lady, sweep for miles in every direction—north up the ragged California coastline; east to where the snowcapped Sierra Nevada form a slender, ragged, silvery scribble at the skyline; south over San Francisco Bay and its glittering city; and west across the Pacific Ocean, past the shadowy Farallon Islands to the curving horizon. When sunshine bathes the forested slopes of the peak, a hike on the Gravity Car and Old Railroad Grades offers the perfect opportunity to appreciate these gifts.

Fog rolls back across the lower shoulder of Mount Tamalpais, revealing San Francisco Bay.

When fog envelops the mountain in cold mists and brisk winds, other gifts become apparent. Mount Tam rises from suburbia, but a hiker on a fog-shrouded ridge is virtually alone in viewless wilderness. On these old grades, however, it's impossible to get disoriented, no matter the lack of visibility. Head up and you reach the summit. Head down and you land in Mill Valley. These are venerable routes that have been traveled for more than a hundred years.

At the turn of the twentieth century, the roads were part of the Mill Valley & Mount Tamalpais Scenic Railway Company, which operated "The Crookedest Railroad in the World" on the mountain. Passengers riding the winding line to the summit rounded 281 curves, savored spectacular views, and perhaps took a hike along the rolling crest or relaxed at the mountaintop tavern, then rode the rails back down to Mill Valley. The main line, abandoned in 1930, and the gravity car line, which sped

▶ The historic West Point Inn offers accommodations for hikers and cyclists wishing to spend the night on the mountain. It is operated by the volunteer West Point Inn Association. Contact the inn by writing PO Box 796, San Anselmo, CA 949791; e-mail westpointinnassociation@gmail.com; or visit the website at www.westpointinn.com.

travelers down the mountain in open-air, engine-free conveyances at an impressive 10 to 12 miles per hour, with a "gravity man" on the brakes, are now incorporated into popular hiking and mountain-biking routes.

The Old Railroad Grade makes a steady, 9-mile ascent, a round-trip journey that is arguably too long for a comfortable day hike but is popular with mountain bikers. This route incorporates sections of the Old Railroad Grade and the Gravity Car Grade in a pleasant loop that links Mountain Home, one historic stop on the line, with the West Point Inn, a second historic stop. An option, you can continue up the grade to the summit and visit the Gravity Car shed, as well as loop around East Peak, which boasts stellar views.

Begin the hike at the trailhead for the Gravity Car Grade, wedged between the Mountain Home Inn on the south and the Throckmorton Fire Station on the north.

Old Railroads May Die, but the Grades Remain

Towns in the North Bay were once connected by a thriving network of rail lines operated by a variety of railroad companies; the heyday was the turn of the twentieth century, also the zenith for the Mount Tamalpais Scenic Railway. Among the most unusual: an experimental prismoidal monorail line built in the 1870s, linking San Pablo Bay with Schellville, south of Sonoma. Other roads were more prosaic—narrow-gauge lines that formed practical links between towns and cities in Marin and Sonoma Counties. The Northwestern Pacific Railroad became the "umbrella" railroad in the area, swallowing smaller operators to monopolize the lines linking the bay to Santa Rosa, Monte Rio on the Russian River, and distant Eureka near the Oregon border.

Most of the lines were abandoned as the automobile ascended, and much of the track was torn up and repurposed as part of the war effort in the early 1940s. But some of the old grades have acquired new popularity as rail-trails, from a shoreline run in Tiburon to a popular bike path through the heart of the city of Sonoma.

And passenger rail service using the Northwestern Pacific right-of-way is not dead. As of 2015, work on development of the SMART (Sonoma-Marin Area Rail Transit) rail line progresses. The SMART line will once again link cities and towns within the neighboring counties, offering an alternative commuter route to car-clogged US 101. It won't wind up the slopes of Mount Tamalpais or into the San Geronimo Valley or out to Glen Ellen, but it will ride on the legacy of the golden era of rail travel in the Bay Area.

▶ The Mountain Home, at the base of the Gravity Car Grade, has hosted Tamalpais travelers since 1912, including such luminaries as writer Jack London and members of the Grateful Dead. Once rustic, the inn now operates as an upscale bed-and-breakfast. For more information about the inn, located at 810 Panoramic Hwy. in Mill Valley, call (415) 381-9000 or visit www.mtnhomeinn.com.

The old grade, wide enough for hikers and cyclists to share amicably, winds gently uphill through stands of redwoods that break to offer views across San Francisco Bay. These views, which encompass Mount Diablo on clear days, get only better as you climb. The redwood groves are watered by springs that, even in summer and drought, sustain gardens of fern and moss, as well as the brilliant burst of orange offered by the tiger lily in season.

Just beyond the 1-mile mark, the route negotiates the Double Bow Knot, where the historic railroad grade bends back on itself in tight curves as it gains more than 100 feet in elevation. Less than 0.5 mile beyond, pass the Hoo-Koo-E-Koo Road, which breaks off to the right (northeast); stay left (west) on the obvious railroad grade.

As you climb, the forest gives way to low-growing coastal scrub, thick with the blooms of sticky monkey flower and scotch broom in the spring, dry and silvery in summer and fall. Pass the Hogback Road intersection and climb into the Fern Creek draw, where a spring-fed waterfall tumbles trailside, stunning when augmented by winter rains. Pass the Fern Canyon Trail and the Miller Trail, both tucked in the woods on the right (north) side of the trail, as you ascend.

The climb finishes with views spreading in a half-moon from the Pacific to the East Bay as the route winds through scrub to the West Point Inn. The inn has offered hospitality to mountain visitors since it was built in 1904, its name derived from its location as the westernmost point on the railroad grade. Travelers on the railroad could pick up a stage here that would take them down to Stinson Beach. These days, the inn offers rustic accommodations to mountain visitors and is the perfect setting for hikers and cyclists to stop, rest, and enjoy the spectacular views.

When you are ready to complete the loop, pick up the Nora Trail, which drops down from the picnic area at the front of the inn. The narrow, switchbacking path cruises through several gullies spanned by small bridges as it drops to meet the Matt Davis Trail. Follow the pleasant Matt Davis Trail, well shaded and well graded, down to its junction with the Hogback Fire Road, which leads back down to the Mountain Home and trailhead.

Miles and Directions

0.0 Start at the Gravity Car Grade trailhead, passing the gate and climbing on the obvious former rail bed.

0.2 Pass a side road that breaks left. Stay right on the Gravity Car Grade, passing a sign advising dogs be kept on leashes.

Gravity Car and Old Railroad Grade Loop (Marin Municipal Water District)

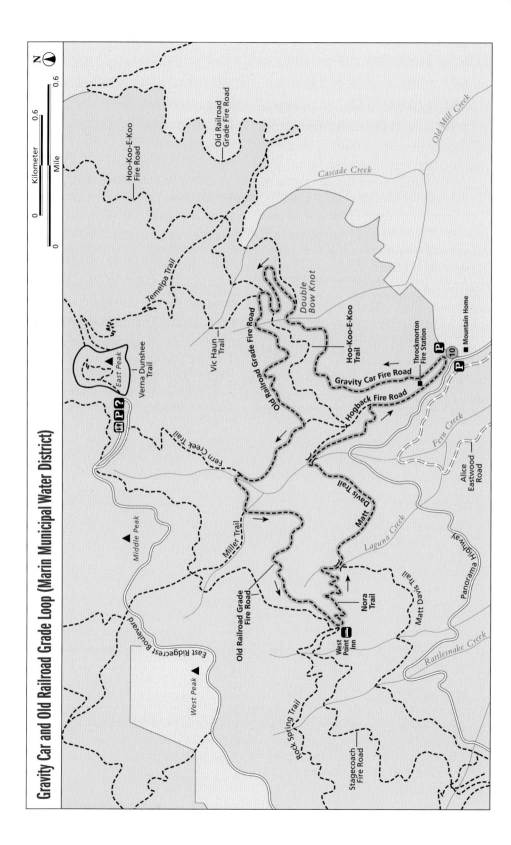

0.7 Pass a spring in a redwood grove.

0.9 Pass a second spring.

1.1 Reach the junction of the Gravity Car Grade and the Old Railroad Grade at the Double Bow Knot. Continue uphill on the Old Railroad Grade.

1.5 At the junction with the Hoo-Koo-E-Koo Fire Road, stay left on the Old Railroad Grade. The junction with the Vic Haun Trail to the East Peak follows shortly; again, stay left on the obvious grade.

2.1 Pass the junction with the Hogback Fire Road. Stay right on the Old Railroad Grade.

2.5 Reach the intersection with the Fern Creek Trail. Stay left on the Old Railroad Grade, passing a 10-foot waterfall in a fern grotto.

2.7 The Miller Trail breaks to the right in a redwood grove. Stay left on the Old Railroad Grade.

3.5 Reach the West Point Inn. Take in the views, then pick up the Nora Trail, which departs from the picnic sites below the inn's decks.

3.8 Cross the first of several small bridges that span ravines as the trail switchbacks down the mountainside.

4.1 Reach the junction with the Matt Davis Trail at the fifth bridge. Go left onto the Matt Davis Trail (a right turn will take you to the Bootjack campground).

4.8 Cross yet another bridge—this one more substantial, with a dam above and a cascade below.

4.9 At the junction with the Hoo-Koo-E-Koo Trail to the Double Bow Knot, stay right (straight) on the Matt Davis Trail toward the Mountain Home.

5.2 At the intersection with the Hogback Fire Road above the water tank, head right down the Hogback roadway.

5.4 Pass through a gate above the Throckmorton Fire Station, then follow the small hogback ridge toward the Panoramic Highway.

5.6 Arrive back at the trailhead.

Options: The top of Mount Tamalpais is a worthwhile goal, with the Verna Dunshee Trail encircling the top of East Peak and offering panoramic views of the Bay Area. To reach the peak, you can continue hiking up the Old Railroad Grade beyond the West Point Inn. Round the switchback, passing behind the inn's cabins, and head east, climbing through wooded ravines that stretch down toward Mill Valley. Another couple miles of easy climbing, during which you will pass the Miller and Tavern Trail junctions, leads to the end of the grade proper on East Ridgecrest Boulevard. Go right (east) on the paved roadway to the summit area parking lot. A visitor center, restrooms, the Gravity Car shed, and the Verna Dunshee trailhead are found here.

A fragment of the railroad is on the west side of East Peak, leading into the Gravity Car shed. The Verna Dunshee Trail, a 0.7-mile paved loop, cruises around the peak, offering dramatic panoramic views of the Bay Area when the weather is clear. An overlook juts out from the mountainside, offering vistas south, beyond the Double Bow Knot, to the greater Bay Area and beyond. A short path also leads to the summit lookout. GPS for East Peak parking area: N37 55.639' / W122 34.797'

11 Redwood Creek to Ridgetop Loop

Linking the deep forest alongside Redwood Creek with ocean views and rolling meadows, this loop is great choice for a hiker who wants to sample all Muir Woods has to offer.

Start: Entrance to Muir Woods National Monument
Distance: 5.1-mile loop
Hiking time: 3–4 hours
Difficulty: Moderate due to climbs
Trail surface: Pavement on interpretive trail, dirt trail, dirt road
Best seasons: Spring and fall
Other trail users: Cyclists on Deer Park Fire Road
Canine compatibility: Dogs not permitted in national monument
Land status: Muir Woods National Monument
Fees and permits: Entrance fee
Schedule: Hours change seasonally; monument opens at 8 a.m. daily and generally closes around sunset.
Trailhead amenities: Information, restrooms, water, gift shop, and cafe. The paved interpretive trail alongside Redwood Creek is wheelchair and stroller accessible.

Maps: USGS San Rafael; Muir Woods National Monument Map available online; Mount Tamalpais State Park map available online at www.parks.ca.gov/?page_id=471
Special considerations: Muir Woods is massively popular, so expect traffic congestion, full parking lots, and crowded trails, especially on weekends. To avoid traffic and parking woes, take the Muir Woods Shuttle (schedule at marin transit.org/routes/66.html). The shuttle runs weekends and holidays from Apr through Oct.

If hiking in the rainy season or after a significant storm, check with rangers to make sure that the bridge over Redwood Creek at the base of the Dipsea Trail is passable.
Trail contact: Muir Woods National Monument, Mill Valley, CA 94941-2696; (415) 388-2595; www.nps.gov/muwo. Golden Gate National Parks Conservancy; (415) 561-3000; www.parksconservancy.org.

Finding the trailhead: To reach Muir Woods from US 101, take the Stinson Beach/CA 1 exit. Follow the frontage road west to the stoplight at CA 1 (also known as the Shoreline Highway). Go left (west) on the highway, which winds through the southernmost reaches of Mill Valley to another stoplight at Tamalpais Junction, the intersection of CA 1 and Almonte, at 0.5 mile. Turn left (west), staying on the Shoreline Highway. The road winds through residential areas for 2.7 miles to its intersection with the Panoramic Highway. CA 1/Shoreline Highway continues straight (west) to Stinson Beach; make a sharp right (north) turn on the Panoramic Highway. Climb the Panoramic Highway for 0.8 mile to its intersection with Muir Woods Road at Four Corners (large signs indicate destinations here). Turn left (west) on Muir Woods Road, dropping steeply to the parking area at 1.5 miles. GPS: N37 53.563' / W122 34.366'

The Hike

Muir Woods National Monument protects a stunning pocket of old-growth redwoods in a steep canyon on the slopes of Mount Tamalpais. These ancient trees escaped the

Ancient sequoias line the trail alongside Redwood Creek in Muir Woods National Monument.

logging frenzy that decimated other redwood forests in the North Bay in the 1800s, spared by seclusion and inaccessibility. The monument is a fitting legacy for the park's namesake, naturalist and wilderness advocate John Muir.

Muir Woods was the gift of a wealthy Marin County resident who aspired to Muir's conservationist ideals. William Kent's legacy includes not only Muir Woods but also neighboring Mount Tamalpais State Park and portions of Marin County's watershed. Thankfully, Kent's vision extended outside this small California county: Kent was among the congressmen who sponsored the bill that established the National Park Service in 1916.

Kent and his wife purchased the land that would become the national monument in 1905 and planned to develop it as a resort, served by a gravity car that spilled off the Mill Valley and Mount Tamalpais Scenic Railway Company's "Crookedest Railroad in the World." But those plans were threatened by a water company that wanted to condemn Redwood Canyon, dam the creek, and bury the old-growth redwoods under a reservoir. To protect the forest, Kent donated the 295 acres he'd purchased for $45,000 to the federal government, and in 1908 President Theodore Roosevelt declared the donation a national monument.

Later, another Roosevelt would be recognized beneath the dark canopy of Muir Woods. Franklin Delano Roosevelt died before the opening conference of the newly chartered United Nations in 1945, but on May 19 of that year, delegates from the UN gathered in Muir Woods to dedicate a plaque honoring his memory.

While the history is fascinating, the undeniable and well-deserved focus of Muir Woods is the coast redwood forest. These woods are part of a complex ecosystem that stretches west from the California shoreline to the eastern reaches of China. The Pacific Ocean, with its cooling winds and nurturing fog, is the fulcrum of the system. *Sequoia sempervirens* thrive on moisture. In most California winters, rainstorms regularly soak the redwood forests that line the north coast. But in summer, the marine influence of the Pacific becomes all-important, as the grand trees are nurtured by dense fog that sweeps in off the ocean almost daily, shrouding them in cooling mist that condenses on the leaves and boughs and falls to the forest floor like rain.

Nourished by the fog and hardy by nature, the trees in Muir Woods reach heights of more than 240 feet and measure as much as 12 feet in diameter. Though their cousins, the giant sequoias, are the largest living things on earth, the coast redwoods grow taller, with the tallest measured at nearly 370 feet. The forest supports a variety of other flora as well, including several varieties of fern, redwood sorrel, trillium, huckleberries, azaleas, miners lettuce, and cow parsnip. Alders grow on the banks of Redwood Creek, and fragrant bay laurel, flowering buckeye, bigleaf maple, and hazelnut also contribute to the abiding shade on the canyon floor.

More than a century after Kent and Muir walked in these woods, hikers clog the interpretive trail alongside Redwood Creek; on summer weekends the paved route is a human highway. You stand a good chance of seeing someone hug a tree—the green spell of the forest invites that. Without doubt you'll see hikers standing open-mouthed with their heads tilted back, staring upward, devices pointed into the canopy.

But climb the steep Ben Johnson Trail onto a ridge overlooking the Pacific, and you'll leave most of the crowds behind. From the ridge, on a clear day, you can look south over the Marin Headlands to San Francisco, and west out across the ocean to the Farallon Islands and beyond.

▶ The Dipsea Trail, famed for its steeps and its stairs, is the venue for an annual footrace from Mill Valley to Stinson Beach. The first Dipsea Race was run in 1905.

Of course, on a foggy day, you aren't going to see much.

The route begins on the Interpretive Nature Trail, quickly passing the Kent Tree, the gift shop and cafe, and restrooms. The trail forks at Bridge 1, which is on the left (west). You can take either fork—the trail loop will reconnect at Bridge 3—but the right-hand path is described here. The trail, lined with benches, interpretive signs, and short fences that keep hikers on track, follows Redwood Creek north. Pass the Founders Grove and the Pinchot Tree, named for Gifford Pinchot, first chief of the USDA Forest Service, then the junction with the Ocean View Trail and, at about 0.3 mile, Bridge 2. If you are on the left side, you'll pass the Bicentennial Tree and Bohemian Grove before reaching Bridge 2.

The trail splits and rejoins in Cathedral Grove, then passes over a boardwalk that ends near the Fern Creek Trail intersection at 0.8 mile. Remain on the paved route, passing the trail to Camp Alice Eastwood on the right.

At about the 1-mile mark, reach the end of the nature trail at Bridge 4. Cross the bridge and climb a short flight of stairs onto the Ben Johnson Trail (the Hillside Trail branches left if you want a shorter hike). The Ben Johnson Trail climbs moderately and relentlessly out of Redwood Canyon. Oaks, bays, and madrones mingle with the redwoods as you gain altitude. The steep path is augmented with short staircases of log and rock and is edged by redwoods whose exposed roots have been polished by hikers' boots. A series of footbridges span seasonal streams, and the trail passes beneath a fallen giant.

Just as you begin to think the climb will never end, the spur to the Dipsea Trail intersects on the left (the Stapelveldt Trail continues straight, passing into Mount Tamalpais State Park and on to the Pantoll Ranger Station). Turn left (south) on the spur trail, and climb a thigh-throbbing set of stairs and switchbacks to the ridgetop and the intersection with the Deer Park Fire Road.

▶ Alice Eastwood, whose name appears on several trails described in this guidebook, was a self-taught botanist and longtime curator of the botany collections in the California Academy of Sciences.

While the better-known Dipsea Trail parallels the fire road on its southwest side (and intersects the road a number of times on the descent), the broader dirt track, part of the Bay Area Ridge Trail, is a fine walk-and-talk choice. It's also lovely, shaded by mingled oaks, redwoods, and firs.

The road makes a roller-coaster run along the ridgetop, then drops into an open area with dramatic ocean views that sweep south to Lands End and west across the steep ridges to the ocean. As you descend through alternating clearings and forest, views open south and east as well, across the bay to Angel Island, the Bay Bridge, and the distant hills of the East Bay. Fragrant coastal scrub now dominates, wildflowers mingled with the grasses and coyote brush in spring.

Farther along, the Dipsea Trail begins to loop back and forth across the broader track. You can skip off onto the trail to vary the descent, tunneling through bowers of brush and negotiating uneven singletrack, or remain on the fire road. Keep an eye out for the trail sign at the 4.5-mile mark, where the Dipsea breaks off to the left and descends back into Muir Woods. If you stay on the fire road at this point, you will continue southeast to the Muir Woods Road.

The Dipsea drops as earnestly as the Ben Johnson climbed, with stairs and roots demanding concentration. The undergrowth is a complex of fern and poison oak, with oaks and bay laurels arching overhead. The descent is relatively short, however, dropping 0.5 mile to the Redwood Creek crossing, with the overflow parking area for the national monument just beyond. A plank footbridge spans the creek easily in summer, when the water is down, but when the creek is swollen with winter rain, the crossing is at best challenging and at worst (though relatively infrequently) impossible.

Redwood Creek to Ridgetop Loop (Muir Woods National Monument)

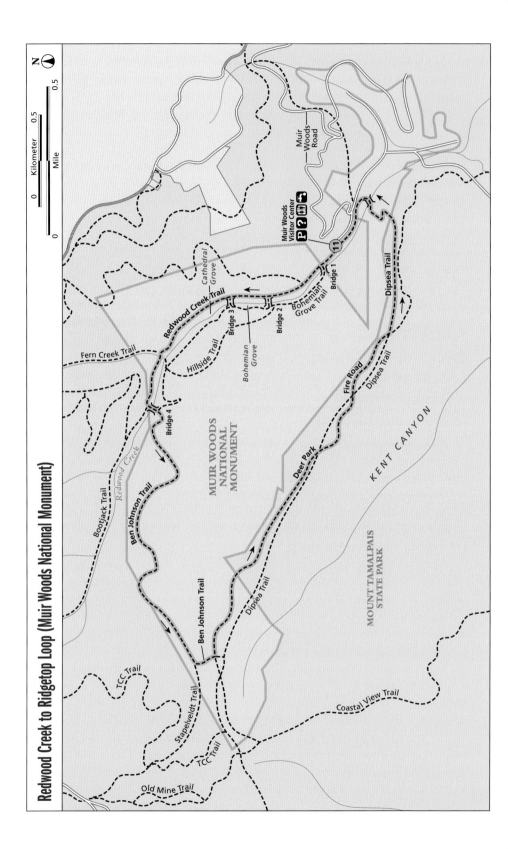

Check with the rangers to make sure passage is safe if you are traveling this route in the rainy season.

A short flight of stairs leads up to the overflow parking lot. If you've parked near the trailhead, turn left (north) on the paved path to return to the visitor center.

Miles and Directions

0.0 Start on the paved interpretive trail, following the pavement up the right-hand side of Redwood Creek.

0.2 Pass the Founders Grove.

0.5 Reach Cathedral Grove.

0.8 At the junction with the Fern Creek Trail, stay left on the paved trail.

0.9 Pass the trail to Camp Alice Eastwood and stay left to Bridge 4.

1.0 Reach the junction with the Ben Johnson and Bootjack Trails at Bridge 4. Cross the bridge and head up on the Ben Johnson Trail. About 200 feet beyond, pass the junction with the Hillside Trail, staying right on the Ben Johnson Trail.

1.5 Cross a seasonal stream via a split-log bridge, then a second, more vigorous stream via another bridge.

2.5 Reach the junction with the spur trail to the Dipsea.

3.0 Arrive at the junction with the Dipsea Trail and the Deer Park Fire Road. Turn left to follow the fire road.

3.4 Views open across the Pacific and the mouth of the Golden Gate. As the trail continues, vistas encompass San Francisco Bay as well.

3.9 The Dipsea crosses the fire road for the first time. Four more intersections follow at intervals of 0.1 mile or less.

4.5 The Dipsea Trail breaks off the Deer Park Fire Road to the left, with a sign directing hikers down toward Muir Woods. Stay left on the Dipsea and head steeply downhill.

5.0 Cross the bridge over Redwood Creek, then climb a short flight of steps to the parking area. Turn left to follow the paved path back toward the main entrance.

5.1 Arrive back at the trailhead.

12 Hill 88 and Rodeo Lagoon

This long route in the Marin Headlands serves up an intriguing mix of grand views, challenging terrain, and twentieth-century military installations to explore.

Start: Trailhead in Fort Cronkhite
Distance: 6.6-mile loop
Hiking time: 3-4 hours
Difficulty: Strenuous
Trail surface: Pavement, dirt road, dirt trail, sand
Best season: Spring and fall
Other trail users: Mountain bikers, trail runners
Canine compatibility: Dogs must either be leashed or under voice control. In some areas pets are prohibited entirely to protect sensitive resources. Dog droppings must be picked up. Contact Golden Gate National Recreation Area for the most current pet regulations.
Land status: Golden Gate National Recreation Area (GGNRA)
Fees and permits: None
Schedule: Sunrise to sunset daily

Trailhead amenities: Restrooms, water, picnic sites
Maps: USGS Point Bonita; GGNRA map available online at www.nps.gov/goga/planyour visit/upload/map-mahe-140402-2.pdf
Special considerations: The Coastal Trail is subject to erosion and the National Park Service reroutes the trail as necessary. Watch for clearly marked detours. Be careful on cliffs and at the beach; staying on the trail will keep you free of eroding cliff edges and sneaker waves.
Trail contact: Golden Gate National Recreation Area, Fort Mason, Building 201, San Francisco, CA 94123-0022; (415) 561-4700; nps.gov/ goga. The Marin Headlands Visitor Center is in the Fort Barry Chapel at the intersection of Field and Bunker Roads near Rodeo Lagoon; (415) 331-1540; open daily 9:30 a.m. to 4:30 p.m.

Finding the trailhead: From San Francisco, head north on CA 1 or US 101 to the Golden Gate Bridge. Immediately after crossing the bridge, take the Alexander Avenue exit. Turn left at the first stop, go under the freeway, and then turn right onto Conzelman Road, following the signs for the GGNRA and Marin Headlands. (If you are headed southbound on US 101, take the Alexander Avenue/Sausalito exit, the last exit before the Golden Gate Bridge, and turn left, then quickly right onto Conzelman Road.) After climbing steeply into the headlands for 1.5 miles—the views are spectacular—turn right onto McCullough Road and head downhill, away from the ocean. Turn left onto Bunker Road, and drive past Field Road, the Marin Headlands Visitor Center, and Rodeo Lagoon to the end of the road at Fort Cronkhite, where you'll find a large parking lot and the trailhead. GPS: N37 49.937' / W122 32.336'

If you want to take public transportation from San Francisco, Bus 76X of the San Francisco Municipal Railway (Muni) runs to Fort Cronkhite on Sat and Sun and some holidays. Contact Muni for schedules, fares, and accessibility at sfmta.com or tripplanner.transit.511.org.

The Hike

What makes the Marin Headlands so appealing to hikers also made them appealing to the military. When the fog is out, views across the Pacific are endless and unimpeded, perfect for watching a sunset or for scouting the approach of enemy ships.

A walk along Rodeo Beach is a nice way to end the climb up Hill 88.

The shoreline is mined with rocks and endlessly slapped by dangerous surf, rendering it both inaccessible and ruggedly lovely. And the slopes are so challenging that only clever trail-building has rendered them manageable on foot; an enemy fighter would have battled harsh inclines and biting brambles to approach any of the military emplacements above.

This long loop-plus-spur through the headlands links the natural world with the military. At waypoints along the loop, which combines four trails—the Coastal Trail, the Wolf Ridge Trail, the Miwok Trail, and a portion of the Lagoon Trail—you can check out World War II–era batteries and radio installations, fabulous views, and raptors soaring on currents rising from the coastal valleys.

Start by climbing away from Fort Cronkhite, busy with surfers and picnickers, on the paved Coastal Trail. The Tennessee Point Trail leads to an overlook on the point, passing through the fragrant mix of sage, coyote bush, sticky monkey flower, and poison oak that composes coastal scrub, punctuated in season with blooms of lupine, blue dick, iris, and brilliant California poppies. The trail ends on a bluff top, from which

▶ The Marine Mammal Center, located in Fort Cronkhite, rescues and rehabilitates ill, injured, and abandoned marine mammals. More than 20,000 seals, sea lions, otters, whales, dolphins, and other marine mammals have been treated at the center since 1975. A nonprofit organization, the center depends upon memberships, donations, and volunteers. It is open daily from 10 a.m. to 5 p.m.; closed Thanksgiving, Christmas, and New Year's Day. Admission is free. For more information, visit marinemammalcenter.org or call (415) 289-7325.

The Military Legacy

As a guidebook writer, I spend a lot of time alone on the trail, which gives me ample opportunity to muse. Most of the time I think about the beauty of the wilderness around me, or about family and friends, or I just daydream. Every outing, even on trails I revisit, is unique in the nature of my contemplation.

The hike to Hill 88 on the headlands is a favorite, and I've spilled many thoughts along these lovely, wide-open paths. Most profoundly, I happened to hike this route just after the terrorist attacks of 9/11. It seems so long ago now. The contrast was striking: On my most recent hike, in 2015, I noted my envy of the raptors circling on the upcurrents from the valleys below. But back then, instead of using trail intersections or viewpoints as landmarks, I gauged my progress by the derelict remnants of America's wars.

When I wrote about this hike in 2002, I described standing amid the weather-beaten military installations atop Hill 88, their hospital-green paint peeling away and stained with rust. I had a hard time focusing on the spectacular views or the raptors surfing the wind currents. Instead, I was struck by how much we had invested in the tools of warfare, and how quickly those investments—from hand axes to cannons to chemical and biological weapons to nuclear warheads—had become obsolete.

The ruins of war dating back centuries are scattered throughout the Golden Gate National Recreation Area, stacked atop each other—clunky, crumbling reminders of the white elephant humankind has nurtured for thousands of years. Our military legacy is built sturdily into these hills facing the sea. Now protected by law, now enlivened by graffiti, it does not fail to provoke.

you can look west out over the Pacific and south past Rodeo Cove, with the Point Bonita Lighthouse white and bright on its rocky perch. The casemated gun platforms of Battery Townsley are carved into the hillside above the trail, and small sea stacks are pummeled by the surf along the coast below.

Retrace your steps back to the paved Coastal Trail and climb to Battery Townsley, where social trails invite exploration of the fortification. The concrete gun emplacements here were built during World War II; a tunnel leads out to gun emplacement #1, with impressive views.

▶ In their last incarnation, the fortifications at the Marin Headlands were outfitted for the Cold War. At the Nike Missile Site in the Rodeo Valley, artifacts of the nuclear age are preserved and, more spectacularly, on display. You can tour the facility, which is open to the public on a limited basis. Visit nps.gov/goga for more information.

Beyond the battery the Coastal Trail abandons the pavement for twisting single-track pathways and staircases. The route is well marked but subject to change, as erosion may force rerouting. And the views continue to be stellar; be sure to turn around on occasion to look down into the Rodeo Valley and south along the coastline.

As you approach the crest of Wolf Ridge, you'll travel on pavement again and meet the Wolf Ridge Trail. To make the final grunt to the top of Hill 88, take the paved roadway to the right, climbing through a colonnade of rusty fence topped with barbed wire. The trail ends on a flat hilltop amid a cluster of Cold War–era radar installations used to guide the Nike missiles that could be launched from Site 88 in the Rodeo Valley.

Views from all points on the flat-topped hill are spectacular, sweeping from Mount Tamalpais out to the glittering Pacific, south to the Golden Gate, and east past sparkling San Francisco and across the bay. The installations were colorful with graffiti in 2014; the park may remedy this someday, returning the buildings to the hospital green of earlier years or to some other color. Birds catch the wind currents rising from the valleys and ravines: turkey vultures, gulls, and a variety of raptors. Hawk Hill, also known as Battery 129, is nearby, where birders gather in flocks during spring and fall migrations to count and observe those raptors.

From Hill 88 retrace your steps to the Wolf Ridge Trail, which descends steeply into a cooler, moister, shadier microclimate. This section of trail is steep but boasts views down onto the Tennessee Valley Trail and, farther off, the houses of Mill Valley scattered across the hillsides. Mount Tamalpais, the Sleeping Lady, dominates the skyline.

The Wolf Ridge Trail meets the Miwok Trail in a saddle; continue to descend toward Rodeo Valley via the Miwok Trail. The route is straightforward and shadeless, passing through sun-soaked coyote brush and sage, and the broad track is easily shared with the mountain bikers who frequent it. The Gerbode Valley opens below and to the left; in the mid-1960s, a huge residential community was planned for the area, but fortunately saner minds prevailed.

▶ Rodeo Beach and Lagoon are renewed annually. In winter, powerful waves cross the beach and enter the lagoon, mixing salt water with freshwater cascading down the hillsides of the headlands and creating ideal habitat for salt-tolerant plants and animals. As the waves mellow in spring, they leave behind enough sand to reestablish the beach, re-creating the separation between lagoon and ocean.

Views open cross Rodeo Lagoon as the trail nears the top of Hill 88.

The trail drops in the bottomlands at the mouth of the Gerbode Valley. The bright green, wind-whipped reeds and sedges of the Rodeo Lagoon marsh border the route, and the sounds of traffic on Bunker Road encroach. The final leg of the trail takes you along the southern shoreline of Rodeo Lagoon, which ripples in an incessant ocean breeze and fosters an abundance of wildlife, from egrets to salamanders, and the rare brown pelican, which has made a comeback from endangered status. The trail deposits you onto Rodeo Beach, where families and surfers play. Cross the beach to close the loop at the trailhead.

Miles and Directions

0.0 Start at the western end of the parking lot at Fort Cronkhite. Pass through a gate and onto the old asphalt road. At the sign, turn left onto the Coastal Trail (signed "Hikers Route; Tennessee Point Trail" on the GGNRA map), which climbs onto the hillside. You'll double back on this trail to take the right-hand trail/road (signed "Bikers Route; Coastal Trail") to reach Battery Townsley and beyond.

0.7 Pass through a gate.

0.8 Pass through a bower of Monterey pine to a large overlook on the flat-topped bluff of Tennessee Point. When you've taken in the views, return as you came to the junction with the Coastal Trail. The social trails that lead up into the hills toward Battery Townsley may be tempting, but they are not maintained, and using them damages habitat.

Hill 88 and Rodeo Lagoon (Golden Gate National Recreation Area)

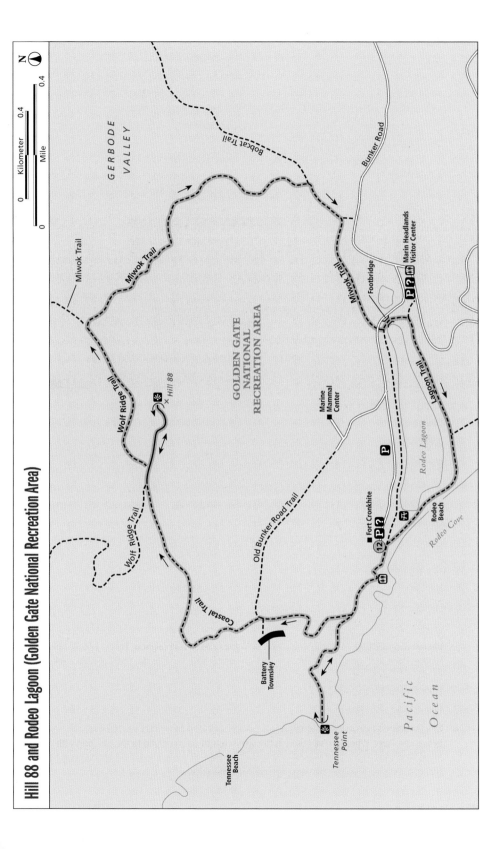

1.4   Back at the junction, turn left onto the paved Coastal Trail.

1.9   Reach Battery Townsley. To explore the site, walk through the tunnel out to the emplacement for gun #1, a massive hollow in the hillside with unimpeded views of the approach to the Golden Gate. Backtrack to the Coastal Trail and continue to climb.

2.0   At the junction with Old Bunker Road, which drops down to the Marine Mammal Center, stay left on the Coastal Trail.

2.1   Pass through a saddle. Follow the paved road uphill to the right to the next sign for the Coastal Trail.

2.2   Take the Coastal Trail (a set of stairs) up and to the left. Do not follow the road; a landslide has taken it out a few curves ahead.

2.4   Reach the top of the staircase and continue to the right on the signed Coastal Trail. At the next junction, with a barrier, stay right on the signed, paved Coastal Trail.

2.9   On the crest of the ridge, pass the Wolf Ridge Trail sign (on the left), which you will return to after you've gone to the top of Hill 88. Follow the paved road uphill to the right, toward the gate.

3.2   Arrive on the summit of Hill 88. Check out the views and fortifications, then retrace your steps to the Wolf Ridge Trail. Turn right and begin descending the dirt Wolf Ridge Trail, which circles around the backside of Hill 88.

4.2   At the bottom of the steep descent, the trail levels out, briefly climbs, then makes a short descent to the signed junction with the Miwok Trail. Turn right onto the Miwok Trail and continue to descend.

5.3   At the junction with the Bobcat Trail, which leads into Gerbode Valley, stay right on the Miwok Trail. Pass a marshy area on the left; the trail ends beside an old warehouse on Bunker Road.

5.8   Cross Bunker Road and turn left, following the trail to the far (south) side of Rodeo Lagoon.

5.9   At the junction of the Coastal and Lagoon Trails, turn right and head down the stairs on the Lagoon Trail. Cross the footbridge, then head up a second flight of stairs below the visitor center. Go right to stay on the Lagoon Trail.

6.2   Reach Rodeo Beach. Go right through the sand toward Fort Cronkhite and the parking area.

6.6   Arrive back at the trailhead.

13 Point Bonita Lighthouse

The scenic drama of California's coastline, along with facets of San Francisco's gold rush–era history, is concentrated on the short hike to the lighthouse on Point Bonita.

Start: Lighthouse parking area at end of Field Road
Distance: 1.0 mile out and back
Hiking time: About 1 hour
Difficulty: Easy
Trail surface: Pavement
Best season: Year-round provided the weather is calm (and preferably sunny)
Other trail users: None
Canine compatibility: Dogs not permitted
Land status: Golden Gate National Recreation Area (GGNRA)
Fees and permits: None
Schedule: Access to lighthouse is on Sat, Sun, and Mon only, 12:30 to 3:30 p.m. On weekends docents lead interpretive hikes to the lighthouse; they also limit the number of visitors that can enter the tunnel and cross the bridge to ensure visitors' safety.
Trailhead amenities: Restrooms, shuttle stop, information signboard. There is limited parking at the trailhead, with more available at Battery Mendell, 0.1 mile west on Field Road.
Maps: USGS Point Bonita; GGNRA map available online at www.nps.gov/goga/planyourvisit/upload/map-mahe-140402-2.pdf
Trail contact: Golden Gate National Recreation Area, Marin Headlands Visitor Center, Fort Barry, Building 948, Sausalito, CA 94965; (415) 331-1540; www.nps.gov/goga/pobo.htm

Finding the trailhead: From US 101 on the north side of the Golden Gate Bridge, take the Alexander Avenue/Sausalito exit (the last exit before you get onto the bridge if headed southbound; the first as you leave the bridge if headed northbound). Follow Alexander Avenue for 0.2 mile to Bunker Road. Turn left onto Bunker Road and go about 3 miles, through the one-way tunnel, to the junction with Field Road. Turn left onto Field Road, and go 0.8 mile to the signed parking area and trailhead. Alternatively, you can follow scenic Conzelman Road to the lighthouse; beyond Hawk Hill, Conzelman Road is one way headed downhill, one of the loveliest and most exposed short stretches of roadway in the Bay Area. GPS: N37 49.322' / W122 31.758'

The Hike

White and red and a vast glittering blue: Where the Marin Headlands drop into the Pacific, the white walls and red roofs of the Point Bonita Lighthouse stand watch. On a calm, sunny day, the turbulence of the surf roiling against the rocky foundation of the lighthouse only hints at the ferocity that can batter these rugged bluffs, and at the treacherous currents and unpredictable tides that have sent an armada to deep green graves.

The lighthouse, built in the middle of the nineteenth century, is an outpost of peacetime on a landscape otherwise built up with houses of war. The trail that leads down to the light begins on a bluff dotted with bunkers that, during World War II, were used by sentinels watching for foreign invaders. The hard architecture of Battery

A suspension bridge connects the Point Bonita Lighthouse to the mainland.

Mendell hulks in the hillside just to the north, and radio towers used by the Marines rise from the lighthouse's original site. But the light itself, relocated to the very tip of Point Bonita in 1877, reflects only humankind's desire to assuage the natural dangers of a rugged coastline.

One of three lighthouses erected to help guide a flood of ships through the Golden Gate during the gold rush, the Point Bonita light is still operational, radiating a powerful beacon through a Fresnel lens that penetrates as far as 23 miles out to sea. The light is augmented by a foghorn, which in its earliest incarnation was a cannon and is now electric. While the system of lights and horns has guided countless vessels safely to harbor, the tankers, cargo ships, tugboats, tour boats, and pleasure craft that now share the crowded waters at the mouth of San Francisco Bay glide over the wrecks of hundreds of wooden ships that went down before—and after—the light's installation in 1855.

A steep paved interpretive trail leads 0.5 mile down to the lighthouse, which is open to the public on a limited basis. The trail begins on a hill topped with bunkers

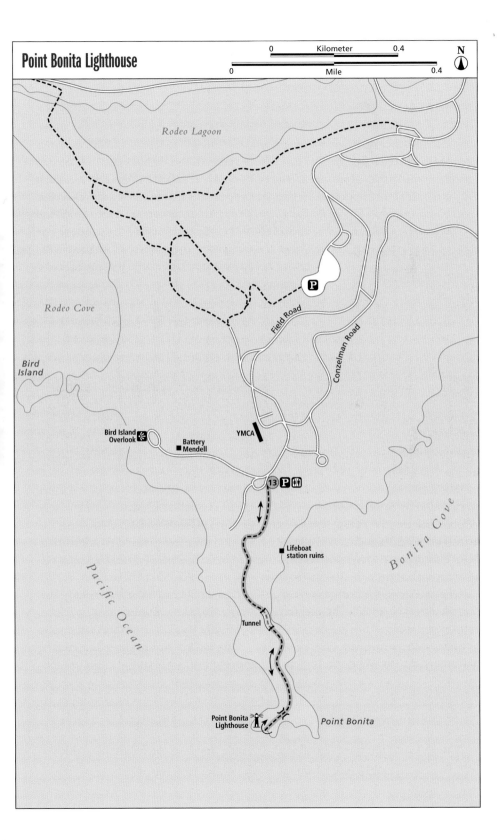

Point Bonita Lighthouse

0 Kilometer 0.4
0 Mile 0.4

N

Rodeo Lagoon

P

Field Road

Conzelman Road

Rodeo Cove

Bird Island

Bird Island Overlook

Battery Mendell

YMCA

13 P

Lifeboat station ruins

Bonita Cove

Pacific Ocean

Tunnel

Point Bonita Lighthouse

Point Bonita

but descends swiftly into a more natural world, with the steep scrubby hillsides below the trail dropping sharply into the cove below.

The trail swings south at a sharp curve at about 0.1 mile and passes beneath the radar towers. Monterey pines sink into the gulch that drops into the cove below. The path drops to a bridge that spans a saddle; here the wind whips through a break in the rock wall that shelters the trail on its west side. Through the break you can look out onto the rocky coastline; on the left, the remnants of the Point Bonita Life-Saving Station—sun-bleaching pilings—stretch into the water. The boathouse, from which "surfmen" went out to rescue shipwrecked sailors, was destroyed by a landslide, but you can still see the marine railroad tracks used to get the rescue boats in and out of the waters of the cove.

▶ The first lighthouse for the Golden Gate was built on Alcatraz Island in 1854.

The trail continues to the historic hand-hewn tunnel; orange lichen stains the cliffs that frame the opening. As you approach, check out the gardens growing on the cliffs to your right: Cabbage, fennel, sage, and other herbs were grown by the lighthouse keepers on these rocky slopes, and their feral descendants can still be seen. Chinese immigrants carved the 118-foot-long tunnel from the rock in 1876; before it was built, a narrow walkway led around the east side of the sheer rock face.

Beyond the tunnel the trail crosses another gap and the lighthouse comes into view. Pass an outbuilding and cross another bridge before you arrive at the broad viewpoint—the exposed foundation of the light-keeper's residence. From here, a whitewashed suspension bridge spans a break in the cliff to the lighthouse itself. This reinforced reconstruction of the original bridge was completed 2012, replacing the bridge that was built in 1955 after the land bridge linking the light to the mainland collapsed. It's no place for those with a fear of heights: Suspended over jagged rocks and a thrashing surf, the span shimmies in the incessant wind and under the weight of those treading its narrow walkway. But it's also a great thrill. Before you cross the bridge (or after, depending on your agenda), check out the views of the Golden Gate Bridge to the east. Views north up the rugged coast are also spectacular, and if the weather is clear, you'll be able to look out west to the Farallon Islands.

The trail—and the continent—end at the squat lighthouse. More light than house, the cylindrical building holds interpretive displays, including nautical maps and charts and a description of the Fresnel lens. Views from the lighthouse are much the same as those at the viewpoint on the east end of the suspension bridge. Once you've explored, return as you came.

Miles and Directions

- **0.0** Start on the signed paved trail.
- **0.3** Pass through the hand-carved tunnel.
- **0.5** Reach the lighthouse. Explore, then return as you came.
- **1.0** Arrive back at the trailhead.

San Francisco

Battery Crosby, the strait of the Golden Gate, and the Marin Headlands from the Coastal Trail

14 Mount Livermore

The top of Mount Livermore, the highest point on Angel Island, commands unimpeded panoramic views of San Francisco Bay. Called the "Ellis Island of the West Coast," Angel Island's historical roots date back to Spanish colonial times.

Start: Ferry terminal in Ayala Cove
Distance: 5.4-mile loop
Hiking time: 3–4 hours
Difficulty: Moderate due to distance and a steep pitch to summit
Trail surface: Pavement, dirt service road, dirt trail
Best season: Year-round, weather permitting
Other trail users: Cyclists on Perimeter Road and Fire Road
Canine compatibility: No dogs allowed
Land status: Angel Island State Park
Fees and permits: You must purchase a ferry ticket to reach the island.

Schedule: Day hikers must adhere to the ferry schedules, but those camping on the island can access the trails 24 hours a day, every day.
Trailhead amenities: Restrooms, picnic sites, water, trash cans, cafe, bike rentals, tram tours, information at visitor center
Maps: USGS San Francisco North; trail map in park brochure available at visitor center or online at www.parks.ca.gov/pages/468/files/angelisland2.pdf
Trail contact: Angel Island State Park, PO Box 318, Tiburon, CA 94920; (415) 435-1915; www.parks.ca.gov/?page_id=468. The Angel Island Conservancy works in tandem with the state parks department; the website is angelisland.org.

Finding the trailhead: Ferry service to Angel Island is available from San Francisco via the Blue and Gold Fleet, departing from Pier 41 near Fisherman's Wharf and from the Ferry Building near downtown. For schedules and fares, call (415) 705-8200 or visit www.blueandgoldfleet.com/ferry/angel-island. Ferry service is also available from Tiburon in Marin County via the Angel Island-Tiburon Ferry, which departs from the Tiburon Ferry Terminal in downtown Tiburon. For schedules and fares, call (415) 435-2131 or (415) 435-1531, or visit www.angelislandferry.com. GPS: N37 52.103' / W122 26.086'

The Hike

The largest island in San Francisco Bay was destined to loom large in the region's history. A climb to the top of Mount Livermore, the island's high point, offers bird's-eye views of the remnants of the military, quarantine, and immigration facilities located on the island's perimeter, as well as vistas across the bay in every direction as far as the eye can see, especially when the fog is out.

Located just across the Raccoon Strait from the mainland of what is now Marin County, the island served as hunting and fishing grounds for the Coast Miwok Indians; while there may not have been permanent settlements, the island stretched the natives' ability to harvest the bounty of the bay. Ayala Cove is named for Spanish

The Sunset Trail offers views across the bay to the Golden Gate.

explorer Juan Manuel de Ayala, who anchored his ship, the *San Carlos*, in the sheltering cove on an expedition to map the newly "discovered" San Francisco Bay.

The island's identity as a military outpost began in the Civil War era. Batteries were built around the island to defend against the potential rebel threat. After that war ended, the army post on the island, known as Camp Reynolds, was used as a staging area for soldiers headed to the Indian Wars.

As military operations on the island expanded and changed, so did its facilities. Fort McDowell served as a recruitment depot starting in World War I and, when that conflict ended, as a discharge depot. During World War II, the island's military installations facilitated the embarkation of 300,000 soldiers bound for the Pacific Theater, according to park literature. During the Cold War, a Nike missile site was established on the island.

▶ Chinese immigrants awaiting entry painted or carved poems in the walls of Angel Island's immigration station that are still visible today. The station is now a museum, open daily from 11 a.m. to 3 p.m. Tours are available.

From the late nineteenth century into the 1940s, a quarantine station operated in Ayala Cove, then called Hospital Cove. Ships and passengers arriving in San Francisco from overseas were screened for communicable, and often deadly, diseases such as smallpox. If contagion was detected, the patients were isolated in one of the forty buildings that cluttered the hills surrounding the cove.

Angel Island's most controversial claim to historical fame is its immigration station, where hundreds of thousands of hopeful travelers were processed in the early twentieth century. The immigration station also enabled enforcement of the Chinese

Looking north across Raccoon Strait to Mount Tamalpais from Mount Livermore on Angel Island

Exclusion Act of 1882, discriminatory legislation intended to stop the inflow of Chinese immigrants. Never mind Chinese contributions to culture, industry, and commerce in San Francisco and beyond: Not a single railroad mogul, banking baron, or construction tycoon could have achieved his goals without them. But the Chinese—and others, a large number from Asia—were no longer wanted, and Angel Island was where they were held up, some detained in barracks on the island for months. While deportation was always an option, the majority were eventually allowed to enter the country. The immigration station is now a National Historic Landmark and museum.

A climb to the summit of Mount Livermore, which allows glimpses of what remains of the immigration station and some of the military sites, begins in Ayala

Mount Livermore (Angel Island State Park)

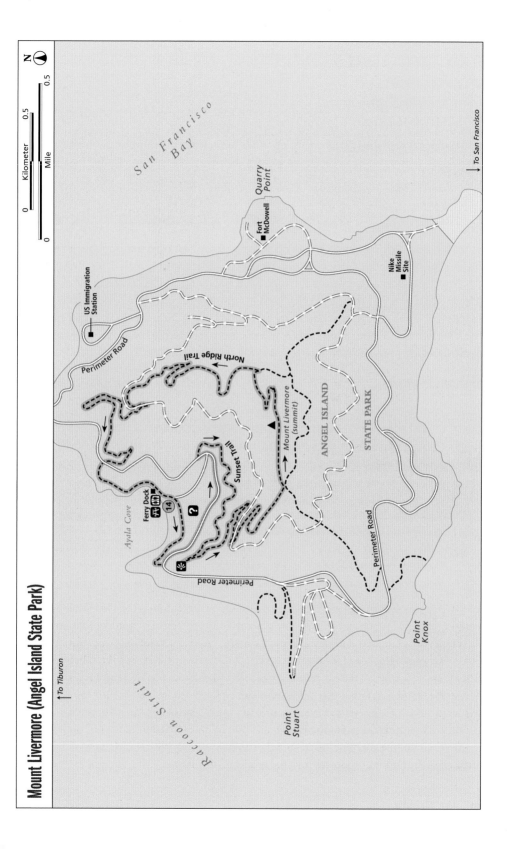

Cove, passing the visitor center before climbing up onto the paved Perimeter Road. A brief jog on the pavement leads to the Sunset Trail, which climbs easily and offers great views west of Mount Tamalpais and the Golden Gate Bridge.

As the route approaches the summit, it sweeps onto the island's south face, with the city skyline and Bay Bridge dominating the viewscape. The bay's two other prominent islands, Alcatraz and Treasure, are also visible. A final steep pitch leads to the summit, from which, on a clear day, you can see south to Mount Diablo and beyond, and north to Mount Saint Helena and beyond. You can also watch all the activity in the bay: sailboats flying with the wind, ferries rumbling to and fro, freighters lumbering into port, fishing boats heading out toward the gate.

The descent follows the North Ridge Trail, which again offers sweeping views of Mount Tamalpais and the North Bay before it plunges into the oak woodlands that shade the island's east slopes. Breaks in the canopy allow hikers to look down onto the whitewashed buildings of the US Immigration Station. The trail then curls into Ayala Cove, dropping down steps to end at the ferry terminal.

Miles and Directions

0.0 From the ferry, follow the paved road to the visitor center.

0.2 Climb stairs onto the paved service road and go right, past the medical officers' housing.

0.4 Following signs to the Perimeter Road, head up a gravel service road, past a utility station.

0.5 Reach the Perimeter Road at the top of the steps. Go left on the Perimeter Road.

1.0 At the signed junction, go right on the dirt Sunset Trail.

1.7 From an overlook at a switchback, enjoy great panoramic views that swing from the Golden Gate past Sausalito, across the Raccoon Strait to Tiburon and Mount Tamalpais, and north to the Richmond–San Rafael Bridge.

2.2 Arrive at the junction with the Fire Road. Go right on the Fire Road for about 100 yards to the junction with the signed trail to Mount Livermore.

2.7 At the unsigned trail junction, head up and left toward the summit. This is the steepest part of the ascent. The last stretch is a bit of a bushwhack, with social trails lacing through coyote bush, but the destination is always in sight.

2.9 Reach the summit. Take in the views from a bench, picnic table, or concrete slab (remnants of military facilities on the summit), then pick up the North Ridge Trail, which descends off the east side of the mountain.

3.3 At the junction with the Sunset Trail, switchback to the left to stay on the North Ridge Trail. Fort McDowell (East Garrison) is visible below.

4.4 At the junction with the Fire Road, go left on the roadway for about 25 yards. The signed continuation of the trail is on the right.

5.2 Cross the Perimeter Road, and take on the staircase that drops toward Ayala Cove.

5.4 Arrive back at the trailhead at the ferry terminal.

15 Batteries to Bluffs and the Golden Gate Bridge

The bluffs overlooking the strait of the Golden Gate are studded with military installations built between the Civil War and the Cold War. This trail links the batteries to the Golden Gate Bridge and a beach tucked at the base of windswept cliffs composed of serpentine rock.

Start: Battery Chamberlin on Baker Beach

Distance: 4.1-miles out and back with linking loops

Hiking time: 2–3 hours

Difficulty: Moderate due to stairs leading to and from Marshall Beach

Trail surface: Dirt, sand, pavement

Best season: Year-round

Other trail users: Cyclists (except on stretch to and from Marshall Beach), trail runners

Canine compatibility: Dogs must either be leashed or under voice control, depending on where you are walking in Golden Gate National Recreation Area (GGNRA). In some areas, pets are prohibited entirely to protect sensitive resources. Dog droppings must be picked up. Contact GGNRA headquarters at Fort Mason for the most current pet regulations. Given the crowds around the Golden Gate Bridge, bringing your dog along is not recommended.

Land status: Presidio of San Francisco

Fees and permits: None

Schedule: Sunrise to sunset daily

Trailhead amenities: Restrooms, trash cans

Maps: USGS San Francisco North; trail map available at park visitor centers or online at www.nps.gov/prsf/planyourvisit/upload/Pad-Map-9-15_color_print1.pdf

Special considerations: Improvements to the Batteries to Bluffs Trail were ongoing in 2015; be prepared for realignments. The easternmost reaches of Baker Beach are clothing-optional. Stay to the high ground if you'd like to avoid this part of the shoreline.

Trail contact: Golden Gate National Recreation Area, Fort Mason, Building 201, San Francisco 94123-0022; (415) 561-4700; www.nps.gov/goga

Finding the trailhead: From the southbound lanes of US 101 at the Golden Gate Bridge, pass through the far right toll booth, take an immediate right at the 25th Avenue exit, and continue onto Merchant Road. From Merchant Road turn right at the first stop sign onto Lincoln Boulevard. Follow Lincoln Boulevard for about 1 mile to Bowley Street. Turn right onto Bowley Street and continue to the junction with Gibson Road. Turn right onto Gibson and follow the road into the parking lot along Baker Beach at Battery Chamberlin. GPS: N37 47.589' / W122 28.996'

The Hike

Military installations along the Batteries to Bluffs route were erected over the better part of a century, and represent a physical time line of protection for the port of San Francisco from the Civil War to World War II. As the design of each battery was rendered obsolete by advances in military technology, it was replaced, each iteration gaining substance and incorporating the latest in weaponry. Though remarkably—and

The remains of Battery Boutelle overlook the strait of the Golden Gate.

thankfully—no shots were fired on an enemy from the dozens of batteries that line the coast north and south of the mouth of San Francisco Bay, they testify to the region's strategic importance.

And then there's the Golden Gate Bridge, built in the 1930s to connect San Francisco with Marin County. Other bridges around the world garner the same superlatives—they are historic, beautiful, iconic—but the Golden Gate Bridge supersedes them all. The setting, the architecture, the interaction with fog and sunshine, its unexpected color—all set the bridge apart.

This hike links the batteries to the bridge, and also to a pair of beaches tucked below the bluffs on the south side of the Golden Gate. The route begins at Battery Chamberlin, which overlooks Baker Beach and the mouth of the strait. A restored "disappearing" gun rises from the first of several emplacements; this weapon was designed to drop out of sight after discharging so that artillerymen could safely reload it. On the first weekend of the month, a park ranger and volunteers in period uniform are on hand to describe how the gun operated.

Fun Facts about the Golden Gate Bridge

Some fun facts from goldengatebridge.org, the website of the Golden Gate Bridge Highway and Transportation District, which oversees the bridge:

- The Golden Gate was named by famed explorer John C. Fremont, the Pathfinder, who likened it to the harbor in Istanbul dubbed the "Golden Horn."
- The bridge took three years to build, opening to pedestrian traffic on May 28, 1937, and to vehicle traffic the following day.
- The Halfway-to-Hell Club was made up of nineteen men whose lives were saved by the safety net that was slung under the bridge during construction. Eleven men lost their lives helping to build the bridge, including ten who died in a single day when the net failed to hold.
- On the bridge's opening day, the *San Francisco Chronicle* described it as a "$35 million steel harp."
- The bridge is designed to move (flex, or "deflect") a total of about 16 feet (10.8 feet down and 5.8 feet up), and at the center of the span, it can sway about 27 feet.
- When it was completed in 1937, the suspension span on the Golden Gate Bridge was the longest in the world. Today, at 4,200 feet, it ranks ninth.

From the beach and battery, the Coastal Trail climbs through a stand of Monterey pine to Lincoln Boulevard, then runs alongside the busy, scenic, two-lane roadway for a stretch. At the top of the climb, the Pacific Overlook—outfitted with benches, excellent views of the Golden Gate Bridge, and interpretive signs, including one that describes the geologic evolution of the Golden Gate—sprawls alongside the trail. The Batteries to Bluffs Trail intersects the Coastal Trail in a stand of trees just beyond the overlook; it breaks left, toward the bluffs, and then curls right to parallel the coastline. Pass two bricked entrances to Battery West, which dates back to the post–Civil War era, one of the oldest in the Presidio. These days its camouflage is complete, with coastal scrub having recolonized its roof and sides so that, barring the entrances, it looks more like a long mound than a structure.

The trail leads next to Battery Godfrey, a more modern concrete structure. Here you can take one of three paths: one route hugs the edge of the bluff; the middle trail (the Bowman Trail) runs along the "fronts" of Batteries Boutelle and Marcus Miller, and the wide Coastal Trail is the farthest inland. The Coastal Trail curves northward, toward the Golden Gate, via a wide pedestrian bridge at the far end of Battery Marcus Miller.

Beyond the batteries, the Golden Gate Bridge becomes the primary focus. At 1.5 miles, the Coastal Trail merges with the paved path that leads right (east) onto the pedestrian walkway/bikeway of the bridge and left (northeast) under the huge iron girders that support it. A trail sign here indicates that the route is also part of the Juan Bautista de Anza National Historic Trail, as well as the Bay Area Ridge Trail.

Follow the pavement to the left (north, then east), dropping down under the roadbed of the bridge. This is a highlight of the hike: The sound of the cars passing overhead is hollow, muffled, and echoing; the architecture

The crumbling earthworks of Battery East date back to the Civil War era.

is massive, solid, and insulating. An interpretive site on the west side of the span includes a re-creation of the metalwork that supports the bridge at the southern and northern anchorages. Watch for speeding cyclists.

As you emerge from the shadow of the bridge on the east side of the Golden Gate, Fort Point comes into view below and to the left (north). Built on the site of a Spanish fort dating back to colonization, Fort Point and its sister fort on Alcatraz Island were armed in 1861 to deter enemies intent on stealing the wealth of the city after the discovery of gold in 1848, and from the rebels during the Civil War.

The trail forks at an interpretive sign as you approach the mounded earthworks of Battery East, of the same construction as Battery West. Stay right, following the heavily used path into Strauss Plaza. A stop for just about every tourist who ever comes to San Francisco, and the jumping-off point for a walk across the bridge and back, the plaza is often packed with people. It is named for prolific bridge-builder Joseph Strauss, chief engineer for the Golden Gate. A huge, kaleidoscopic diorama depicts the various stages of the bridge's construction, as do other exhibits in the plaza. The Roundhouse Gift Center, the Bridge Cafe, and restrooms are also found here. Paths lead eastward from the plaza as well, through Battery East to Crissy Field, Fort Point, and the Golden Gate Promenade.

On the return, the route takes the Batteries to Bluffs Trail rather than the Coastal Trail back to Baker Beach. At the end of Battery West, take the signed path that plunges via staircases down the bluff side. The well-constructed stairway, with landings, is relatively easy, through those with knee problems may take issue. Views open out to sea, with Lands End pinching the opening of the Golden Gate from the south, and Point Bonita from the north.

At the base of the stairway, take the short side trail to the right down to Marshall Beach, a small half-moon of sand with—you guessed it—superlative views. The Batteries to Bluffs Trail heads uphill from this point, again via a well-built stairway, and tops out on the apron of Battery Crosby. This fortification, like Battery Chamberlin, was outfitted with a disappearing gun.

The trail heads up toward Lincoln Boulevard from the battery; once adjacent to the roadway, head downhill to the Sand Ladder Trail. As promised by the name, this is a steep, sandy plunge down the bluff side via "stairs" built using round timbers and wire railings. The sand ladder ends on Baker Beach; turn left and walk down the beach back to Battery Chamberlin and the trailhead.

Miles and Directions

0.0 Start by walking through Battery Chamberlin, protected by a chain-link fence. Walk up and along the concrete aprons fronting the four gun emplacements, then bear right and up on the obvious Coastal Trail.

0.4 The broad path leaves the woods to parallel Lincoln Boulevard. Follow the roadside path uphill, enjoying views (fog permitting) across the channel to the Marin Headlands.

0.5 Pass the signed trail on the left for the Sand Ladder, part of the return route. About 100 yards beyond, a signed trail breaks left to Battery Crosby, also along the return run. Stay right on the roadside trail.

0.8 Reach the Pacific Overlook, outfitted with benches, interpretive signs, and expansive views across the strait to the Golden Gate Bridge and the Marin Headlands. The Juan Bautista de Anza National Historic Trail to Rob Hill and beyond joins from the right.

1.0 At the junction with the Batteries to Bluffs Trail, go left. The Coastal Trail continues to the right. Go about 300 feet then turn right, remaining on the Batteries to Bluffs Trail. The trail to the left drops down to Marshall Beach, which is, again, part of the return route. The earthworks and brick entryways of Battery West, regrettably marred by graffiti, are on the left, overgrown with coastal brambles.

1.2 Reach Battery Godfrey, the first concrete installation. The wide concrete apron atop the battery faces the Golden Gate and makes a marvelous bench from which to enjoy the views. Battery Godfrey melds into Battery Boutelle; Battery Marcus Miller comes next, followed by Battery Cranston. The trail splits, enabling hikers to explore at will, staying right to check out the structures themselves, and staying left, atop the concrete aprons, to enjoy views across the gate. The wide, gravel Coastal Trail is farthest inland. A pedestrian bridge, completed in 2015, links the Coastal Trail to the coastal bluff at far end of Battery Marcus Miller. Continue on the broad Coastal Trail.

1.5 Leave the batteries behind as the route meets the busy, paved trail on the final approach to the Golden Gate Bridge.

1.7 The trail drops under the roadbed of the bridge.

2.0 On the bay side of the bridge, stay right on the paved pathway that leads into busy Strauss Plaza.

Batteries to Bluffs and the Golden Gate Bridge
(Presidio of San Francisco)

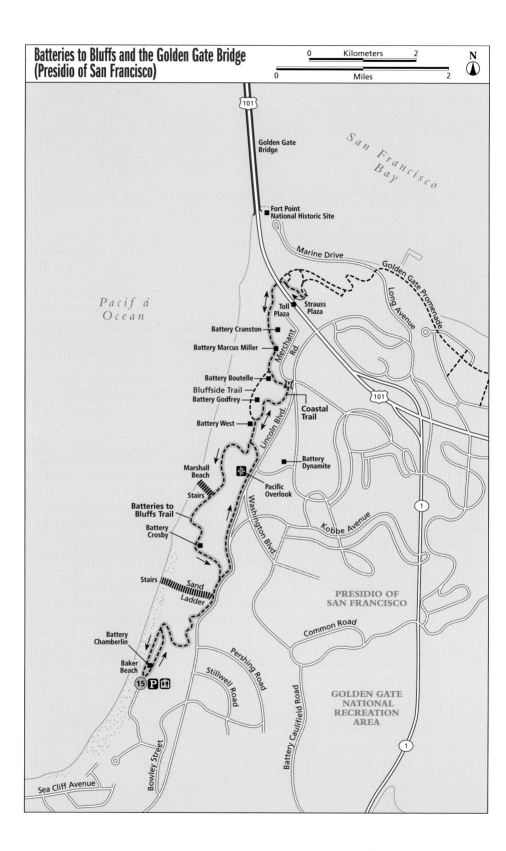

3.0 At the end of the battery row, beyond Battery West, stay right on the signed Batteries to Bluffs Trail, which negotiates a steep descent of the bluff via well-built stairways.

3.3 Take the trail to Marshall Beach, with unbeatable views of the Golden Gate and the Marin Headlands. After you've checked it out, begin the brief but steep climb up more staircases to Battery Crosby.

3.5 The climb deposits you in front of the gun emplacements of Battery Crosby. Take in the views, then follow the relatively flat path back to the Coastal Trail alongside Lincoln Boulevard.

3.7 Turn right onto the Coastal Trail. Within 100 yards, turn right again onto the signed Sand Ladder Trail, which drops straight onto Baker Beach.

3.8 Turn left on the beach and walk through the sand back toward Battery Chamberlin.

4.1 Arrive back at the trailhead.

Options: There are a number of ways to extend your exploration of the Golden Gate and its defensive batteries. The most obvious—something every visitor to the City by the Bay should do—is to walk across the bridge. This is not, by any stretch of the imagination, a hike, though the arc of the suspension span does mean there's minimal elevation gain and loss as you cross. The sidewalk is literally right next to the lanes of traffic, with cars whizzing by at 45 miles per hour (or more); the smell of exhaust is inescapable. On sunny weekends, the walk is packed with tourists. But everything that's enervating is forgiven when you reach the first tower, where the splendid architecture and views vie for center stage. Look up to where the top of the tower scrapes the fog. Gaze out across the bay and down onto the strait, where ferries and sailboats skim the turbulent water. Grip a cable, place your palm on the steel, feel the vibration under your feet, run your hand along the low railing that separates you from a long, long drop to the sea. It's a timeless experience. An out-and-back walk across the bridge adds about 3.4 miles to the round-trip distance.

You can also continue beyond the Strauss Plaza turnaround by heading down to the historic sites along the Golden Gate Promenade, including Fort Point and Crissy Field, home base for record-setting flights at the turn of the twentieth century.

16 Golden Gate Promenade and Crissy Field

A walk along the Golden Gate Promenade parallels the long, grassy expanse of historic Crissy Field and leads to Fort Point.

Start: 1 block off Marina Boulevard, just west of St. Francis Yacht Club, near Crissy Field Center

Distance: 3.4 miles out and back

Hiking time: 2–3 hours

Difficulty: Easy

Trail surface: Crushed granite

Best season: Year-round

Other trail users: Cyclists, trail runners

Canine compatibility: Dogs must either be leashed or under voice control, depending on where you are walking in Golden Gate National Recreation Area (GGNRA). Pets are prohibited to protect sensitive resources in the marsh. Some owners allow their animals to run unrestrained on Crissy Field's lawns and on East Beach. Dog droppings must be picked up. Contact GGNRA for the most current pet regulations.

Land status: Golden Gate National Recreation Area

Fees and permits: None

Schedule: Trail open all day, every day, year-round. Warming Hut open 9 a.m. to 5 p.m. Mon through Fri and 9 a.m. to 7 p.m. Sat and Sun; call (415) 561-3040 for information. Greater Farallones National Marine Sanctuary Visitor Center open 10 a.m. to 4 p.m. Wed through Sun.

Trailhead amenities: Because you can access the trail from a long stretch of parking lots, no amenities may be immediately available. Restrooms, picnic areas, and a visitor information center can be found along the promenade.

Maps: USGS San Francisco North; GGNRA and Presidio of San Francisco brochures and maps available at park visitor centers and online at www.nps.gov/prsf/planyourvisit/upload/Pad-Map-9-15_color_print1.pdf

Special considerations: This trail can be very congested, especially on sunny days. Please be considerate.

Trail contact: Golden Gate National Recreation Area, Fort Mason, Building 201, San Francisco, CA 94123-0022; (415) 561-4700; www.nps .gov/goga

Finding the trailhead: From the Golden Gate Bridge, go south on US 101/Presidio Parkway (Doyle Drive) to the Marina exit. Stay in the left-hand lanes after you come off the bridge, then again in the left-hand lanes (following signs for the Marina) as you approach the Palace of Fine Arts. Once off Doyle Drive, go left onto Mason Street. The shoreline parking lot is just west of the St. Francis Yacht Club. Additional parking is available in the lots between Mason Street and the shoreline, just west of where Mason meets Marina Boulevard.

The San Francisco Municipal Railway (Muni) provides bus service to the Presidio. Contact Muni for information (sfmta.com or tripplanner.transit.511.org). The PresidioGo Shuttle provides service within the Presidio, as well as routes that link downtown to the park. Visit presidiobus.com for information. GPS: N37 48.384' / W122 26.900'

The Hike

Stretching between the south towers of the Golden Gate Bridge and the Marina District, the Golden Gate Promenade lies between East Beach on San Francisco Bay and historic Crissy Field. It's a fun, busy, scenic stroll that encompasses great views of the Golden Gate Bridge for most of its outgoing distance and city skyline views on the return. Fort Point, built to deter raiders with an eye on San Francisco's gold-rush wealth and potential attacks during the Civil War, is the turnaround point.

The wide, flat, multiuse trail is invariably crowded with hikers, runners, moms and dads pushing strollers, cyclists, folks in wheelchairs, and dog walkers. Sailboarders and kayakers launch from the beach, mingling with sailboats on sunny, windy days, and kites fly where once biplanes took wing. Even if the fog doesn't burn off, the promenade puts on a show.

Heading west along the path from the easternmost parking areas near the St. Francis Yacht Club, a spur breaks off to the left (south) to the Crissy Field Center. You can use this cutoff to link up with a paved path on the south side of the restored marsh, designated for faster travelers on bikes or skates. The restored marsh area, once part of the military airfield and now a thriving natural habitat, is to the trail's left (south) and lined with interpretive signs. Other trails branch right (north) to the beach, also restored since the Presidio passed from the US Army to the National Park Service. Concrete benches along the promenade and overlooking the beach offer opportunities to sit and watch the parade of humanity that clogs the popular route.

▶ Planes that took off from Crissy Field participated in the dedication of Lassen Volcanic National Park in 1931.

The boardwalk leading to the Golden Gate Overlook breaks off the promenade to the right (north) at 0.6 mile, and a narrow dirt track heads left (south) onto the huge, grassy platform on the left, a re-creation of the historic Crissy airfield. Crissy Field was a hub of military aviation during the 1920s and early 1930s, strategically situated so that pilots tasked with patrolling the West Coast for enemy ships that might not be seen from fortifications on land could get aloft expeditiously. The airstrip was built on an area that had been used as a dump in the late 1800s; in 1915 the tidal flats were filled in preparation for the Panama Pacific International Exposition.

▶ The old hangars alongside Crissy Field are occupied by a variety of businesses, part of an innovative public-private partnership that sustains the Presidio of San Francisco as a national park. The Presidio Trust, a first-of-its-kind federal agency established in 1996 by an act of Congress, oversees management of the park and facilitates use of its structures by both for-profit and not-for-profit private entities. The trust's mandate was to ensure funding for the park without using taxpayer money; that goal was reached in 2013. The success of the model has resulted in its emulation to ensure preservation of underfunded and/or threatened parklands elsewhere in California.

Looking across the grass at Crissy Field toward the Palace of Fine Arts and San Francisco skyline

After the exposition, the US Army selected the site for an Air Coast Defense Station, and the airfield was born.

In addition to flying reconnaissance, aviators from Crissy Field also took aerial photographs, went out on search-and-rescue missions, and patrolled for forest fires. A number of record-setting flights began or ended on the grass runway, including the first "Dawn to Dusk" transcontinental flight in 1924 and the first flight from the mainland to Hawaii.

By the mid-1930s, however, Crissy Field's desirability as a "first-line air base" was waning. Fog and wind had always plagued the fliers. Its demise was certified upon completion of the Golden Gate Bridge in 1937, as the structure compromised flight lines. After the air corps moved north to Hamilton Field in Marin County, Crissy Field was used as barracks, its hangars as classrooms, and its then-paved runways for medical flights. The airfield became part of the Golden Gate National Recreation Area when the Presidio was turned over to the National Park Service in 1994. Restoration included replacing the pavement with grass, which was the preferred surface in the early days of flight, softening the landings.

▶ Crissy Field is named for Major Dana H. Crissy, onetime commander of Mather Air Field in Sacramento, who died on October 1919 while attempting one of the nation's first transcontinental flights.

As the promenade continues west, arcing toward the Warming Hut and Fort Point

Fort Point

The history of a defensive post at Fort Point dates back to colonization by the Spanish, who, with the help of local natives, erected a defensive structure known as Castillo de San Joaquin on the site in the early 1790s. That fort was razed to make way for the present edifice—three tiers lined with casements and living quarters, plus a barbette tier and lighthouse—built between 1853 and 1861 by the US Army Corps of Engineers. The fort was designed to house 126 cannon, with casements for thirty guns on each tier, and was intended to defend San Francisco Bay in the event of an invasion that never materialized.

The fort became obsolete quickly. By 1900 both men and cannon were removed, and the fort was used for training, storage, and as an operational base during the construction of the Golden Gate Bridge in the 1930s. It was manned again during World War II, as part of the defensive network erected around the mouth of the bay, then again fell into disuse. Its current revival as a National Historic Site began in 1970, and today it is one of the biggest attractions within the Golden Gate National Recreation Area.

Fort Point is open for tours every day except Wednesday from 10 a.m. to 5 p.m.; it is also closed on Thanksgiving, Christmas, and New Year's Day. The fort's bookstore is open on the same days that the fort is open. Both self-guided and volunteer-led tours are available. For more information, visit www.nps.gov/fopo or call (415) 556-1693.

Pier, the beach gives way to a rockier shoreline. Pass the Greater Farallones National Marine Sanctuary Visitor Center at the 1-mile mark. The center, which houses hands-on exhibits and hosts educational programs, is housed in a historic lifeboat station. Beyond the sanctuary, visitor center spur trails lead to the West Bluff picnic area, which sports tables, interpretive signs, an amphitheater of concrete risers, and little hillocks that serve as windbreaks.

The Warming Hut and the Fort Point Pier (aka Torpedo Wharf) are at 1.3 miles. The pier is often crowded with anglers, some bustling from one line to another, while others seem content to use their poles as an excuse to take in the great views of the Golden Gate Bridge and Fort Point. The Warming Hut houses a cafe and bookstore, with restrooms in an adjacent structure. Informational and interpretive billboards are stationed around the building. The Coastal Trail breaks off to the left (south) from the

Golden Gate Promenade and Crissy Field (Presidio of San Francisco)

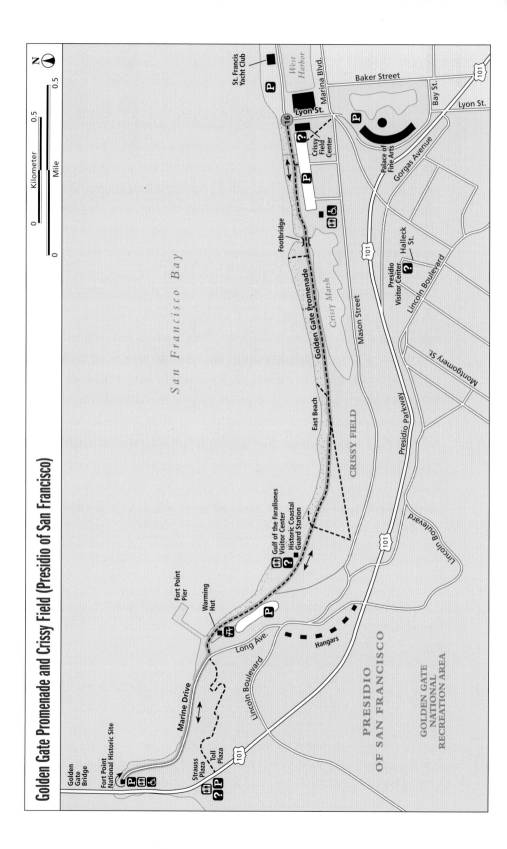

The Golden Gate Bridge towers over Fort Point at the end of Marine Drive and a walk on the Golden Gate Promenade.

west side of the hut, climbing stairs to Battery East, Strauss Plaza at the southern end of the Golden Gate Bridge, and military fortifications on the west side of the bridge.

The Golden Gate Promenade proper ends at the Warming Hut, but you can continue west on Marine Drive, the access road to the Fort Point National Historic Site. Located at the end of the rock-faced seawall below the southern terminus of the Golden Gate Bridge, the fort is open for tours and is well worth a visit.

Return as you came, with the city skyline forming the viewscape to the right and the bay, including Alcatraz and Angel Islands, on the left.

Miles and Directions

0.0   Start by heading west from the East Beach parking area on the crushed gravel path.

0.1   Pass the side trail to the Crissy Field Center and reach the border of the marsh.

0.2   Cross a bridge that spans the marsh's outlet stream.

0.6   Pass the boardwalk to the Golden Gate Overlook; the trail parallels Crissy Field.

1.0   Pass the Greater Farallones National Marine Sanctuary Visitor Center.

1.3   Arrive at the Warming Hut and Fort Point Pier.

1.7   Reach Fort Point and the end of the line. Retrace your steps to the trailhead.

3.4   Arrive back at the trailhead.

17 Ecology Trail and Lovers Lane

Located in the heart of the historic Presidio of San Francisco, this route climbs through restored natural habitat to a scenic overlook, drops past a spring used by the native Ohlone, and rambles along a lane where Presidio soldiers once walked with their sweethearts.

Start: Intersection of Sheridan Avenue and Montgomery Street on southwest corner of Main Post parade ground in the Presidio
Distance: 2.9-mile lollipop
Hiking time: 1–2 hours
Difficulty: Easy
Trail surface: Sidewalk, dirt trail, paved pathway
Best season: Year-round
Other trail users: Trail runners, mountain bikers
Canine compatibility: Dogs must either be leashed or under voice control, depending on where you are hiking in Golden Gate National Recreation Area (GGNRA). Dog droppings must be picked up. Contact GGNRA for the most current pet regulations.
Land status: Presidio of San Francisco
Fees and permits: Parking fee levied for Main Post lot

Schedule: Sunrise to sunset daily
Trailhead amenities: None. Restrooms, water, trash cans, and information are all available at the Presidio Visitor Center, located as of 2015 in Building 36 on Lincoln Boulevard on the Main Post. The visitor center is open Thurs through Sun from 9 a.m. to 4 p.m.
Maps: USGS San Francisco North; GGNRA and Presidio of San Francisco brochures and maps available at park visitor centers and online at www.nps.gov/prsf/planyourvisit/upload/Pad-Map-9-15_color_print1.pdf
Trail contact: Presidio of San Francisco, Golden Gate National Recreation Area, Building 201, Fort Mason, San Francisco, CA 94123; (415) 561-4323; www.nps.gov/prsf. Golden Gate National Parks Conservancy, Building 201, Fort Mason, San Francisco, CA 94123; (415) 561-3000; www.parksconservancy.org.

Finding the trailhead: The trailhead is just south of the Presidio's Main Post. From the junction of Van Ness and Lombard Streets, turn onto Lombard and go 11 blocks to Broderick Street (stay in the left-hand lane). Just after Broderick, as traffic curves to the right, stay straight on Lombard. Continue 1.5 blocks and enter the Presidio through the Lombard Gate. Turn right onto Presidio Boulevard at the first stop sign. Continue straight through several stops—you are now on Lincoln Boulevard—to the foot of the parade ground parking lot.

From the southbound lanes of the Golden Gate Bridge, pass through the far right tollbooth and take an immediate right at the 25th Avenue exit, onto Merchant Road. Turn left at the first stop sign onto Lincoln Boulevard, and continue on Lincoln as it twists and turns through the Presidio for about 1.5 miles to the main parade ground. Park in the huge lot on the former parade grounds.

The San Francisco Municipal Railway (Muni) provides bus service to the Presidio. Contact Muni for information (sfmta.com or tripplanner.transit.511.org). The PresidioGo Shuttle provides service within the Presidio, as well as routes that link downtown to the park. Visit presidiobus.com for information.

The corner of Sheridan and Montgomery, at the south end of the row of brick barracks, has been pegged for the trailhead, but you can pick up the route anywhere along Moraga Avenue, which borders the south side of the Main Post. GPS: N37 47.974' / W122 27.589'

The Hike

A hike on the Ecology Trail and Lovers Lane captures the scenic and historic diversity of the Presidio in a neat package. It tracks through a dark forest of eucalyptus, pine, and cypress to wide vistas at Inspiration Point, showcases a pocket of rare native habitat, drops to a spring used by the Ohlone and later by the Spaniards who established the Presidio, and finishes along a lane that linked the Presidio to Mission Dolores and the city outside the military compound from colonial times onward.

The route starts and ends on the Main Post, flanked on the west by a row of impressive brick barracks that now house a variety of nonmilitary operations: The unique public-private partnership between the National Park Service and private enterprise, fostered by the Presidio Trust to fund park operations, is showcased here. Among those private businesses is the Inn at the Presidio, a boutique hotel housed in the former Pershing Hall, located southeast of the barracks row. The hall is named for Brigadier General John Joseph Pershing, commander of the American expeditionary force in Europe during World War I. Tragically, the general lost his wife and three children in 1915, when their house on the post was consumed by fire.

The Ecology Trail proper starts behind the inn, passing through a gate and climbing into a stand of eucalyptus. The first 0.25 mile or so involves a rather vigorous ascent, then the pitch eases in a redwood grove. Passing the trail that drops toward El Polin Spring, the route climbs more gently through a restored expanse of the serpentine grasslands that once covered this area. The flora accommodated by this habitat includes eleven rare and endangered plants, including Presidio clarkia and Marin dwarf flax. Restoration and maintenance of this fragile ecosystem is ongoing; be sure to remain on the trails.

Beyond the junction with the Mountain Lake Trail, the Ecology Trail ascends a brief but steep pitch and staircase to the overlook at Inspiration Point. A broad flagstone platform outfitted with benches and banked with interpretive signs, Inspiration Point offers views across the Presidio's treetops to San Francisco Bay, Alcatraz Island, and Angel Island. Mostly nonnative, more than 100,000 trees were planted on the Presidio as part of a beautification project in the 1800s.

To continue to Lovers Lane, retrace your steps on the Ecology Trail to the El Polin Spring Trail. Switchback down the wide path that drops into the El Polin Spring picnic area, located near the head of Tennessee Hollow. A water source for the Ohlone, and later the Spanish and Mexican forces at the Presidio, the spring and surrounding area has been rehabilitated with native plantings and artful stonework.

▶ While the National Park Service is dedicated to restoring native habitats, like the serpentine grasslands below Inspiration Point, it also is committed to preserving the historical plantings, including portions of the forest of Monterey pine, Monterey cypress, and eucalyptus that shade parts of the Presidio.

The History of the Presidio in 500 Words or Less

The Presidio was established by the Spanish in 1776, part of the initial thrust of missionaries and soldiers into what would become Alta California. The colonists also established Mission San Francisco de Asís (Mission Dolores) and Yerba Buena, a secular pueblo, on the shores of the magnificent harbor.

While the native Ohlone and neighboring tribes had long utilized the plentiful resources surrounding San Francisco Bay—even on the windy, sandy tip of the peninsula—the Spanish recognized the bay's strategic significance. Their first line of defense for their northern California frontier was the Castillo de San Joaquin at the mouth of the Golden Gate, the narrow strait that renders the bay a desirable and defensible port. The rest of the Presidio was composed, in those first days, of brush and tule huts surrounded by a palisade that housed, according to one historian, about 40 soldados and nearly 150 settlers. Adobe would replace wood and mud within a few years, with a chapel, a guardhouse, officers' residences, barracks, warehouses, and other buildings protected inside a defensive wall. But visitors consistently described the Presidio as derelict, with one commenting that it resembled a cattle pen.

The Presidio would pass into the hands of the new Mexican government in 1821, following Mexican independence. It suffered from a failure to thrive under that leadership as well, with the pueblo of Yerba Buena drawing off resources. Mariano Guadalupe Vallejo,

Gentle switchbacks lead out of the spring area toward the Mountain Lake Trail. This route doesn't climb to that formal trail, however. Instead, follow a sandy path (labeled on some maps as a second Mountain Lake Trail) that passes below the Julius Kahn playground and above the Paul Goode Field. The track leads into a mixed forest of eucalyptus and Monterey pine, a restored part of the aging Presidio forest.

A brief climb leads to paved Lovers Lane, which is lined with light poles and cuts a straight shot northwest toward the Main Post. Bordered on the east by stands of eucalyptus and on the west by a row of homes once occupied by enlisted men and their families, this is a busy corner of the Presidio. But it is still possible to imagine what it may have been like to stroll arm in arm with a sweetheart on the narrow path.

A quaint brick footbridge spans El Polin Creek at the end of the lane, and the route climbs briefly to Presidio Boulevard. Pass four homes built in the 1880s in the Queen Anne/Stick architectural style before turning left onto Funston Avenue. Officers' Row, then commandante of the Presidio, moved most of the garrison north to Sonoma so he could better monitor the Russian settlement at Fort Ross. By 1846, when Captain John Montgomery raised the Stars and Stripes, the Presidio's fortifications had mostly disintegrated into lumps of adobe.

The discovery of gold in the Sierra Nevada heralded a long renaissance for the Presidio. Under American command, layers of fortifications would be built on the prime real estate, reflecting the state of military technology in each war the nation endured. The Civil War saw construction of earthwork batteries, with Fort Point erected on the site of the old castillo. Those structures were obsolete by the time of the Spanish-American War, so new batteries were built. Presidial troops were dispatched to Mexico to find the rebel Pancho Villa, and fought on the battlefields of World War I. Crissy Field was activated in 1921, supplementing already impressive coastal defenses with air power. During World War II, the Presidio served as headquarters for the Western Defense Command. During the Cold War, installations of the Nike missile system were built along the San Francisco coastline, and the Presidio served as headquarters.

When more sophisticated weapons rendered Nike missiles obsolete, the age of coastal defense ended. The Presidio was no longer relevant to America's civil defense. The US Army handed the property off to the National Park Service in 1994, and its 200-year history as a military post came to an end.

composed of the oldest structures on the Presidio, lines this block. At the junction of Funston and Moraga, turn right and follow the sidewalk back to the trailhead.

Miles and Directions

0.0 Start on the corner of Sheridan and Montgomery, walking 2 blocks up Montgomery to the intersection with Moraga Avenue. Turn left onto Moraga, passing the Officers' Club and the post chapel as you follow the sidewalk.

0.2 At the junction of Moraga and Funston, go right onto Funston, passing the parking lot for the Inn at the Presidio, to the signed start of the Ecology Trail. Stay on the main trail as you ascend into the woodland, ignoring side paths and passing a gated roadway.

0.8 Reach the restored serpentine grasslands. Stay right (south) at the junction with the trail leading down to El Polin Spring, climbing on the Ecology Trail toward Inspiration Point.

The Officers Barracks, now housing private and public enterprises, front on the Presidio's historic Main Post.

0.9   At the junction with the Mountain Lake Trail, stay right on the Ecology Trail, climbing the staircase to reach the overlook. Enjoy the views, then retrace your steps to the junction with the El Polin Spring Trail.

1.0   Back at the El Polin Spring junction, drop down the switchbacks to El Polin Spring.

1.3   Arrive at the El Polin Spring picnic area. Housing for Presidio residents is to the left, and the city streets can be seen above the head of Tennessee Hollow. Check out the restoration and read the interpretive signs, then climb the switchbacks leading out of the hollow. Go left on the signed connector to the Mountain Lake Trail, the Julius Kahn playground, and the Bay Area Ridge Trail.

1.5   Circle the parking lot below the playground (which is out of sight, but you can hear children playing), and take the first left onto the broad, unsigned sandy path that runs behind the ball field.

2.0   Ignore an unsigned path that breaks left, and climb into a clearing in the West Pacific Grove, where a stand of elderly Monterey cypress was replaced with one hundred seedlings of the same species in 2009. Take the path to the left toward Lovers Lane.

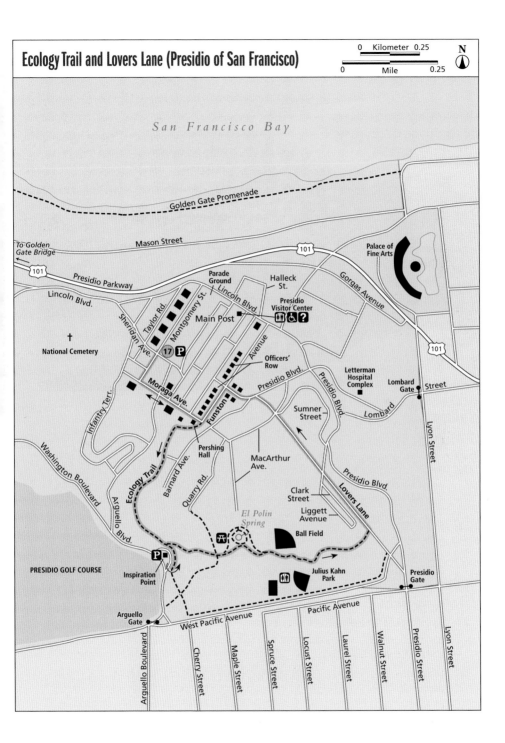

Ecology Trail and Lovers Lane (Presidio of San Francisco)

0 Kilometer 0.25

0 Mile 0.25

N

San Francisco Bay

Golden Gate Promenade

Mason Street

101

To Golden Gate Bridge

101

Presidio Parkway

Lincoln Blvd.

Parade Ground

Halleck St.

Lincoln Blvd

Palace of Fine Arts

Gorgas Avenue

Taylor Rd.

Sheridan Ave.

Montgomery St.

Main Post

Presidio Visitor Center

17 P

National Cemetery

Avenue

Officers' Row

101

Moraga Ave.

Presidio Blvd.

Letterman Hospital Complex

Lombard Gate

Street

Lombard

Lyon Street

Infantry Terr.

Funston

Sumner Street

Presidio Blvd.

Washington Boulevard

Ecology Trail

Barnard Ave.

Pershing Hall

Quarry Rd.

MacArthur Ave.

Arguello Blvd.

El Polin Spring

Clark Street

Liggett Avenue

Presidio Blvd.

Lovers Lane

PRESIDIO GOLF COURSE

P

Inspiration Point

Ball Field

Julius Kahn Park

Presidio Gate

Arguello Gate

West Pacific Avenue

Pacific Avenue

Arguello Boulevard

Cherry Street

Maple Street

Spruce Street

Locust Street

Laurel Street

Walnut Street

Presidio Street

Lyon Street

Restoration efforts at the Presidio of San Francisco have included improvements of the habitat around El Polin Spring.

2.1 Reach Lovers Lane, the oldest historic trail in San Francisco. Turn left and follow the paved path downhill. The homes on the left side of the trail were built in the 1930s to house the families of enlisted men.

2.3 Cross Liggett Avenue.

2.5 Cross MacArthur Avenue.

2.6 Cross the footbridge over El Polin Creek and climb to Presidio Boulevard. Go left onto Presidio, then left again onto Funston Avenue.

2.7 Reach the junction of Moraga and Funston Avenues. Turn right toward the Main Post parade ground.

2.9 Arrive back at the trailhead and parking area.

▶ As part of the short-lived Bear Flag Revolt, during which California was declared an independent republic, a band of rebels including John C. Frémont and Kit Carson "invaded" the castillo at Fort Point. It was an easy win, as the adobe fortification had been long abandoned by the Mexican forces stationed at the Presidio.

18 Coastal Trail at Lands End

The trails at Lands End knit natural beauty with San Francisco history perfectly, melding evocative vistas of the Golden Gate and the Pacific with rambles through the ruins of Sutro Baths and Adolph Sutro's end-of-the-continent estate.

Start: Merrie Way parking lot near Lands End Lookout visitor center
Distance: 5.0 miles out and back, including spurs to the labyrinth, Sutro Baths, and Sutro Heights Park
Hiking time: 3–4 hours
Difficulty: Easy
Trail surface: Pavement, dirt trail, crushed gravel, staircases
Best season: Year-round
Other trail users: Trail runners
Canine compatibility: Leashed dogs permitted
Land status: Golden Gate National Recreation Area (GGNRA)
Fees and permits: None
Schedule: Sunrise to sunset daily

Trailhead amenities: Restrooms, water, trash cans, information, and cafe in Lands End Lookout visitor center
Maps: USGS Point Bonita and San Francisco North; GGNRA brochure and map available in park visitor centers and online at www.nps.gov/goga/planyourvisit/maps.htm
Special considerations: Remain on trails. Straying off-route may bring you dangerously close to crumbling cliffs and a long fall.
Trail contact: Golden Gate National Recreation Area, Fort Mason, Building 201, San Francisco, CA 94123-0022; (415) 561-4700; nps.gov/goga. Lands End Lookout visitor center, 680 Point Lobos Ave.; (415) 426-5240.

Finding the trailhead: From US 101/CA 1 at the Golden Gate Bridge, follow Lincoln Boulevard south, then west, for about 1.5 miles to where it becomes El Camino Del Mar in upscale Sea Cliff. Continue west on El Camino Del Mar for 0.9 mile to its intersection with Legion of Honor Drive. Turn left, passing the Palace of the Legion of Honor, to Clement Street. Go right (west) on Clement Street for 0.9 mile to its intersection with 48th Avenue and El Camino Del Mar. Go left on El Camino del Mar for less than 0.1 mile to Point Lobos Avenue. Turn right (west) on Point Lobos Avenue, and then quickly turn right again into the Merrie Way parking lot.

From within the city, take Geary Boulevard west toward the Pacific Ocean. As you approach the sea, veer right, with traffic, onto Point Lobos Avenue. Continue on Point Lobos for 0.75 mile to the Merrie Way parking lot.

From cities south on the peninsula, follow I-280 northbound and stay in the left-hand lanes, taking the Golden Gate Bridge/19th Avenue exit. Continue north on CA 1, following 19th Avenue, for about 4 miles to Irving Street. Turn right onto Irving and go 1 block. Turn left onto 18th Avenue and go 1 block. Turn left onto Lincoln Way and drive 2 miles to the Pacific Ocean. Turn right onto the Great Highway and follow the oceanfront road past the Cliff House and onto Point Lobos Avenue. About 1 block past the Cliff House, turn left into the Merrie Way parking lot.

San Francisco Municipal Railway (Muni) provide access to the Merrie Way junction on Point Lobos Avenue. Contact Muni for information at sfmta.com or tripplanner.transit.511.org.

The trailhead is on the north side of the parking lot. GPS: N37 46.843' / W122 30.706'

The Hike

The appeal of Lands End never ebbs: the bloom of a wild iris amid the coastal scrub, sunset on the labyrinth on Eagle Point, a fleeting glimpse of a shipwreck on the rocks just offshore, watching the fog roll back through the towers of the Golden Gate Bridge. Add the historic sites passed along the way—Sutro Baths near the trailhead, Sutro Heights Park, the Mile Rock beacon, and, just off the route, the Palace of the Legion of Honor, the Cliff House, and the USS *San Francisco* Memorial—it's historic hike perfection.

The Lands End trail follows the route of the Cliff House and Ferries Railway, which at the turn of the twentieth century transported visitors to resort attractions built on Point Lobos by self-made millionaire and onetime San Francisco mayor Adolph Sutro. Sutro, who these days might be called a successful serial entrepreneur, made his fortune in the Nevada silver boom by building a tunnel that ventilated and drained the mines of the Comstock Lode. Back in San Francisco, Sutro purchased more than 2,000 acres on the headlands at Point Lobos and went on to build the Sutro Baths, refurbish the then-ramshackle Cliff House, and establish a public park, complete with exotic plantings and statuary, at Sutro Heights. The remnants of what drew thousands to the point in Sutro's day continue to attract thousands more than a century later.

The route described here is a simple out-and-back along the Coastal Trail, finished with an exploration of Sutro Baths and Sutro Heights Park. But obvious additions include visits to the museum at the Palace of the Legion of Honor, the *San Francisco* memorial, and the nearby Cliff House.

Begin by heading north on the broad, clear, well-trod pathway. Views from the Coastal Trail Overlook reach across the mouth of the Golden Gate to Point Bonita, with its white beacon and suspension bridge vibrant against the browns and greens of the Marin Headlands. You can also see the now-humble Mile Rock buoy, resembling a white soup can with an orange stripe, that sounds off to warn ships of hazards along the coastline. A three-tiered light station once stood on the rock, resembling a "steel wedding cake"; this sea-battered sculpture was removed in the 1960s.

The Coastal Trail becomes dirt and gravel beyond the overlook and passes through coastal scrub and the occasional grove of Monterey pines as it traverses the wooded headlands, with views opening onto the strait, the steep hills beyond, and to the Golden Gate Bridge. A staircase leads right up toward the Veterans Administration building at about the 1-mile mark; just beyond, take the trail that leads down to the labyrinth on Eagle Point.

▶ San Francisco's Palace of the Legion of Honor, which houses an extensive collection of French sculptor Auguste Rodin's sculptures, along with works created by other notable artists, is modeled after the Palais de la Légion d'Honneur in Paris. The museum is at 100 34th Avenue; for information, call (415) 750-3600 or visit legionofhonor.famsf.org.

The Golden Gate Bridge falls square in the viewfinder from the Coastal Trail on Lands End.

A pair of gun emplacements dating back to the battery days flank the labyrinth, built with polished stones, bathed in sea breezes, and resonant with the sounding of the buoy. Originally put in place in 2004, the labyrinth has been repeatedly vandalized, most recently in August 2015. But the vandals can't destroy the spot's meditative beauty, no matter whether the rocks are in place. From the labyrinth, the path drops to the west, down to little Mile Rock Beach, then circles up to a landing of sorts above the labyrinth before regaining the main route.

▶ **The memorial to the USS *San Francisco* commemorates the men who died on the cruiser in the Battle of Guadalcanal in November 1942 and is made from the battle-scarred bridge of the ship.**

Back on the Coastal Trail, continue to trace the bluffs to the Painted Rocks Cliff. The only physical challenge of the route is the staircase that climbs from here, eventually topping out alongside the Lincoln Park Golf Course.

Errant golf balls can be found trailside along the final stretch of the Lands End section of the Coastal Trail, which parallels the links. The California Palace of the Legion of Honor, one of the best museums in San Francisco, is just uphill and is a nice addition to a day's exploration.

Trail's end is at the Eagle Point Overlook, at the border with the tony Sea Cliff neighborhood. Enjoy the views and then retrace your steps to Merrie Way. At the west end of the parking lot, trails dive down to the ruins of Sutro Baths, remnants of the grand resort that attracted generations of San Franciscans beginning at the turn of the twentieth century. In this amazing endeavor, Adolph Sutro built six pools that could be filled with ocean water at high tide (a seventh pool was filled with freshwater). The pools, which could accommodate up to 10,000 people, were heated

The Cliff House

My family's Cliff House picture hangs in my brother's office now. It's a classic shot of the second Cliff House incarnation—the Gothic-style structure built by San Francisco millionaire Adolph Sutro and opened in 1896. The image originally hung in the dark living room of my grandparents' West Portal home; it was spooky, mysterious, and romantic, the building perched on the edge of the earth, lit by a ghostly sun, with the sea kissing its rocky foundations.

That Cliff House was destroyed by fire in 1907, but a new Cliff House stands in its place, still fulfilling the role that inspired its construction in the first place. Now remodeled in a neoclassic style, the building overlooks Seal Rocks, where California sea lions and harbor seals regularly gather to sun, swim, and entertain visitors.

The seals, which had been attracting sightseers since the middle of the nineteenth century, initially inspired a New York investor to build a resort at the site in 1863. The first Cliff House was a relatively low-key structure and drew some of the finest families in San Francisco to its dining rooms, as well as presidents Theodore Roosevelt and William McKinley. Sutro would purchase the restaurant in 1883, adding to his land holdings on Lands End.

That first structure was heavily damaged when a schooner carrying dynamite ran aground on the rocks below the building and exploded. Sutro rebuilt the Cliff House, but his spectacular turreted structure stood on the site for a little more than ten years before it too was destroyed by fire. The third Cliff House, more modest but boasting those same spectacular end-of-the-continent views, was opened in 1909 by his daughter, Emma, and acquired by the GGNRA in 1977. The present iteration, which has been extensively remodeled, houses a restaurant, bar, and gift shop.

to different temperatures and enclosed in a massive glass house. Other amenities at the baths included an amphitheater, restaurants, museums, and galleries. The baths' popularity fell off during the Great Depression, and, despite various efforts to revive the fun, including conversion to an ice-skating rink, the resort fell into disuse. The structure was destroyed by fire in 1966 and the site acquired by the GGNRA in 1973.

From the baths, climb up to and then across Point Lobos Avenue to Sutro Heights Park, where Sutro built a conservatory, overlooks, and elaborate gardens dotted with statues of Roman gods and goddesses. The site is stunning, with views sprawling west across the Pacific and south down Ocean Beach and the more ragged coastline beyond. A broad promenade circles the park, with paths and staircases leading onto an overlook with expansive views.

The paved paths in the park lead back to Point Lobos Avenue; cross the street to return to the trailhead off Merrie Way.

Miles and Directions

0.0 Start by heading north on the broad, well-signed main path, which switches back up to the Coastal Trail proper. Other trails diverge, but the main route is obvious.

0.2 Pass the staircase to the USS *San Francisco* Memorial and Fort Miley on the right. The historic batteries, dating back to 1901, and the memorial are well worth a visit. This will add about 0.2 mile to the out-and-back distance.

0.3 Reach the viewing platform at the Coastal Trail Overlook, which offers views of the Golden Gate and the Mile Rock beacon. The Point Bonita Lighthouse can be seen across the strait. The pavement ends; continue on the dirt track.

0.6 Two intersections—one with a staircase and the second with a paved road—offer access to the Veterans Administration Hospital to the right. Stay left on the Coastal Trail.

0.7 At the junction, go left down the steep trail to the labyrinth. To reach the labyrinth, stay right at the "landing." You'll return via the trail to the left.

0.9 Walk the labyrinth. Then descend to Mile Rock Beach.

1.0 Arrive on the beach. Take in the sights, then circle back to the main Coastal Trail via the path and steps to the right as you face the bluff, completing a short loop to the landing. Retrace your steps from here.

1.4 Back on the Coastal Trail, go left to continue.

1.5 Reach the fenced-off access route to Painted Rocks Cliff (heed warning signs against climbing here) and ascend the staircase. A couple of rock benches on the climb offer rest for weary legs and lungs. The trail resumes its flat, easy demeanor above; stay left to continue.

1.6 The trail skirts the fairways of Lincoln Park Golf Course.

2.2 Reach the Eagle Point observation deck and the turnaround point. Retrace your steps to Merrie Way.

4.4 Back at the trailhead, cross the parking lot to the trails that lead down into the ruins of Sutro Baths.

4.5 Reach the baths and overlooks. Once you've explored, pick up the obvious traversing trail that leads up to Point Lobos Avenue, on the right as you face the bluffs.

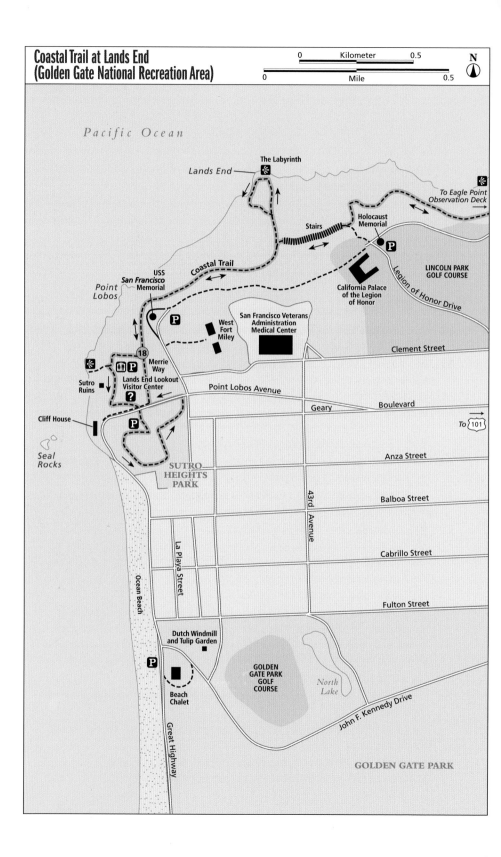

Coastal Trail at Lands End
(Golden Gate National Recreation Area)

0   Kilometer   0.5
0   Mile   0.5

N

Pacific Ocean

The Labyrinth

Lands End

To Eagle Point
Observation Deck

Holocaust
Memorial

Stairs

P

LINCOLN PARK
GOLF COURSE

Coastal Trail

USS
San Francisco
Memorial

Point
Lobos

P

California Palace
of the Legion
of Honor

Legion of Honor Drive

West
Fort
Miley

San Francisco Veterans
Administration
Medical Center

Clement Street

18

Merrie
Way

P

Sutro
Ruins

Lands End Lookout
Visitor Center

?

Point Lobos Avenue

Geary   Boulevard

To 101

Cliff House

P

Anza Street

Seal
Rocks

SUTRO
HEIGHTS
PARK

Balboa Street

43rd Avenue

La Playa Street

Cabrillo Street

Fulton Street

Ocean Beach

Dutch Windmill
and Tulip Garden

GOLDEN
GATE PARK
GOLF
COURSE

North
Lake

P

Beach
Chalet

John F. Kennedy Drive

Great Highway

GOLDEN GATE PARK

The Cliff House hovers over the ruins of Sutro Baths.

4.7 Cross Point Lobos Avenue and the Sutro Heights Park parking lot, climbing the paved path to a small white gazebo. At the gazebo turn right, following the promenade around the perimeter of the park. On the south side, a staircase climbs onto the overlook, where you can take in the views.

4.9 Descend from the overlook and take any of several paths across the park to the entrance on Point Lobos Avenue opposite Merrie Way, guarded by the statues of two lions.

5.0 Arrive back at the trailhead.

Option: It's easy to link a hike along Lands End with a walk along Ocean Beach, which stretches south from Point Lobos. A 2-mile-long out-and-back addition will take you past the historic Cliff House restaurant; the deck behind the house looks down onto Seal Rocks and its namesake pinnipeds. You'll also pass the former site of Playland at the Beach, an amusement park torn down and replaced with housing in the early 1970s, and the refurbished Dutch Windmill at the west entrance to Golden Gate Park. The turnaround is the Beach Chalet, which houses stunning murals by Lucien Labaudt and a restaurant and brewpub.

19 City Walk

The Embarcadero, the piers, the Exploratorium, Fisherman's Wharf, Coit Tower, the Transamerica Pyramid, buildings that survived the fire that destroyed downtown San Francisco during the 1906 earthquake: This long urban hike encompasses all that and more.

Start: Front of San Francisco's Ferry Building
Distance: 7.2 miles out and back with loops
Hiking time: 4–5 hours
Difficulty: Strenuous due to length and stair climbs on Telegraph Hill
Trail surface: Pavement, sidewalk, staircases
Best season: Year-round. You have better chances of fog-free days in fall.
Other trail users: Trail runners, cyclists
Canine compatibility: Leashed dogs permitted, but because these thoroughfares are typically packed with sightseers, bringing a dog along is not recommended. Be sure to pick up dog droppings.
Land status: City of San Francisco
Fees and permits: None
Schedule: All day, every day
Trailhead amenities: Restaurants, restrooms
Maps: USGS San Francisco North
Trail contact: San Francisco Convention and Visitors Bureau, 900 Market St., Hallidie Plaza, San Francisco, CA 94102-2804; (415) 391-2000; sanfrancisco.travel

Finding the trailhead: The Ferry Building is located on the Embarcadero at the foot of Market Street. Parking anywhere in San Francisco can be a nightmare, but a number of public parking garages and lots can be found downtown near the Ferry Building, the most significant at the Embarcadero Center. Arrive early in the day to get a spot. Your best bet: public transportation. Bay Area Rapid Transit (BART) trains and San Francisco Municipal Railway (Muni) buses stop at or near the Ferry Building; contact Muni for information about schedules, stops, and fares (sfmta.com or tripplanner.transit.511.org).

If you must drive and are headed westbound on I-80, take the Fremont Street exit and proceed to the intersection of Market, Fremont, and Front Streets. Cross Market and drive 3.5 blocks on Front Street to Clay Street. Turn right onto Clay and drive a couple of blocks to Drumm Street, which offers access to the Embarcadero parking garages.

From the Golden Gate Bridge, follow US 101/Presidio Parkway east onto Lombard Street. At the intersection of Lombard and Van Ness, go left onto Van Ness and drop onto Bay Street. Turn right onto Bay Street and follow it to its end on the Embarcadero. Turn right onto the Embarcadero and head south along the waterfront for about 1 mile to Washington Street. Turn right onto Washington Street and go 1 long block to Drumm Street. Turn left onto Drumm to access the Embarcadero parking garage.

From the south, both US 101 and I-280 lead into downtown. From the intersection of Market, Third, Kearny, and Geary Streets, follow Kearney north to Clay Street. Turn right onto Clay and proceed to Drumm. Turn right onto Drumm to reach the Embarcadero garage. GPS: N37 47.676' / W122 23.589'

The Hike

What's cool about urban hiking in San Francisco is that the city is completely foot-friendly. You can walk everywhere—and even better, you can walk for miles in any direction and catch public transportation back to your starting point.

Choosing some part of the city for an optimal hike through history presents a challenge—no matter what's chosen, something historic is passed by. This hike, for example, is bounded by Market Street, the heart of downtown, Chinatown, the shopping district surrounding Union Square, and North Beach—all places with worthy stories that can be explored by veering a couple of blocks west or south of the route described. Oh well. Add or subtract as you see fit, or head off someplace completely different, like the Castro, Noe Valley, West Portal, Japantown . . .

The hike begins at the landmark Ferry Building, hub of the Port of San Francisco on the Embarcadero. Despite the Spanish name, the port did not take shape until the gold rush, and the story goes that the current bay-front is built on the bones of ships that were abandoned by crews bound for the Sierra Nevada to seek riches in the gold mines. Over several decades at the turn of the twentieth century, the ragged shoreline was fortified with a seawall to accommodate deepwater vessels. At this point the Embarcadero became industrialized, frequented by longshoremen working the piers. By the 1960s the shipping industry had moved across the bay to the Port of Oakland, and the piers became ramshackle, smelling of the sea and tobacco smoke and machinery oil.

These days the piers north of the Ferry Building have been revitalized as a destination; the Embarcadero is thronged with tourists on weekends. Restaurants, boutiques, and galleries have been installed in "storefronts." The Exploratorium, the renowned hands-on science museum that once resided at the Palace of Fine Arts near the Presidio, is at Pier 15. Openings between the piers lead onto boardwalks on the water, including the Bay Trail public promenade, its lamp-lined wooden planks leading out over the bay.

A waterfront park separates the end of the Embarcadero from the beginning of Fisherman's Wharf, long a mainstay of San Francisco's tourist industry and home to the city's commercial and recreational fishing fleets. A carnival atmosphere dominates this stretch of the walk, with street performers attracting circles of spectators. Museums, an aquarium, the Pier 39 shopping arcade, cafes and restaurants, a floating national historic park, access to ferries and bay cruises, Ghirardelli Square, and the Cannery—it's all contained within a half-mile stretch a few blocks thick.

▶ If you need to stoke the fires before and/or after your hike, the Ferry Building has been transformed into a marketplace, its cavernous interior lined with shops selling chocolate, coffee, deli sandwiches, fine cheeses, and other delights. On Tuesday, Thursday, and Saturday, a farmers' market is set up outside.

Coit Tower tops Telegraph Hill.

The party atmosphere diminishes on the arc of sand and grass fronting Aquatic Park, site of the San Francisco Maritime Museum. Swimmers with the legendary South End Rowing Club and Dolphin Club do laps in the chilly water, while families picnic on the grass. Stroll out to the tip of the Municipal Pier to punch fresh air into your lungs at the turnaround: There's a climb ahead.

Telegraph Hill is a green exclamation mark on this otherwise urban hike. After following Bay Street back to the Embarcadero, cut through Levi's Plaza, a small park surrounding the headquarters of Levi Strauss & Co., founded in gold rush–era San

Francisco. Two sets of historic steps lead to the summit of the hill from Levi's Plaza; you'll head up via the Filbert Street steps and come down via the Greenwich Street steps. Coit Tower crowns Telegraph Hill: Built using a bequest by Lillie Hitchcock Coit, who was rescued as a child from a hotel fire in San Francisco, the tower was erected in honor of firefighters and is designed to resemble a fire nozzle. Views from the top of the tower are panoramic, and the murals at the base were painted by twenty-five California artists during the 1930s.

▶ **You'll likely hear them even if you can't spy them. Flocks of wild parrots have roosted in the gardens around the Filbert and Greenwich stairs on Telegraph Hill since the early twentieth century.**

Back on Levi's Plaza, the walk follows Battery Street into the historic Jackson Square neighborhood, where antiques shops and design studios line the sidewalks. Many of these buildings survived the 1906 earthquake and fire. This is also where you'll get a sense of what the Barbary Coast may have been like: narrow streets permeated by the sea-smell of the nearby waterfront and roamed in the night by raucous young men looking to blow the small fortunes they'd wrestled from the gold fields on women and whiskey.

Pass the base of the Transamerica Pyramid, integral to the San Francisco skyline, and then skim the edge of the downtown business district to the Embarcadero Center. The center occupies 4 square blocks; staircases and walkways link the shops and restaurants housed on the lower floors. The route ends on Justin Herman Plaza opposite the Ferry Building; cross the Embarcadero to arrive back at the trailhead.

Miles and Directions

0.0 Start at the Ferry Building, heading north toward Fisherman's Wharf. Pass Pier 1, home of the Port of San Francisco.

0.3 At Pier 7, break toward the water to stroll down the Bay Trail public promenade, enjoying views of the Bay Bridge and Treasure Island. The ferry *Santa Rosa* is permanently docked at nearby Pier 3. Retrace your steps to return to the Embarcadero.

0.6 Pass the Exploratorium at Pier 15. As you proceed down the Embarcadero, you'll pass Piers 19–23, which hosted the America's Cup in 2012-13. A cruise ship terminal is at Pier 27.

1.1 Pass Pier 33, dock of departure for ferries to Alcatraz Island.

1.3 Arrive at Waterfront Park, which forms a nice, open separation between the Embarcadero and Fisherman's Wharf.

1.4 Reach Pier 39 and turn right, following the crowds through the mall. The pier also is home to the Aquarium of the Bay, which offers close encounters with sea life behind glass. An expansive view of San Francisco Bay opens at the end of the pier, including Alcatraz Island, Angel Island, Treasure and Yerba Buena Islands, and the Bay Bridge. The wooden docks on the west side of Pier 39 host a noisy pride of sea lions—as many as 200 of them.

1.5 Back on the Embarcadero, continue past the dock for the Blue & Gold Fleet. At Pier 41, a boardwalk heads out over the water, passing a relief map of San Francisco Bay.

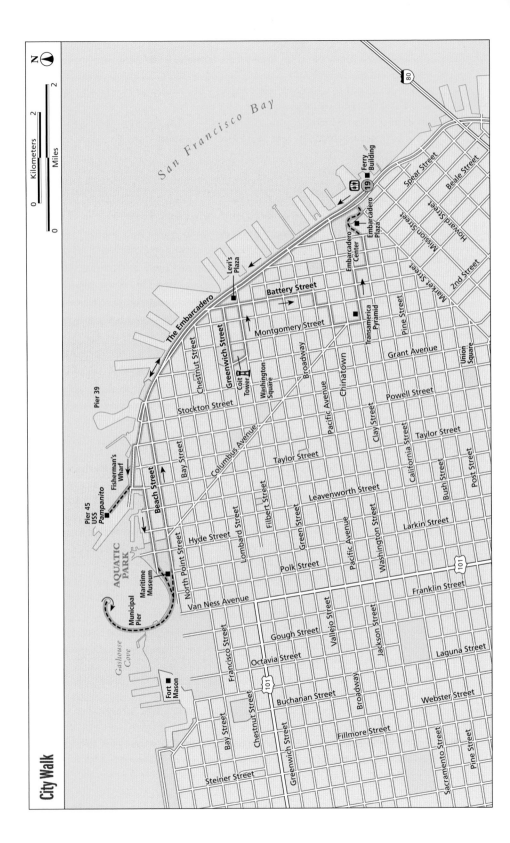

City Walk

N

San Francisco Bay

Gashouse Cove

Fort Mason

AQUATIC PARK

Municipal Pier

Maritime Museum

Pier 45
USS *Pampanito*

Fisherman's Wharf

Pier 39

Beach Street

North Point Street

Hyde Street

Van Ness Avenue

Bay Street

Stockton Street

Chestnut Street

Columbus Avenue

Filbert Street

Lombard Street

Green Street

Taylor Street

Leavenworth Street

Polk Street

Pacific Avenue

Washington Street

Larkin Street

Franklin Street

Gough Street

Octavia Street

Vallejo Street

Jackson Street

Broadway

Laguna Street

Webster Street

Buchanan Street

Fillmore Street

Greenwich Street

Chestnut Street

Francisco Street

Bay Street

Steiner Street

Pine Street

Sacramento Street

Greenwich Street

The Embarcadero

Levi's Plaza

Battery Street

Montgomery Street

Greenwich Street

Coit Tower

Washington Square

Broadway

Pacific Avenue

Chinatown

Clay Street

California Street

Taylor Street

Bush Street

Post Street

Grant Avenue

Powell Street

Union Square

Transamerica Pyramid

Embarcadero Center

Embarcadero Plaza

Ferry Building

19

Market Street

Pine Street

2nd Street

Spear Street

Beale Street

Howard Street

Mission Street

80

101

101

Kilometers   0   2   4

Miles   0   2

1.8 Explore Pier 45, home of the USS *Pampanito*, a World War II fleet submarine, and the SS *Jeremiah O'Brien*, a Liberty ship listed on the National Register of Historic Places. Tours of both are offered. The pier is also home to the Musée Mecanique, which houses a collection of historic arcade games.

1.9 The Embarcadero ends on Taylor Street. Walk a block up Taylor to Jefferson Street, passing open-air seafood markets. Turn right onto Jefferson and continue past the Jefferson Street lagoon.

2.5 Reach the old brick Cannery, a former packing plant that now houses restaurants and stores. The Hyde Street Pier, home to the "floating" San Francisco Maritime National Historical Park and its collection of historic ships, is located downhill from the corner of the Cannery. The Maritime Museum is just ahead, overlooking Aquatic Park.

3.0 Follow the arcing path between the beach and the stone steps/benches of Aquatic Park to Van Ness Avenue. Head down the last block of Van Ness to the Municipal Pier. Pass the gate, and proceed out to the pier's end, enjoying wonderful views of the San Francisco skyline, Alcatraz Island, the Golden Gate, and the hills of Marin. Retrace your steps.

3.5 Back on Van Ness, pick up the paved path that links left to Beach Street.

4.0 Continue down Beach Street, passing the Maritime Museum; taking a break here to check out the exhibits is recommended.

4.2 Pass Ghirardelli Square, home of the famous chocolate factory. The turntable for the Hyde Street cable car line is located at the corner of Beach and Hyde. Continue down Beach Street.

5.1 Beach Street ends on the Embarcadero at Waterfront Park. Turn right onto the Embarcadero.

5.5 Arrive at the intersection of Battery and Lombard Streets and the Fog City Diner. Continue down Battery Street to the entrance of Levi's Plaza. Turn left into the park and follow the curved path through the plaza to Sansome Street at the base of Telegraph Hill.

5.6 Climb Telegraph Hill using the Filbert Street steps. The stairs pass through the Grace Marchant Garden and cross quaint Napier Lane, one of the city's remaining boardwalks. You'll also cross Montgomery Street, passing a mass of bougainvillea with fluorescent purple blooms in season.

6.1 The stairs deposit you on Telegraph Hill Boulevard at the base of Coit Tower. Follow the road around to the entrance of the tower; there's a viewing platform here as well, in the event you don't want to pay for the ride to the top of the tower. Checking out the murals at its base is free, however, and well worth the time.

6.2 Upon leaving the tower, turn right, cross Telegraph Hill Boulevard, and start down the Greenwich Street stairs, marked with a street sign.

6.4 The stairs descend to Montgomery Street. The shuttered landmark restaurant Julius' Castle is on the left, and an overlook offers views of Fisherman's Wharf, a portion of Alcatraz, Treasure Island, and the Bay Bridge. To continue, go right up Montgomery for about 30 paces; a sign marks the beginning of the 300 block of Greenwich Street. At the sign take a sharp left, passing under a walkway for the apartment building.

6.6 Arrive back on Sansome Street. Cross Levi's Plaza to Battery and turn right. Continue 5 blocks to Pacific Avenue.

6.8 Turn right onto Pacific and walk 1 block to Sansome Street. Cross Sansome, then Pacific, and continue on Sansome to Jackson Street. Turn right onto Jackson and walk through the Jackson Square Historic District. In 1906, while the rest of downtown San Francisco went

The tall ship Balclutha, *with Coit Tower behind, from the Municipal Pier*

up in smoke following the earthquake, this enclave was spared, so the buildings date back to gold rush–era San Francisco.

6.9 Turn left onto Montgomery Street and walk 1 block to Washington Street, passing the historic Belli Building, believed to be the oldest surviving building in downtown San Francisco. Cross Washington to the base of the Transamerica Pyramid. Go left on Washington for half a block to the entrance of Transamerica Redwood Park. Turn right and walk through the park, shaded with redwoods, to Clay Street. Turn left onto Clay Street.

7.0 Follow Clay 1.5 blocks to Battery Street. Pass a bronze plaque that marks the site of the *Niantic*, which had been beached on the waterfront and was used as offices, stores, and a warehouse in the fast-growing young city. Cross Clay, cross Battery, and proceed a partial block on Battery to One Embarcadero Center.

7.1 Proceed through the 4 blocks of Embarcaderos, which are linked via walkways, sidewalks, and staircases.

7.2 Climb down steps from Four Embarcadero into Justin Herman Plaza. Cross the Embarcadero to the Ferry Building and the trailhead.

▶ One (or two) of San Francisco's most popular street performers worked on Fisherman's Wharf for three decades. The "Bushman," disguised as—you guessed it—a bush, would lie in wait for an oblivious tourist, then leap up, throwing out his arms. Watching the victim jump in surprise proved great entertainment for onlookers.

20 Golden Gate Park

Follow garden paths and manicured trails linking premier attractions in San Francisco's hallmark park.

Start: In front of Conservatory of Flowers, near eastern edge of park
Distance: 3.0 miles
Hiking time: About 2 hours
Difficulty: Easy
Trail surface: Pavement, dirt trails
Best season: Year-round
Other trail users: Trail runners, cyclists
Canine compatibility: Leashed dogs permitted. Pick up dog droppings.
Land status: Golden Gate Park
Fees and permits: None for trails, but fees charged to tour de Young Museum, California Academy of Sciences, Japanese Tea Garden, and San Francisco Botanical Garden
Schedule: Sunrise to sunset daily

Trailhead amenities: None at trailhead, but restrooms, trash cans, water, a snack bar, and bicycle, Segway, and boat rentals are available at the Boathouse on Stow Lake and elsewhere in Golden Gate Park.
Maps: USGS San Francisco North; online at www.golden-gate-park.com/map.html
Special considerations: John F. Kennedy Drive is closed to auto traffic for half days on Sat and all day Sun from Stanyan Street to Park Presidio/CA 1. No parking is permitting along the side of the road either.
Trail contact: Golden Gate Park, www.golden-gate-park.com. San Francisco Convention and Visitors Bureau, 900 Market St., Hallidie Plaza, San Francisco, CA 94102-2804; (415) 391-2000; sanfrancisco.travel.

Finding the trailhead: From I-80 westbound and/or US 101 northbound near downtown, follow US 101 to the Fell/Laguna exit. Drive about 1.5 miles west on Fell Street. At Stanyan Street, Fell turns into John F. Kennedy Drive. Continue 0.25 mile on John F. Kennedy Drive to the Conservatory of Flowers.

From the San Francisco peninsula, take I-280 north to the Golden Gate Bridge/19th Avenue exit (stay in the left-hand lanes of the freeway). Continue north on CA 1 almost 5 miles, following 19th Avenue, then Park Presidio, through Golden Gate Park. On the north side of the park, turn right onto Fulton Street, go 3.5 blocks, and turn right onto 10th Avenue. At the next stop sign, turn left onto John F. Kennedy Drive and go 0.5 mile to the Conservatory of Flowers.

From the Golden Gate Bridge, stay right on the Park Presidio/19th Avenue off-ramp and drive about 2 miles south on Park Presidio Boulevard. One block before Golden Gate Park's northern boundary, turn right onto Cabrillo Street, and then make an immediate left turn onto 14th Avenue. Drive 1 block and turn left onto Fulton Street. Cross Park Presidio and continue on Fulton for 3.5 blocks. Turn right onto 10th Avenue. At the next stop sign, turn left onto John F. Kennedy Drive and go 0.5 mile to the Conservatory of Flowers. GPS: N37 46.333' / W122 27.616'

A number of San Francisco Municipal Railway (Muni) buses stop within walking distance of the trailhead. Contact Muni (sfmta.com or tripplanner.transit.511.org) for schedules. A park shuttle runs on Sat, Sun, and major holidays; a fee is charged.

The Hike

A narrow swath of green separates the Sunset District of San Francisco from the Richmond. Stretching 3 miles from Stanyan Street to the sea, and a mere 8 city blocks wide, Golden Gate Park has been, for more than a century, the city's favorite escape. You can do anything here, from walking in the woods to wandering through galleries of fine art.

CA 1 divides the 1,017-acre park roughly in half, with the eastern section arguably more popular, and certainly more packed with historic structures and gardens. The closer you get to the Pacific, the more "rugged" the environs. This is where you'll find the buffalo paddock, the polo greens, and the golf course, as well as trails linking the greenway to the sands of Ocean Beach.

Along this looping tour, paths lead from garden to garden, hitching the Conservatory of Flowers to the rhododendron dell to the Japanese Tea Garden to the San Francisco Botanical Garden, and finally to the rose garden. The route also cruises through the Music Concourse, flanked by the de Young Museum and the California Academy of Sciences, and includes a cruise around Stow Lake.

Golden Gate Park was conceived when San Francisco was in the throes of the great building and population boom that followed the gold rush. Building a park on the tip of the peninsula was not an easy task, given that the landscape was dominated by windblown sand dunes. It had inauspicious beginnings, at least for an open space now known for its magnificent gardens and towering trees. When the site was first selected in the 1860s, the acreage was little more than sand dunes whipped by ocean winds. Undeterred, civil engineer William Hammond Hall, the park's designer and first superintendent, set to work, starting with a survey and then embarking on an arduous plan to turn what was perceived as a wasteland into a world-class public space.

The transformation began with the planting of imported beach grasses, lupine, and barley, which stabilized the dunes. Then more than 200,000 trees were planted. The Conservatory of Flowers was erected, in 1878, while Hall was in charge: It is the oldest building in the park. Closed following a battering winter storm in 1995, the conservatory reopened after a $25 million restoration in 2003.

The park's second champion, Scottish garden designer John McLaren, continued Hall's work during his sixty-year tenure as superintendent. He also was responsible for the installation of some of the park's most popular attractions, including Stow Lake and Huntington Falls.

▶ The Conservatory of Flowers houses permanent and rotating horticultural exhibits, showcasing exotic orchids, bromeliads, ferns, aquatic plants, and others. It is open Tuesday through Sunday from 10 a.m. to 4 p.m.; a fee is charged. Guided tours are available. For more information, call (415) 831-2090 or (415) 666-7001, or visit www.conservatoryofflowers.org.

Stow Lake attracts boaters, walkers, and duck feeders.

The route begins at the Conservatory of Flowers, then traverses the rhododendron garden to the Music Concourse. On the concourse, orderly rows of plane trees shade benches, and a band shell dominates the eastern end. But the dominant features are the two museums flanking the plaza. You could spend hours touring both. The de Young houses a permanent collection of fine art, as well as traveling exhibits that have featured the works of masters like Monet, van Gogh, and Rembrandt. The California Academy of Sciences features exhibits showcasing the natural world, including a three-story rain forest exhibit and a living roof. The academy is also home to the Steinhart Aquarium and the Morrison Planetarium.

Beyond the concourse lies the Japanese Tea Garden, and beyond that the San Francisco Botanical Garden. Again, hours can be lost: The grace of the tea garden, built for the 1894 California Mid-Winter Exposition and modeled after rural Japanese gardens, is enchanting; and nearly a mile of interlocking paths cruise through the outdoor exhibits in the botanic garden, planted with more than 8,000 different species.

▶ Formerly known as the Strybing Arboretum, the San Francisco Botanical Garden features exhibits from New Zealand, South America, and Asia, as well as plantings native to California. The garden also hosts the Helen Crocker Russell Library of Horticulture, with its 27,000-volume reference collection. For more information, call (415) 661-1316 or visit sfbotanicalgarden.org.

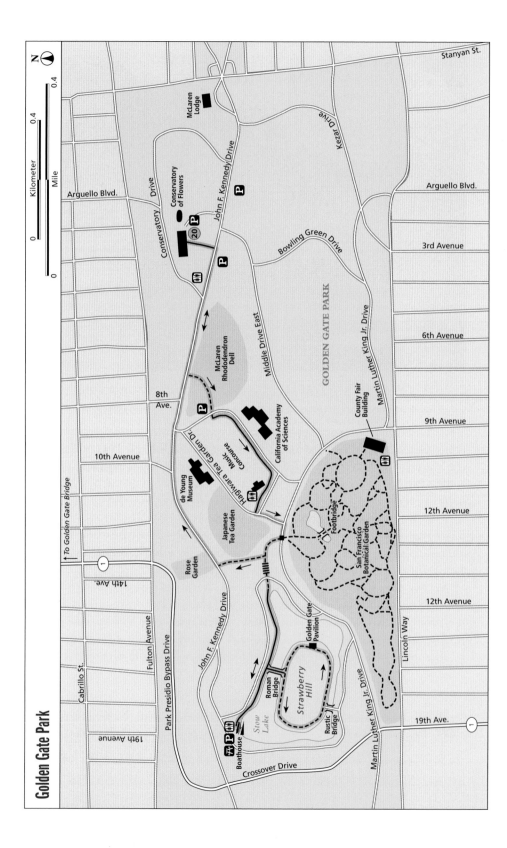

Golden Gate Park

N

Kilometer
0   0.4
Mile
0   0.4

Stanyan St.

McLaren Lodge

Conservatory Drive

Conservatory of Flowers

20

John F. Kennedy Drive

Arguello Blvd.

P

P

Kezar Drive

P

Bowling Green Drive

Arguello Blvd.

3rd Avenue

McLaren Rhododendron Dell

Middle Drive East

GOLDEN GATE PARK

6th Avenue

8th Ave.

P

California Academy of Sciences

Music Concourse

Hagiwara Tea Garden Dr.

County Fair Building

Martin Luther King Jr. Drive

9th Avenue

10th Avenue

de Young Museum

Japanese Tea Garden

Footbridge

12th Avenue

To Golden Gate Bridge

1

14th Ave.

Rose Garden

San Francisco Botanical Garden

12th Avenue

Fulton Avenue

Cabrillo St.

Park Presidio Bypass Drive

John F. Kennedy Drive

Golden Gate Pavilion

Lincoln Way

19th Avenue

Stow Lake

Roman Bridge

Strawberry Hill

Rustic Bridge

Martin Luther King Jr. Drive

19th Ave.

1

P

Boathouse

Crossover Drive

The Conservatory of Flowers, rehabbed after being damaged by a storm, is a glass-house beauty.

Stow Lake is the next stop on the loop: It draws picnickers, parents with strollers, and kids and elders who feed the placid ducks while others explore the lake by paddleboat. Strawberry Hill, the lake's island, is reached via a footbridge, and a nice trail circles through the forest at its base. Man-made Huntington Falls spills from the summit into the lake near the Golden Gate Pavilion, a gift from San Francisco's sister city, Taipei, Taiwan. At the lake's boathouse, you will find restrooms, a snack bar, and boat, rickshaw, and bicycle rentals. The boathouse is a great place to take a breather: Kick back and watch the turtles sun themselves on half-submerged logs.

To loop back to the Conservatory of Flowers, head left at the bottom of the staircase you climbed to reach Stow Lake, and walk out to John F. Kennedy Drive. The rose garden is on the far side of the road; no charge to wander here. From the rose garden, follow John F. Kennedy Drive back to the trailhead.

Miles and Directions

Note: *Mileage does not include tours of the Conservatory of Flowers, any of the museums, the Japanese Tea Garden, or the San Francisco Botanical Garden.*

0.0 Start at the Conservatory of Flowers on John F. Kennedy Drive. Check out the exhibits and the formal plantings that surround the glasswork, then use the pedestrian tunnel that runs under John F. Kennedy Drive to reach the paved path alongside the busy drive.

0.4 At the large wooden sign, go left into the John McLaren Rhododendron Dell. Follow the paths, staying right, through agapanthus, rhododendron, and blankets of raspberries.

0.6 The rhododendron garden empties onto the Music Concourse. The California Academy of Sciences is on the left as you face the band shell; the de Young Museum is on the right. Walk through the concourse, past the fountain, then pass behind the band shell to reach Hagiwara Tea Garden Drive.

0.9 Cross Hagiwara Tea Garden Drive to the gate to the Japanese Tea Garden. A fee is charged to tour the site. Turn left, and walk down Hagiwara Tea Garden Drive to its junction with Martin Luther King Jr. Drive.

1.0 Use the crosswalk on Martin Luther King Jr. Drive to reach the Friend Gate of the San Francisco Botanical Garden. Again, there's a fee to tour. To continue to Stow Lake, cross back to the tea garden side of Martin Luther King Jr. Drive and go left on the asphalt path, heading up into a grove of trees. Pass a no-longer-used exit from the tea garden, and veer left at the next intersection. Head uphill and away from the tea garden.

1.5 Climb the set of concrete stairs to the roadway that encircles Stow Lake. Cross the road and turn right, following the asphalt path along the shoreline.

1.7 Take the paved path/road that veers across the concrete Roman Bridge. Cross the bridge and turn right onto the broad dirt trail that circles the base of Strawberry Hill. Stay right on the flat path to circumnavigate the island; paths and stairways lead left and steeply to the summit.

2.0 Pass the stone Rustic Bridge, the Golden Gate Pavilion, and Huntington Falls before completing the circuit of Strawberry Hill.

2.1 Cross the Roman Bridge and turn left to the boathouse. When you are ready to move on, retrace your steps to the asphalt path that drops from the lakeside and descend the concrete stairs.

2.3 Turn left at the bottom of the stairs and walk to John F. Kennedy Drive.

2.4 Cross the roadway via the crosswalk to the park's extensive rose garden. After you've smelled the roses, follow the sidewalk that parallels John F. Kennedy Drive back toward the Conservatory of Flowers.

3.0 Arrive back at the trailhead.

21 Summit Loop Trail

From the summit of San Bruno Mountain, panoramic views radiate in all directions, with the San Francisco skyline shimmering to the north.

Start: Upper parking lot by information signboard
Distance: 3.3-mile loop
Hiking time: About 2 hours
Difficulty: Moderate due to length and elevation changes
Trail surface: Dirt trail
Best season: Year-round, though you are least likely to encounter view-obscuring fog in autumn.
Other trail users: Trail runners, mountain bikers
Canine compatibility: No dogs allowed
Land status: San Bruno Mountain State and County Park
Fees and permits: Parking fee
Schedule: Park opens daily at 8 a.m. and closes at or before sunset depending on season. Check park website at parks.smcgov.org/ locations/visiting-san-bruno-mountain-state-county-park for seasonal hours.
Trailhead amenities: Information signboard, restrooms, trash cans, picnic tables
Maps: USGS San Francisco South; San Bruno Mountain State and County Park map online at parks.smcgov.org/ san-bruno-mountain-park-trails
Special considerations: Fog, rain, and wind can make conditions downright arctic on the summit, so be prepared for changing conditions. Rain can also render portions of the trail muddy and slick.
Trail contact: San Mateo County Parks Department, 455 County Center, 4th Floor, Redwood City, CA 94063-1646; (650) 363-4020; parks.smcgov.org/ san-bruno-mountain-state-county-park

Finding the trailhead: To reach the trailhead from the northbound lanes of I-280 in Daly City, take the Eastmoor Avenue exit to Junipero Serra Boulevard. Go right (northwest) on San Pedro Road for 0.3 mile to East Market Street. Follow East Market Street, which becomes Guadalupe Canyon Parkway, for 2.2 miles to Radio Road and the entrance to San Bruno Mountain State and County Park on the left (north).

From the southbound lanes of I-280, exit at Eastmoor Avenue and turn left (east) on Eastmoor, heading over the freeway to the intersection with San Pedro Road and Junipero Serra Boulevard, then follow the directions above.

From US 101, take the Bayshore Boulevard exit. Head west on Bayshore Boulevard for about 2 miles to the Guadalupe Canyon Parkway. Turn right (west) on Guadalupe Canyon Parkway and proceed to Radio Road and the park entrance on the right (north).

From the entry kiosk, follow the park road past the lower parking area. The road curves under Guadalupe Parkway and climbs to a second, upper lot located 0.2 mile from the kiosk. GPS: N37 41.709' / W122 26.056'

The Hike

There is plenty of history on San Bruno Mountain, which shrugs its massive green and gray shoulders out of the sprawling development that surrounds it. Costanoan

Indian villages were located on its flanks, and after the Spaniards arrived, the slopes were grazed by cattle and sheep. In the Mexican period, the mountain was incorporated into Rancho Canada de Guadalupe la Visitation y Rancho Viejo. In the late nineteenth century, the land was purchased by Charles Crocker, one of the builders of the Central Pacific Railroad, and passed into ownership of the Crocker Land Company after the tycoon's death.

But to be honest, San Bruno Mountain's summit trails are known more for their views, which are among the best in the Bay Area and encompass sister peaks with their own great panoramas: Mount Tamalpais to the north, Mount Diablo to the east, and Montara Mountain to the south. If the fog rolls in—a soggy jacket that San Bruno Mountain wears with great regularity—the vistas shut down and a hiker's attention turns downward and close in, to the little brown birds that flick into and out of the brush, to the tiny pops of magenta and white blooms in the rich bouquet of coastal scrub along the trail's edge. It's a wonderful, overlooked hike.

Through the years various schemes to develop the slopes of the landmark peak were considered, including a plan that, according to one historian, was foiled because of wafting odors from a nearby dump. In the end, due in part to the presence of the endangered mission blue butterfly, the mountain was preserved. Most recently, the name San Bruno evokes not the mountain but a man-made disaster that struck the city around it. In 2010 a gas pipeline burst on a residential street, and the resulting fireball incinerated thirty-five homes and killed eight people.

From the trailhead, go right (west) on the gravel singletrack, heading into the scrub. At the first trail junction, with the Eucalyptus Loop Trail, go left and up into the eucalyptus grove. The right trail is the end of the Summit Loop Trail. As with all loops, you can go either way; it's described here clockwise, with a quick and dirty up and a long, relaxed downhill run.

A switchback lifts you into the scrub, and you'll not find much shade on the rest of the climb (which won't matter if the fog's in). At 0.3 mile the Eucalyptus Loop and the Summit Loop Trail part ways. Go right (southeast) on the Summit Loop Trail.

Switchbacks offer alternating views of San Francisco Bay to the north and Mount Diablo to the east, and sight across the pastel homes of Daly City and southern San Francisco to the Pacific to the west. Those uniform houses are the proverbial "little boxes on a hillside; little boxes made of ticky tacky," described with acid sarcasm in the famous folk tune by Malvina Reynolds, which later became the theme for the TV series *Weeds*.

After traversing into and out of Cable Ravine, the trail intersects the Dairy Ravine Trail and then reaches an overlook with awesome city-from-a-bird's-eye views.

Two quick switchbacks and a ridgetop traverse south toward the summit towers leads to the intersection with the Ridge Trail. Remain on the Summit Loop Trail, which climbs toward the dishes of the tower farm. The summit service road intersects the route at 1 mile. The Summit Loop Trail continues across the road. A sign directs you behind a utility shed, and the trail then switchbacks down to a paved side road.

Summit Loop Trail (San Bruno Mountain State and County Park)

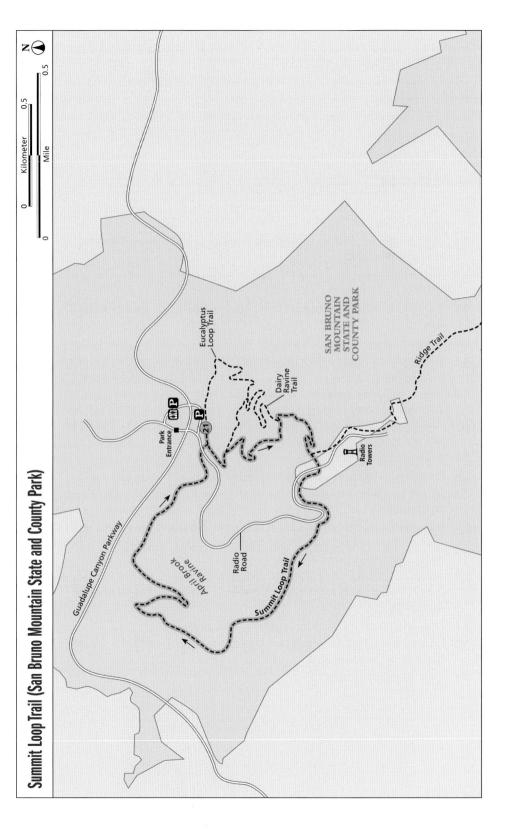

Alternatively, you can follow Radio Road down to the side road, pass the gate, and pick up the signed Summit Loop Trail there.

The path descends gently through the lush scrub, then steepens and sweeps around switchbacks into April Brook Ravine, crossing its soggy bottom via a wooden bridge. On the climb out of the ravine, short boardwalks span the seeps that bleed from the mountainside into the brook. On the final stretch, the trail parallels Guadalupe Canyon Parkway to the trailhead.

Miles and Directions

0.0   Start by heading right from the informational signboard on the signed Summit and Eucalyptus Loop trails.

0.1   Reach the first trail junction and go left (south and up) on the combined Eucalyptus Loop and Summit Loop Trails.

0.3   The Eucalyptus Loop and Summit Loop Trails diverge. Go right (southeast) on the Summit Loop Trail.

0.4   The trail traverses the south face of a brushy ravine and climbs with the radio towers in sight.

0.6   Reach the Dairy Ravine Trail junction. Stay straight (right/east) on the Summit Loop Trail.

0.8   At the intersection with the Ridge Trail, stay right (south) on the Summit Loop Trail toward the tower farm.

1.0   Arrive at the summit service road. A sign indicates the Summit trail continues behind the utility shed. Follow the trail down to the paved spur road. Alternatively, follow Radio Road down to the gated spur road and pick up the Summit Loop Trail behind the gate, on the right side of the spur road.

1.6   Pass a bench.

1.8   Pass a trail marker and a social trail, remaining on the obvious Summit Loop Trail.

2.2   Another social trail leads left (north) to a small rock outcrop; remain right and downhill on the Summit Loop Trail.

2.5   The steepening track heads down switchbacks to the base of April Brook Ravine, where a wooden bridge spans the creek. The trail climbs in a long traverse out of the ravine toward the Guadalupe Canyon Parkway.

2.8   Sweep around the north face of the mountain, climbing parallel to the Guadalupe Canyon Parkway. The trail passes over bridges and through copses of oak, Monterey pine, and eucalyptus.

3.1   Cross a final bridge and climb to the summit service road.

3.2   Cross the road to the Eucalyptus Loop and Summit Trail intersection. Go left (northeast) and down on the Summit Trail.

3.3   Arrive back at the trailhead.

22 Portola Discovery Site on Sweeney Ridge

Follow a steep paved track onto the windswept ridge where Gaspar de Portola and his men became the first Europeans to look down on sprawling San Francisco Bay.

Start: The base of paved Sneath Lane

Distance: 3.6 miles out and back

Hiking time: 2–3 hours

Difficulty: Strenuous given the steady climb and descent

Trail surface: Pavement, dirt roadway, dirt trail

Best season: Year-round. Fall is best for views, as the fog is less likely to roll in.

Other trail users: Mountain bikers, trail runners, equestrians on ridgetop trails

Canine compatibility: Leashed dogs permitted

Land status: Golden Gate National Recreation Area (GGNRA)

Fees and permits: None

Schedule: Sunrise to sunset daily

Trailhead amenities: None

Maps: USGS Montara Mountain; GGNRA Sweeney Ridge map available online at www.nps .gov/goga

Trail contact: Golden Gate National Recreation Area, Building 201, Fort Mason, San Francisco, CA 94123; (415) 561-4323; www .nps.gov/goga. Golden Gate National Parks Conservancy, Building 201, Fort Mason, San Francisco, CA 94123; (415) 561-3000; www .parksconservancy.org.

Finding the trailhead: Approach the trailhead from the north or south via I-280 or Skyline Boulevard (CA 35) in San Bruno. Take the Sneath Lane exit from I-280 and head west to Skyline Boulevard. Sneath Lane heads west from Skyline Boulevard, climbing through a residential area for 1.1 miles to the trailhead parking area. There is parking for about 15 cars at the end of the road. GPS: N37 37.175' / W122 27.250'

The Hike

Explorer Gaspar de Portola, employed by Spain to establish settlements in Alta California to cement its status as a Spanish colony, set off from Mexico with Franciscan padre Junípero Serra in 1769. Leaving Serra behind to set up a mission in San Diego, Portola and his men headed north, looking for Monterey Bay, which had previously been scouted by sea. But because Portola was traveling by land, he passed that bay by, not recognizing the perfect colonial site described by an earlier explorer.

So Portola and the members of his expedition kept walking. And walking. Finally, on November 4, 1769, the exhausted leader and his companions climbed Sweeney Ridge to survey the lay of the foreign land. There they beheld the unexpected—a bay of colossal proportions that was destined to become one of the most important harbors on the California coast.

If Portola surveyed San Francisco Bay from the discovery site that bears his name today, he'd still be amazed, but he'd also be stunned. Much of the pristine expanse of water and wildland that existed in missionary times has long since been filled in and built over. But the top of the ridge still presents panoramic views of the Bay Area; in

California's Sainted Padre

While Gaspar de Portola gets the credit for "discovering" San Francisco Bay, Padre Junípero Serra is, without question, the greatest celebrity of California's missionary period. Born in Mallorca, Spain, in 1713, Serra entered a Franciscan convent as a teenager and was ordained a Franciscan priest in 1738. By the time he departed to serve as a missionary in the New World in 1749, he had earned a doctorate of philosophy and was renowned as both a teacher and preacher.

His penchant for walking (a Franciscan habit, so to speak) began as soon as he arrived in the New World. But on a journey from Vera Cruz to Mexico City, he was bitten on the leg or foot by a nasty bug, and that resulted in a nagging disability that plagued him for the rest of his life. The story goes that Serra walked from mission to mission during his tenure in Alta California, but there's a good chance that is the stuff of legend.

In 1769 Serra was dispatched to Alta California to serve as the *padre presidente* of the string of missions that was to be established there. He envisioned a chain of fifty missions stretching along El Camino Real from Baja California to Alaska, according to one historian, but fell far short of this goal, establishing or overseeing the establishment of only nine. His successor, the less-heralded but equally productive Padre Fermín Francisco de Lasuén, would establish another nine, and others would establish the remainder. In the end, twenty-one missions would line California's El Camino Real.

After devoting his life to missionary work and defense of his neophytes, Serra died in a spartan cell at Mission San Carlos Borroméo (the Carmel Mission) in 1784. He was canonized by Pope Francis in 2015.

fact, that spectacular exposure would later result in the installation of a Nike missile site on the site during the Cold War. And later, local residents would battle to protect the 1,200-foot ridgetop from developers who not only wanted to build houses on the slopes but also run a freeway through it.

A serpentine monument that commemorates the Portola expedition is on the north side of a little clearing atop a knob on the ridgeline. A second monument honoring Carl McCarthy, who escorted more than 11,000 people to the site as part of its

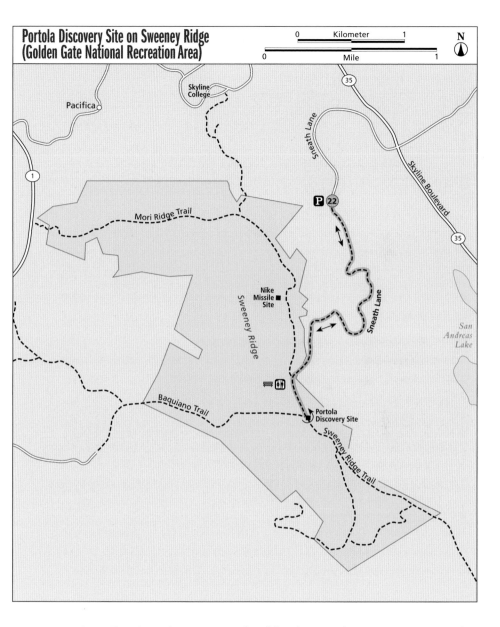

0   Kilometer   1

0   Mile   1

N

Skyline College

Pacifica

Sneath Lane

Skyline Boulevard

35

Mori Ridge Trail

P 22

35

Nike Missile Site

Sweeney Ridge

Sneath Lane

San Andreas Lake

Baquiano Trail

Portola Discovery Site

Sweeney Ridge Trail

preservation effort, is on the opposite side of the clearing; this carries engravings that identify Bay Area landmarks visible on the horizon.

Begin the climb to the discovery site on Sneath Lane, passing around the gate. Head south down the paved road toward the northern reaches of San Andreas Lake, which glitters in the distance. Filled with water from the Sierra Nevada via the gravity-fed Hetch Hetchy pipeline system, the reservoir occupies a portion of the San Andreas Fault's rift zone.

The easy passage ends when the route arcs southwest and begins a long, unbroken ascent to the ridgetop. The pavement winds relentlessly upward through coastal scrub, but because it's exposed, the climb offers views of the reservoir, San Francisco International Airport, and bay. Pass the "fog line" at 0.8 mile; beyond this marker a single faded yellow line runs up the middle of the road.

The trail swings northwest, climbing at a fairly steep pitch, with San Bruno Mountain rising to the northeast. The steepness mellows as the road heads back southwest and passes through a stand of eucalyptus. A final push, this time heading directly west, lands you atop the ridge at the intersection of Sneath Lane and the Sweeney Ridge Trail.

Leave the pavement for the dirt track that heads south toward the Portola Discovery Site, passing a restroom and a bench perched on the edge of the trail that look west over the Pacific. The discovery site is less than 0.1 mile from the trail junction, reached via any of the use trails that mount a knob on the east side of the route.

When your explorations at the site are complete, return as you came.

Miles and Directions

0.0 Start by heading down the paved road beyond the gate.

0.2 Pass a gated side road.

0.3 Start the long climb on the pavement to the ridgetop.

0.8 Pass the fog line.

1.3 Travel through a stand of eucalyptus.

1.7 Reach the summit of the ridge and the intersection with the Sweeney Ridge Trail, with a restroom and bench. Turn left (south) on the unpaved Sweeney Ridge Trail. The paved road to the north leads to water towers and the remains of the Nike missile site.

1.8 Take in the views from the Portola Discovery Site. The Baquiano Trail drops off the ridge to the west. Retrace your steps to the trailhead.

3.6 Arrive back at the trailhead.

Options: If ever an area begged for further exploration, it would be Sweeney Ridge. Aside from the discovery site, you can head north along the ridge to the Nike missile site or west toward the Pacific on either the Baquiano or Mori Ridge Trail.

23 Sawyer Camp Trail

Snaking through the San Andreas Fault's rift valley, the Sawyer Camp Trail is a classic hike on the San Francisco peninsula. It traces the shoreline of the San Andreas Reservoir and ends at the spectacular Jepson Laurel.

Start: Trailhead on Hillcrest Boulevard
Distance: 5.0 miles out and back
Hiking time: 3–4 hours
Difficulty: Easy
Trail surface: Pavement
Best season: Year-round
Other trail users: Cyclists, trail runners, skaters, equestrians
Canine compatibility: No dogs allowed
Land status: San Francisco Public Utilities Commission
Fees and permits: None
Schedule: Sunrise to sunset daily

Trailhead amenities: Water; restroom at San Andreas Lake dam; restrooms, water, picnic sites, and trash cans at Jepson Laurel
Maps: USGS San Mateo; San Mateo County Department of Parks map and guide available at trailhead and online at parks.smcgov.org/sawyer-camp-segment
Trail contact: San Mateo County Department of Parks, 455 County Center, 4th Floor, Redwood City, CA 94063; (650) 363-4020; parks.smcgov.org. Contact park rangers for the Crystal Springs Regional Trail by calling (650) 573-2502. The trail runs through the Peninsula Watershed of the San Francisco Public Utilities Commission; (415) 544-3289; sfwater.org.

Finding the trailhead: From the southbound lanes of I-280 in Millbrae, take the Millbrae Avenue exit. Pass under the freeway and follow the frontage road back north to Hillcrest Boulevard. Turn left (west) on Hillcrest Boulevard and pass back under the freeway to the parking area. From the northbound lanes of I-280, take the Millbrae Avenue/Larkspur Drive exit. Follow the frontage road north to Hillcrest Boulevard and turn left (west) under the freeway. The Crystal Springs Regional Trail intersects Hillcrest; the trailhead for the Sawyer Camp segment is to the left (south) as you face the coastal mountains. GPS: N37 35.336' / W122 24.787'

The Hike

The Sawyer Camp Trail is heralded as one of the most popular on the San Francisco peninsula, and for good reason. It's eminently pleasant—paved, flat, shady, running alongside water and through fragrant woodlands, and wide enough to share with other trail users, whether on foot, bicycle, or skates. No wonder hundreds of thousands of people gravitate to it each year.

But the trail has more to recommend it than just its setting. The geologic history is provocative: The path sits atop the San Andreas Fault. Rocks on one side of the rift valley differ drastically from those on the other, as they ride on entirely separate tectonic plates. Geology and human history collide in this place, as the fault's 1906 rupture represents a defining moment for San Francisco.

The Jepson Laurel is the oldest living laurel in California.

Then there's the natural history. The Jepson Laurel, the largest in the state of California, enjoys a sun-splashed dotage at the turnaround point of this hike. It's a gnarly, tumbledown specimen, fenced off to protect its ancient, delicate root system. But when you read the 600-year-old tree's vital statistics, recorded in 1923 and codified on a stone plaque (at the time it was only the second-largest laurel in the state), you can't help but be impressed. Though the laurel dwarfs the surrounding flora and fauna, some of these smaller creatures are rare and exotic as well. The Peninsula

Watershed's 23,000 acres are home to more than 250 different animal species, including the endangered San Francisco garter snake and the blue elfin butterfly.

The watershed doesn't slack off in the human history department either. Gaspar de Portola, the Spanish explorer who set out to find Monterey Bay in 1769 and instead "discovered" the much larger and more significant San Francisco Bay, camped in the area; a plaque at the trailhead memorializes this event. The trail is named for Leander Sawyer, who, in the mid-nineteenth century, established a camp near the Jepson Laurel. He would go on to run cattle on his property in the valley. The route also served as the main thoroughfare between San Francisco and Half Moon Bay for a time. Much of the original trail was flooded when the Crystal Springs Dam was built in 1888.

▶ The Jepson Laurel measures 22 feet 4 inches in circumference and stands 55 feet tall.

The route is an easy ramble on a paved track in the shade of overarching bay laurels and stately oaks. It has only one minor hill, which leads to and from the San Andreas Lake dam. Otherwise, the trail rolls along the valley floor alongside a portion of the reservoir, with the breath of the not-so-distant Pacific washing over forested Sawyer Ridge to the west. It's just all-around pleasant.

It's also very straightforward. After an inauspicious start, adjacent to the noisy interstate on a path adorned with a power station, power poles, and a sign warning about rattlesnakes, you'll drop to the dam and the lovely lake at the 0.5-mile mark. Cross to the west side of the rift valley, then cruise through the woods past a couple of picnic areas to the Jepson Laurel, where you'll find restrooms, picnic tables, benches, trash cans, and water. This is the turnaround point, but you can continue south to Crystal Springs Reservoir and beyond, if you choose. Otherwise, return as you came.

Miles and Directions

0.0   Start behind the gate on the south side of Hillcrest Boulevard's cul-de-sac.

0.2   Climb the paved road past a power station to an informational billboard and a water fountain.

0.3   The trail descends past a gated road on the left (south). Sweeping curves drop past a bench toward the shimmer of San Andreas Lake.

0.5   Pass a mile marker and signs that denote the area as a state fish and game refuge.

0.8   Arrive on flat land at the east end of the San Andreas Lake dam.

1.0   Cross the dam, passing a plaque describing the San Andreas Fault. On the west side of the lake, another plaque commemorates the dam's completion in 1960. The trail turns left (south) down the rift valley.

1.5   Pass a bench and a mile marker.

1.7   A small picnic area and benches are tucked into a lovely laurel grove on the right (west) side of the trail.

2.0   After passing another bench and picnic ground—this one in an oak grove—reach another mile marker.

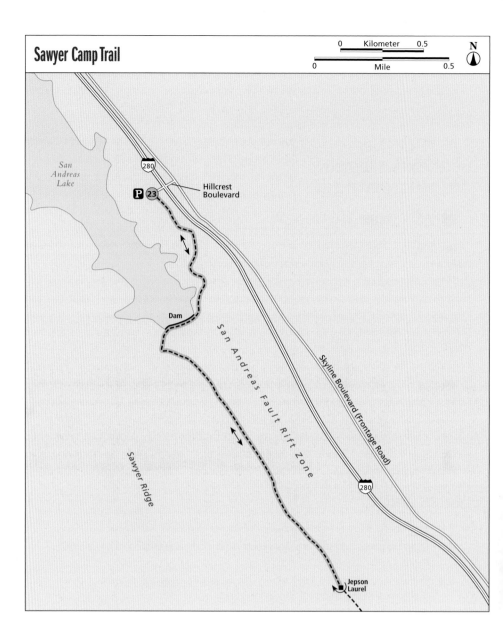

0   Kilometer   0.5

N

0   Mile   0.5

San
Andreas
Lake

280

P 23

Hillcrest
Boulevard

Dam

San Andreas Fault Rift Zone

Skyline Boulevard (Frontage Road)

Sawyer Ridge

280

Jepson
Laurel

2.5 Arrive at the Jepson Laurel, where you'll find informational signs, picnic tables, restrooms, and other facilities. Unless you plan to follow the trail farther south, retrace your steps to the trailhead.

5.0 Arrive back at the roadside parking area on Hillcrest Boulevard and trail's end.

Option: The Sawyer Camp Trail segment is 6 miles long in its entirety and reaches south to Crystal Springs Reservoir. Continue as time and desire allow.

East Bay

The old Giant Powder Company pier on Point Pinole

24 Marsh and South Pasture Trails

The looping trails through Rush Ranch pass a bedrock mortar used by the Patwin tribe and a boneyard of ranch equipment and offer long-ranging views across the Sacramento and San Joaquin River delta.

Start: Signed Marsh trailhead behind museum and visitor center
Distance: 4.1-mile double loop
Hiking time: 2-3 hours
Difficulty: Easy
Trail surface: Dirt ranch roads
Best season: Spring for wildflowers; late fall and winter for migrating birds
Other trail users: None
Canine compatibility: Dogs not permitted
Land status: Solano Land Trust/Rush Ranch
Fees and permits: None
Schedule: Sunrise to sunset daily, year-round

Trailhead amenities: Large gravel parking area, picnic tables, restrooms, signboard with information and maps. Restrooms and information are in nearby visitor center and exhibit room.
Maps: USGS Fairfield South; online at www .rushranch.net; in interpretive trail brochures available at visitor center
Special considerations: Insects, including wasps, can be pesky at Rush Ranch in the dry season. Wear repellent.
Trail contact: Solano County Land Trust, 1001 Texas St., Fairfield, CA 94533; (707) 432-0150; www.rushranch.net; www.solanoland trust.org/RushRanch.aspx

Finding the trailhead: From I-80 eastbound east of Cordelia, take the CA 12/Abernathy Road exit, and continue east on CA 12 toward Rio Vista. Go about 3.5 miles on CA 12 to Grizzly Island Road, and turn right (a left turn at this arterial will put you on Sunset Avenue). Follow Grizzly Island Road for 2.4 miles to Rush Ranch, on your left. GPS: N38 12.530' / W122 01.537'

The Hike

At Rush Ranch, where salt water meets freshwater, coastal plain meets Great Valley prairie, and eucalyptus grove meets open ranchland, the emphasis is on the ecotone. A quote from Richard Louv's "Last Child in the Wilderness," displayed on the wall in the exhibit hall of the ranch's visitor center, explains why:

> Look for the edges between habitats;
> Where the trees stop and a field begins;
> Where rocks and earth meet water.
> Life is always at the edges.

But history is also emphasized on the trails that circle through this former working ranch. The Suisun Marsh was a seasonal hunting and gathering ground for natives known as the Suisuns, a subgroup of the larger Patwin tribe. The indigenous people left one lasting mark on the land: the grinding stone overlooking the marsh.

Retired ranching equipment rests in the boneyard at Rush Ranch.

Other signs of the Suisuns—their tule canoes, shelters, and granaries—have all been reclaimed by time, though for educational purposes re-creations of a Patwin tule house, shade shelter, and granary have been built on the Marsh Trail and are used as part of the ranch's educational program.

The ranch eventually became part of the vast holdings of Hiram Rush, who arrived in California in 1849 and defied conformity by not running off to the gold fields. Instead, Rush ran cattle, and his son, who inherited the ranch, did the same. Significantly, neither the junior nor the senior Rush did much to alter the natural tidal ebb and flow of the Suisun Marsh, leaving the basic underpinnings of the landscape and its rich habitats untouched. It was the pristine nature of the ranch and its

▶ The Rush Ranch Educational Council, a nonprofit organization, supports educational programs at Rush Ranch as well as promotes the ranch's unique environmental and historical attributes. Write to the council at PO Box 2088, Fairfield, CA 94533; call (707) 432-0150; or visit www.rushranch.net.

The Owners of Rush Ranch

Rush Ranch founder Hiram Rush arrived in California in 1849. But he didn't come seeking gold, like so many others. Instead, he arrived with a seed herd of cattle, which he ran on about 5,000 acres; he would eventually acquire more than 50,000 acres in the Suisun Valley and Monterey County. Thousands of head of cattle and sheep were raised on Rush Ranch, and Hiram Rush amassed both wealth and influence in his years on the delta. But he met a tragic and unexpected end when he was killed in a buggy accident on the ranch. He was 60 years old.

Hiram's son, Benjamin Franklin Rush (1852–1940), took over following his father's death, and he too achieved great success. He ran as many as 5,000 head of cattle and sheep on the land. He and wife Anna raised seven children; he also became a publisher and a bank director and was active in valley agricultural societies.

The ranch was acquired by the Solano Land Trust in 1988, with a grant from the California Coastal Conservancy. Its remarkable attributes, including its location within one of the largest estuarine marshes in the western United States, have also resulted in its inclusion in the San Francisco Bay National Estuarine Research Reserve.

unique niche in the shrinking San Francisco Bay delta region that attracted preservation efforts. A signboard in the parking area says it best: The ranch may be "40 miles from the Golden Gate . . . but it's still the edge of the bay."

The edges along the ranch's two loop trails are very different. The Marsh Trail climbs over a hilltop covered in grasses, then slides down to the salt marsh and continues into a managed freshwater marsh. The South Pasture Trail follows a finger of the marsh to where the Suisuns used a large stone as a bedrock mortar for food preparation, then climbs into the uplands, where grazing cattle crop the annual grasses before the stalks crisp in the summer sun. From grassland to marshland the differences in flora are profound—bunchgrass is a stone's throw from pickleweed, which in turn is a few paces from cattail, which backs up to hedges of nonnative blackberry. The fauna, which includes a variety of songbirds, shorebirds, waterfowl, and raptors, as well as river otter, coyote, and raccoon, transitions from habitat to habitat as instinct or opportunity dictates.

But the creatures of Rush Ranch often find what they need at the edges, and that's where they are most often observed. Among the unique (and sometimes endangered) species that can be found on the ranch's more than 2,000 acres are the Suisun shrew and the Suisun Marsh song sparrow; rare plants include the Suisun aster and Jepson's tule pea. The delta smelt, a species of some controversy because the protection of its freshwater-saltwater habitat has allegedly resulted in job losses within California's agricultural community, is also present in the waterways of the marsh.

The Suisun Marsh, one of the largest contiguous estuarine marshes in the western United States, is a fragment of a once-sprawling wetland delta system that reached well into the Central Valley. About 90 percent of that vast marshland has been eroded by the activities of humankind in the last 250 years or so. The water has been corralled by levees and channeled into sloughs; vast tracts have been drained for farmland, and other areas have been filled to provide a foundation for residential and commercial development. At Rush Ranch, you will walk on levees that restrict tidal action on all but 5,000 of the marsh's 85,000 acres.

At about 2 miles each, and given their different emphases, hiking both the Marsh and South Pasture Trails makes for an enlightening day hike. Be sure to pick up interpretive guides for the trails at the visitor center; return them for the next user when you're done.

Begin on the Marsh Trail, which starts directly behind the visitor center in a grove of eucalyptus. Fairly common on ranch properties, the Australian native was intended to serve as a timber crop, but the wood proved unsatisfactory as lumber and the trees were instead employed as windbreaks.

Climb to the top of Overlook Hill, take a seat on a bench, and survey the marsh, which stretches north toward the Vaca range and west toward the steep flanks of Mount Diablo. To the south and east are the Potrero Hills, completely treeless, emerald green in the wet season and hot gold in summer and fall.

Drop to the base of the hill and head into the wetland, following a mown path that threads through reeds and tules; tall, thick hedges of blackberry; and wild fennel that can tower to 8 feet. The thick foliage shelters ducks, red-winged blackbirds, and other resident and migrating birds. Cross a tidal gate, which helps regulate the inflow and outflow of salt water, carefully managed to provide optimum habitat for wildlife.

As you swing east, the Suisun Slough, looking much like a lazy river, comes into view. Beyond the water you can see some of the development around Fairfield; planes taking off and landing at nearby Travis Air Force Base fly low over the ranch on occasion. Interpretive marker 12 identifies Goat Island and Japanese Point, but you wouldn't know unless the marsh has water in it. Stay left on the ranch road, circling the hill to a gate. In winter or early spring, a wildlife pond appears on the left; this dries up later in the year. Climb the two-track trail and cross the grassland back to the main ranch, where you'll pick up the South Pasture Trail at the trailhead under the water tower.

The South Pasture Trail begins in the boneyard, where ranch implements are labeled and being left to do what a rancher would let them do when they were no longer of use: rust and decay. The trail follows a ranch road east toward Mount Diablo; the interpretive guide directs your attention to the summer homes of thousands of solitary native bees that burrow into the ground along the road, creating distinctive "chimneys." Look right to the Notch, a cleft in the rise where dirt was excavated for use in levee building. An interpretive sign describes ongoing research being conducted on the ranch.

At Spring Branch Creek, the marsh extends across the trail up into the swale on the left. Trail signs indicate the crossing with the Spring Branch cutoff, which is an option for a shorter loop. Stay right instead, heading out a short distance to the Indian grinding rock, where Indian women prepared the harvest of the marsh year after year, leaving deep holes in the soft pale rock. An arrow directs you up to an overlook, then down through a gate, where the route wanders onto grazed pastureland.

Walking along the high ground, the views across the tidal plain to the peaks of the coastal ranges are unimpeded. The trail curls to the east and then the south. The property is still grazed; keep your distance and the livestock will do the same. Off in the distance, through a gap in the Potrero Hills, wind turbines slowly spin in the nearly constant breeze.

Low trail markers direct you across the uplands, then down into the swale and across Spring Branch Creek again. Beyond the boardwalk that spans the marsh, the trail rolls back to the boneyard and trailhead.

Miles and Directions

Marsh Trail

0.0 Start at the signed trailhead behind the visitor center.

0.1 Trails merge; proceed toward the hill on the broad dirt ranch road.

0.2 Pass through a fence. Go left, then quickly right, picking up the trail that climbs onto Overlook Hill.

0.3 Reach the top of Overlook Hill. Take in the views, then descend left (west), following signs down to the trail at the base. Go right on the Marsh Trail, passing the mock native structures.

0.4 At the signed trail junction, go left into the marsh.

0.5 Cross the tidal gate.

1.0 At interpretive marker 12, the trail arcs east over a rise, then south toward the Potrero Hills.

1.25 Pass through a gate and go left, circling the hill on the ranch road.

1.5 At the gate, continue straight up the hill on the two-track road toward the ranch.

2.0 Arrive back at the ranch and trailhead.

South Pasture Trail

0.0 Start at the signed trailhead under the water tower in the boneyard. The trail splits immediately; stay right to complete the loop in a counterclockwise direction.

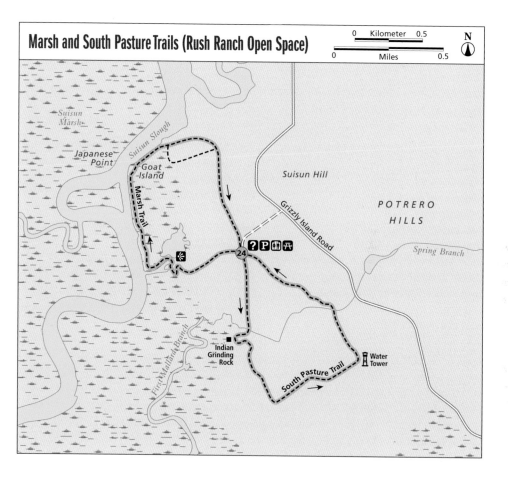

Marsh and South Pasture Trails (Rush Ranch Open Space)

0 Kilometer 0.5

0 Miles 0.5

N

Suisun Marsh

Japanese Point

Goat Island

Suisun Slough

Marsh Trail

Suisun Hill

Grizzly Island Road

POTRERO HILLS

Spring Branch

24

First Mallard Branch

Indian Grinding Rock

South Pasture Trail

Water Tower

0.3 Reach the junction with the Spring Branch Creek Cutoff and the signed trail to the Indian grinding rock.

0.4 Visit the grinding rock, then continue around its base and climb to an overlook with a bench. The South Pasture Trail continues to the right.

0.8 Another bench affords great views of Mount Diablo.

1.0 Reach the water tank. Stay right, on the ranch road that leads to another viewing bench. Go sharply left at the bench (an arrow points the way), heading downhill on the mown track.

1.5 Cross the swale and pass through a stile at the break in the fence line. At the junction with the Spring Branch Creek Cutoff, stay right, following the path across the boardwalk.

1.7 Pass a second fence line via a stile. Follow the ranch road up and over the small hill.

2.0 Reach the boneyard.

2.1 Arrive back at the trailhead.

25 Carquinez Strait Overlook Trail

Pass through swaths of grassland and stands of eucalyptus on this easy trail overlooking the strategic Carquinez Strait.

Start: Signed trailhead at Bull Valley Staging Area
Distance: 1.9-mile lollipop
Hiking time: About 1 hour
Difficulty: Easy
Trail surface: Dirt road, dirt trail
Best season: Spring and fall
Other trail users: Trail runners, mountain bikers
Canine compatibility: Leashed dogs permitted
Land status: Carquinez Strait Regional Shoreline
Fees and permits: None

Schedule: Park hours change by season; consult park website. Generally, trails open sunrise to sunset daily.
Trailhead amenities: Restrooms, trash cans, information signboard with map
Maps: USGS Benicia; online at www.ebparks .org/parks/carquinez#trailmap
Trail contact: East Bay Regional Parks District, 2950 Peralta Oaks Ct., Oakland, CA 94605; (888) EBPARKS or (888) 327-2757; www .ebparks.org/parks/carquinez

Finding the trailhead: From I-80 in Crockett, take the Crockett/Pomona Street exit. Follow Pomona Street through town; it becomes Carquinez Scenic Drive. Follow Carquinez Scenic Drive for 1.6 miles to the Bull Valley Staging Area. From CA 4, take the Cummings Skyway exit toward Crockett. Follow the Cummings Skyway to Crockett Boulevard and turn right. Follow Crockett Boulevard for about 2 miles into Crockett. Turn right onto Pomona Street. Follow Pomona Street/ Carquinez Scenic Drive for 1.6 miles to the staging area and trailhead. GPS: N38 02.942' / W122 11.832'

The Hike

This short loop trail overlooks what once was one of the busiest shipping lanes in the San Francisco Bay Area. The Carquinez Strait links San Pablo Bay to Grizzly Bay and, hence, San Francisco to the Sacramento and San Joaquin River Delta. The strait also presented a short paddle from the East Bay to the North Bay for native people, a relatively easy, protected traverse from one set of oak- and grass-covered hills to the next.

This region of the Bay Area, though growing more residential as time passes, has long been industrial. During the gold rush, men and goods were ferried between San Francisco and Sacramento, gateway to the mining camps, via the strait, which was deep enough to allow passage of tall ships. Gold fever would forever alter the waterways, with detritus from mining operations—tailings, toxins, trash—silting up both river and delta, and threatening livelihoods, travel, and habitat. Most destructive was hydraulic mining, by which water under pressure was used to wash away mountainsides and expose ore. It wasn't until this practice was outlawed, in 1884, that the rivers and delta were able to begin to recover.

The Carquinez Bridge spans the strait.

That recovery is ongoing. Many watersheds in the Sierra Nevada drain into the Sacramento and San Joaquin, and the mining residues they carry—mercury among them—continue to flow through the Carquinez Strait into San Francisco Bay. Those freshwater inflows and the habitats they foster are embattled in other ways as well, with ongoing debates over how to mitigate environmental damage wrought by diversion of river water to agriculture in the Central Valley. The rope being used in the tug-of-war between environmental groups in the Bay Area and farmers in the Great Valley is stretched right through the strait.

The trail begins by winding through open grasslands, which sport a lovely wildflower bloom in season. The Carquinez Bridge is visible to the west, and sailboats,

▶ One leg of Juan Bautista de Anza's epic trek of discovery and settlement included passage along the Carquinez Strait, where he and his entourage reportedly traded with the Ohlone people who lived on the shoreline. The 1,200-mile-long Juan Bautista de Anza National Scenic Trail commemorates the Spanish explorer's 1775–76 journey, which resulted in the establishment of one of the first colonial settlements in what would become Alta California.

Carquinez Strait Overlook Trail (Carquinez Strait Regional Shoreline)

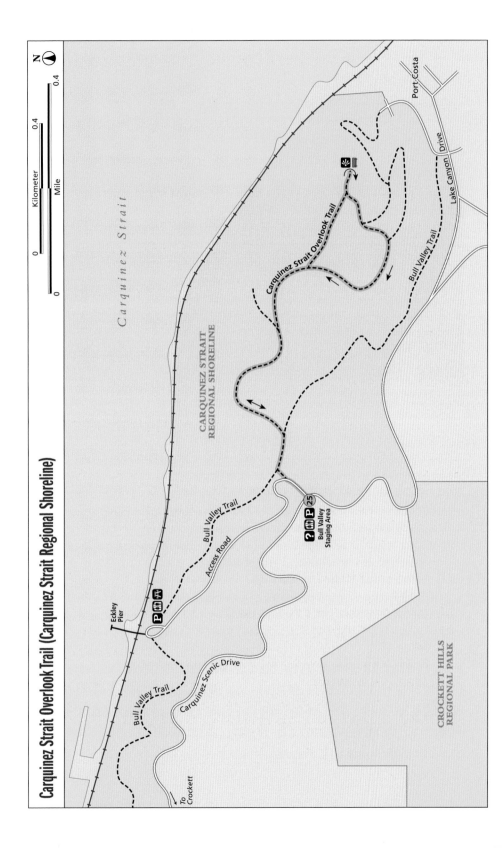

Carquinez Strait

Eckley Pier

CARQUINEZ STRAIT REGIONAL SHORELINE

Carquinez Strait Overlook Trail

Bull Valley Trail

Access Road

Bull Valley Trail

Bull Valley Staging Area

25

Lake Canyon Drive

Port Costa

Bull Valley Trail

Carquinez Scenic Drive

To Crockett

CROCKETT HILLS REGIONAL PARK

N

Kilometer
0   0.4

Mile
0   0.4

▶ The city of Benicia, on the north side of the Carquinez Strait, is named for Francisca Benicia Carrillo, wife of General Mariano Vallejo, a prominent Spanish, and later Mexican, political and military leader in Alta California. The nearby city of Vallejo is named for the general himself.

kayaks, and fishing vessels ply the waterway below; you might even see a seaplane flying low over the strait. The views are decidedly urban, with housing developments and business and industrial parks painted on the hills of Benicia across the strait. You may also find yourself sharing the landscape with cattle, which are placid and will generally move away (or off the trail) as you approach.

The trail enters a large stand of eucalyptus. The loop starts just within the fragrant woodlands; you can go either way, but the route described here goes left (clockwise). After a short passage through the trees, the trail breaks out into the open again. Take a break at the picnic table or bench at the overlook, enjoying views out to the port of Benicia, down onto the tucked-away hamlet of Port Costa, and south toward the distinctive summits of Mount Diablo.

The trail continues around the overlook knob, passing a side path down to Port Costa, and reenters the eucalyptus. Steep draws open to the left, one down onto the road leading into Port Costa, a second thick with eucalyptus. Close the loop, then retrace your steps to the trailhead, enjoying nice views of the Carquinez Bridge on the return.

Miles and Directions

0.0 Start by climbing away from the trailhead on the traversing main track, avoiding spurs that lead up onto the hillside and down toward the Eckley Pier.

0.2 At the Y junction, stay left, following the broad track that parallels the shoreline.

0.3 Pass a bench and overlook.

0.5 Pass an unmarked trail that leads left into a stand of eucalyptus. Stay right on the loop trail, which also enters the large stand of fragrant trees.

0.6 At the junction that marks the beginning of the loop, stay left, circling in a clockwise direction.

0.8 Arrive at the overlook. Take in the views, then continue on the loop trail.

0.9 Pass a side path on the left that leads down toward Port Costa, staying right on the loop trail.

1.3 Back in the eucalyptus, close the loop. Go left to return to the trailhead.

1.9 Arrive back at the trailhead.

Option: After your hike, continue down the park road to the Eckley Pier, with waterfront picnic sites, restrooms, lawns, and fishing from the dock.

26 Mount Wanda

Climb through the hills just south of John Muir's fruit farm to high points named for the naturalist's two daughters.

Start: Mount Wanda trailhead on south side of CA 4 in Martinez
Distance: 3.0-mile lollipop
Hiking time: About 2 hours
Difficulty: Moderate due to steep slopes
Trail surface: Dirt roadway
Best season: Year-round; wildflowers are best in spring.
Other trail users: Trail runners
Canine compatibility: Leashed dogs permitted on Mount Wanda trails. No dogs allowed in visitor center, Muir home, or Martinez adobe unless they are service dogs.
Land status: John Muir National Historic Site
Fees and permits: None
Schedule: Trails on Mount Wanda open daily from sunrise to sunset. Ranger-led night hikes are also offered; check at visitor center. Muir home and visitor center open daily 10 a.m. to 5 p.m., with holiday closures on Christmas, New Year's Day, and Thanksgiving.
Trailhead amenities: None other than parking and trash cans. Restrooms, information, and water are available at the John Muir National Historic Site visitor center, located about 3 blocks north on the north side of CA 4.
Maps: USGS Briones Valley; trail map available online at www.nps.gov/jomu/planyourvisit/maps.htm
Trail contact: John Muir National Historic Site, 4202 Alhambra Ave., Martinez, CA 94553; (925) 228-8860; www.nps.gov/jomu

Finding the trailhead: From CA 4 in Martinez, take the Alhambra Avenue exit. Head south on Alhambra Avenue, passing under the railroad trestle, to the junction with Franklin Canyon Road. Turn right onto Franklin Canyon Road, then immediately left into the parking lot (a stop for public transportation) at the trailhead. GPS: N37 59.358' / W122 07.800'. The John Muir National Historic Site proper is 1 block north of the freeway exit.

The Hike

On an April day in 1895, John Muir headed into the hills above his Martinez fruit farm with his daughters. Of this outing the "father of the national parks" would write: "Took a fine fragrant walk up the west hills with Wanda and Helen, who I am glad to see love walking, flowers, trees, and every bird and beast and creeping thing. . . . A fine fragrant walk, the babies are delighted."

With a freeway having since been built at the base of those west hills, the high points of which bear the names of Muir's daughters, fine and fragrant doesn't become apparent until you have climbed up and away, around the corner and into the draw. But then, in full sunshine, you can appreciate what the father and his children once cherished.

And when the hike is through, you can cool down with a tour of the home where Muir and his wife, Louie, raised their two daughters, and where Muir kept the office in which he would pen books and articles about the wonders of nature he had witnessed and the value of conserving those wonders for future generations. The windows of Muir's "scribble den" open northward across what remains of the family's lucrative fruit ranch. The fortune that Muir amassed from the operation of this ranch would enable the wilderness advocate to pursue his passion for wandering and enable him to compose the books that would become his legacy.

Though the homesite and trails are within easy walking distance of each other, because they are separated by busy thoroughfares and exits from CA 4, it's recommended that hikers park in the lot at the trailhead on the south side of the highway and railroad tracks. From the lot, walk around the corner onto Franklin Canyon Road to the signed trailhead. The hike begins inauspiciously, traversing a hillside shaded with oak and bay and bombarded with the sounds of the nearby roadways. The trail is a gravel road wide enough for hikers to climb side by side; fortunately, the road noise is not so loud as to preclude walking and talking.

John Muir in the Bay Area

Think of John Muir, and Yosemite comes to mind. It was in that grandest of national parks that Muir found his muse; in the Sierra Nevada, his Range of Light, his lengthy careers as a nature writer and conservationist would be ignited.

But Muir had a more prosaic side. It wasn't all about wandering and hobnobbing with presidents and power brokers; he was also a father, husband, and "gentleman farmer." His marriage to Louie Strentzel grounded him, and together they would raise two daughters. He amassed a small fortune in ten years' work on the farm, which paid for the journeys and political work that would follow. Once released from the farm, which his wife recognized was stifling him, he would travel to Alaska on several occasions, to Europe, and to South America.

Muir wrote many of his books in the house on the farm in Martinez, where his "scribble den" is carefully preserved. Many of those works—*The Yosemite, Stikeen, My First Summer in the Sierra*—were written and published after Louie Muir's death in 1905. Muir himself would pass on in 1914, technically from pneumonia but, many say, from heartbreak after losing the battle to save the Hetch Hetchy Valley—his Tuolumne Yosemite—from being dammed to create a reservoir for the city of San Francisco.

Mount Diablo rises above the shoulder of Mount Wanda.

Road noise fades as the trail curls into a drainage and passes another sign, and as you climb you stand a much better chance of hearing the one hundred kinds of birds that reside in or visit the hills above the Muir home. Pass the link with the nature trail, which is part of the return route, and continue up into the grasslands, where the rolling slopes are shaded by the occasional spreading oak. The draw on the left steepens, with an unsigned neighborhood access trail breaking left just below a saddle.

In the saddle below Mounts Helen and Wanda, a web of trails connect. Stay left on the broad path past the bench, then left again and again. The dark shoulders on Mount Diablo rise over the grassy summits. The high point on Mount Wanda is reached via an obvious two-track path that climbs, again, to the left. (**Note:** The USGS quad appears to label this Mount Helen.)

The summit, outfitted with a bench and interpretive sign, offers panoramic views of Mount Diablo to the east, the hills above neighboring Briones Valley to the south, and, on clear days, Mount Saint Helena in the distance to the north.

When ready, descend back into the saddle and, again, stay left at the junctions to drop into the drainage at the headwaters of Strentzel Creek. Pass an interpretive sign, then bear right onto the signed nature trail.

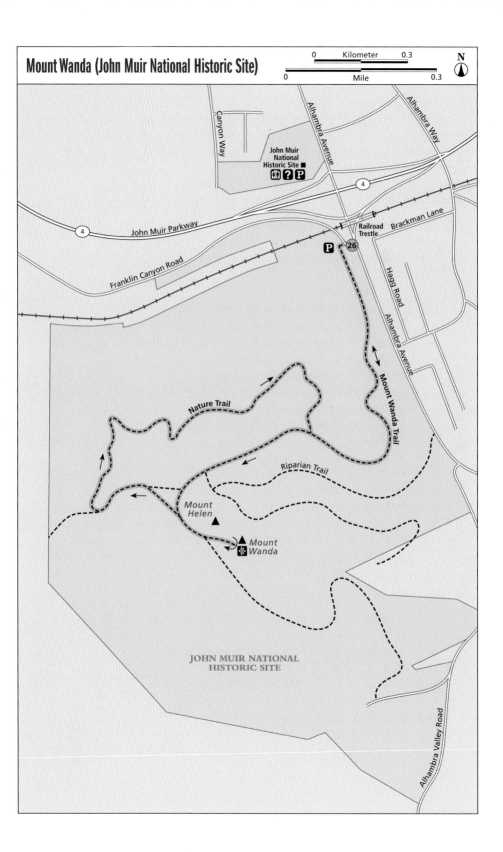

Mount Wanda (John Muir National Historic Site)

0   Kilometer   0.3

0   Mile   0.3

N

Canyon Way

Alhambra Avenue

Alhambra Way

John Muir
National
Historic Site ■

4

John Muir Parkway

4

Railroad
Trestle

Brackman Lane

Franklin Canyon Road

26

Hagg Road

Alhambra Avenue

Nature Trail

Mount Wanda Trail

Riparian Trail

Mount
Helen ▲

▲ Mount
Wanda

JOHN MUIR NATIONAL
HISTORIC SITE

Alhambra Valley Road

The narrow nature trail winds through steep ravines under a thick canopy of oak and bay laurel. Unfortunately, highway noise returns on this stretch of the route, but the path is more rustic and wild than the roadway, looping through folds in the hillsides and crossing small bridges that span seasonal creeks. Posts line the path, keyed to a nature guide available at the historic site's visitor center. ⁓

The nature trail ends back on the gravel Mount Wanda Trail above the draw. Go left onto the roadway and descend to the trailhead.

Miles and Directions

0.0 Start in the parking lot at the corner of Alhambra Avenue and Franklin Canyon Road. Walk around the corner onto Franklin Canyon Road to the signed trailhead.

0.3 Pass a bench and interpretive sign. A spur trail takes off to the right; stay left on the broad, obvious trail.

0.5 Pass a second interpretive sign.

0.7 At the junction with the end of the nature trail, stay left on the wide Mount Wanda Trail.

0.9 At the junction with an unsigned trail breaking left at the head of the draw, stay right on the roadway, continuing to climb. About 100 yards farther, at the bench, stay left, then stay left again.

1.1 A two-track breaks left, climbing toward the summit.

1.2 Reach the top. Take in the views, then return to the saddle, staying left at the junctions to drop into the Strentzel Creek drainage.

1.5 At the signed junction, go right onto the singletrack nature trail.

2.0 Pass a picnic site on the right, staying left to past post #3.

2.3 At the junction with the Mount Wanda Trail, go left and retrace your steps.

3.0 Arrive back at the trailhead.

27 Bay View Trail and Owl Alley Loop

Given that this route loops through the former dynamite works of the Giant Powder Company, there's a temptation to call the hike explosive. But it's not. Instead, this peaceful ramble features stunning views and gentle terrain, with the occasional bunker punching the historic button.

Start: Paved path heading to railroad bridge
Distance: 4.4-mile loop
Hiking time: 2–3 hours
Difficulty: Moderate due only to length
Trail surface: Gravel, dirt path, pavement
Best season: Year-round
Other trail users: Mountain bikers, equestrians, trail runners
Canine compatibility: Leashed dogs permitted
Land status: Point Pinole Regional Shoreline
Fees and permits: Day use/parking fee; dog fee; additional charge if you opt to use shuttle
Schedule: Park open 5 a.m. to 10 p.m. unless otherwise posted
Trailhead amenities: Restrooms, water, information, trash cans, picnic sites, dog waste stations

Maps: USGS Mare Island; East Bay Regional Park District map and brochure to Point Pinole Regional Shoreline
Special considerations: A shuttle runs several times daily (Thurs through Mon) between the park entrance and the picnic areas and fishing pier on the tip of the point. Fishing is permitted off the pier and along the shoreline. Please obey California Fish and Game regulations, posted on the pier. Those fishing from shore must carry a valid fishing license.
Trail contact: East Bay Regional Park District, 2950 Peralta Oaks Ct., PO Box 5381, Oakland, CA 94605-0381; (888) EBPARKS; www.ebparks.org

Finding the trailhead: Point Pinole Regional Shoreline is at 5551 Giant Hwy. in Richmond. From I-80, take the Fitzgerald Drive/Richmond Parkway exit. Follow the Richmond Parkway southwest for 1 mile to Atlas Road. Turn right (west) on Atlas Road, and go 0.8 mile to Giant Highway. Turn left (south) on Giant Highway and travel 0.5 mile to the park entrance on the right (west). GPS: N37 59.475' / W122 21.351'

The Hike

Wandering along the edge of San Pablo Bay, with shorebirds wheeling on the sea breeze, it's difficult to envision Point Pinole as the site of a dynamite factory. Yet the Giant Powder Company churned out explosives on the point in a thriving enterprise that included a company town, railroad, production facilities, and a dance hall. Over nearly one hundred years, Giant Powder produced two billion tons of dynamite at the site. *Ka-boom!*

Dynamite production here is now a relic. These days, bird-watchers, picnickers, hikers, and anglers wander trails that offer peaceful vistas of the bay. A fishing pier juts from the tip of the point, with the ruins of the powder company pier running

Mount Tamalpais and an expanse of San Pablo Bay are framed by eucalyptus boughs.

alongside. The thick eucalyptus forest shelters earthworks and other structures erected to buffer and mix explosions on the property.

The Giant Powder Company found its way to Point Pinole, just north of Richmond, following a series of blasts that destroyed its facilities in San Francisco and Berkeley, according to park literature. Explosions were expected in the manufacture of dynamite, nitroglycerine, and gunpowder, so the location—at the time remote—seemed a safe place to set up shop. The earthworks and eucalyptus served as buffers. The Atlas Powder Company eventually bought out Giant, and when Atlas ceased operations in the 1960s, Bethlehem Steel acquired the property and dismantled the powder works and attendant infrastructure. The East Bay Regional Parks District acquired the land in the early 1970s.

▶ During World War II, women employed at the Atlas Powder Company were known as "Dynamite Dorothys."

The Giant Powder Company may be defunct, but industry continues apace in this part of the Bay Area. Neighboring Point San Pablo is home to a Chevron refinery, with the hills on the approach to the Richmond–San Rafael Bridge dotted with storage tanks. The city boasts a deepwater port and extensive rail lines; in many ways Richmond's history has been shaped by the accessibility of transportation. After the Santa Fe Railroad established its terminus at the port at the turn of the twentieth century, a number of companies began doing business in the then-small burg, including a well-known railcar manufacturer, a chemical company, and a distiller.

When World War II erupted, the Kaiser Richmond Shipyards were built along the city's Southern Shoreline, and Richmond experienced an influx of workers that generated a "boomtown" feel, according to the city's website. In the postwar years, the shipyard's buildings were converted to other industrial uses, including "warehousing" facilities for Ford and International Harvester.

Begin an exploration of Point Pinole by following the paved roadway to a bridge that spans the railroad tracks. The junction with the Bay View Trail is on the other side of the tracks; the trail descends through eucalyptus to the shoreline of the sparkling bay, then turns sharply right to trace the waterline. As you head northwest on the route, views open of Mount Tamalpais and, farther north and more rounded and sprawling, Sonoma Mountain. The trail is mostly exposed, with the grasslands on the uphill side littered with wildflowers in spring and gnarly old eucalyptus providing dollops of shade.

At the 1-mile mark, a beach access trail marks a detour in the Bay View Trail. Follow the signed detour up and right, climbing to an intersection where you'll turn left (northwest), rejoining the Bay View Trail.

A series of intersections in the eucalyptus woodland follows. Take the Biazzi Trail on the right, which hitches up to the Nitro Trail, which then leads to one of the derelict remnants of the powder works. A sign on the building shell reads "Fire Extinguisher Here," a good thing at the time. The Nitro Trail continues around the far side of the building to rejoin the Bay View Trail, which continues within sight of the water toward the point. Pass the Angel Buggy Trail, an unnamed trail, and the remnants of an old packhouse and the trail that borrows its name, staying left on the Bay View at each junction.

The remnants of the Giant Powder Company are scattered along the trails in Point Pinole Regional Shoreline.

Another series of side trails intersects the Bay View Trail as you approach the tip of the point, but the way forward is obvious. Depart from the main track as the pier comes into sight, following an arcing singletrack that passes above a dynamite bunker before dropping to the picnic area and shelter at the start of the fishing pier and its shadow pier, which dates back to the powder works and is now little more than waterlogged timbers.

The return route begins by following the paved Point Pinole Trail, which leads southeast out of the picnic area. Just beyond the shuttle stop, bear left onto the Owl Alley Trail, a route less traveled (most walkers return via Point Pinole Trail). The alley is essentially a dirt service road, wide enough for walking side by side, shaded at the outset by eucalyptus. It dead-ends at the park headquarters and service yard, where the Cooks Point Trail breaks right and climbs to the site of Giant Station, now a sprawling recreational area, complete with a sand volleyball court, barbecues, group picnic areas, a tot lot, a horseshoe pit, restrooms, broad lawns, and views of Mount Tamalpais. A grand old eucalyptus rises above it all.

From Giant Station, a quick downhill stretch on the paved Point Pinole Road returns you to the railroad bridge, then down to the trailhead.

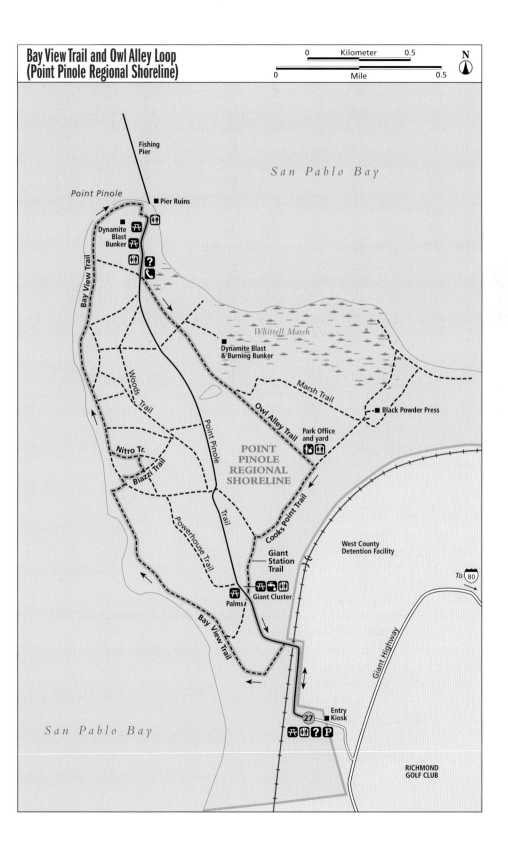

Bay View Trail and Owl Alley Loop
(Point Pinole Regional Shoreline)

0   Kilometer   0.5

0   Mile   0.5

N

San Pablo Bay

Fishing Pier

Point Pinole

Pier Ruins

Dynamite Blast Bunker

Bay View Trail

Whittell Marsh

Dynamite Blast & Burning Bunker

Marsh Trail

Woods Trail

Black Powder Press

Point Pinole Trail

Owl Alley Trail

Park Office and yard

Nitro Tr.

Biazzi Trail

POINT PINOLE REGIONAL SHORELINE

Cooks Point Trail

West County Detention Facility

Powerhouse Trail

To 80

Giant Station Trail

Palms

Giant Cluster

Bay View Trail

Giant Highway

San Pablo Bay

27

Entry Kiosk

P

RICHMOND GOLF CLUB

Miles and Directions

0.0 Start by following the paved Point Pinole Trail up to and across the railroad bridge.

0.2 At the signed junction, turn left onto the Bay View Trail.

0.5 Pass the unsigned Cooks Point Trail. Continue straight on the Bay View Trail.

1.0 Reach the Bay View Trail detour. A quick jog uphill leads to where the trail resumes. At the next signed junction, turn right onto the Biazzi Trail.

1.1 At the junction, turn left onto the Nitro Trail. Explore the hollowed-out building, including the staircase to nowhere, then follow the Nitro Trail around the backside to rejoin the Bay View Trail.

1.4 Turn right onto the Bay View Trail to continue out to the pier.

1.5 Pass the Angel Buggy Trail. Stay left on the Bay View Trail.

1.6 Reach the Packhouse Trail. The timbers and foundation of the packhouse are on the right. Continue straight on the Bay View Trail.

1.9 Pass the junction with the Tramway Trail. Stay straight on the Bay View Trail.

2.2 Where the Bay View Trail breaks right and descends to the picnic sites, stay left on the singletrack, which curls around a dynamite bunker now overgrown with eucalyptus. Take a sharp right at the bench to drop to the picnic area and shelter alongside the paved Point Pinole Trail.

2.4 Turn left onto the Point Pinole Trail to the fishing pier. Take a break on the dock. When you are ready to return, head down the Point Pinole Trail into the picnic area.

2.6 At the junction just beyond the shuttle stop, go left onto the signed Owl Alley Trail, leaving the pavement behind. *Option:* Point Pinole Trail leads more directly back to the trailhead, for a round-trip total of 3.4 miles.

2.8 Pass the China Cove Trail intersection. Remain on the obvious Owl Alley Trail.

3.0 Pass a freshwater pond on the right. The Whittell Marsh opens to the left.

3.1 Pass the junction with the Marsh Trail. Stay right on the wide Owl Alley Trail.

3.4 Arrive at the park offices and yard and the junction with the Cooks Point Trail. Turn right onto Cooks Point.

3.6 Pass the junction with the Sobrante Trail, remaining straight on the Cooks Point Trail. Continue about 200 yards to the junction with the Giant Station Trail and turn left. Look for the old bricks in the trail bed.

4.0 Pass the Giant Station group picnic site, with all the amenities and the grandmother eucalyptus arching overhead. At the junction with the Point Pinole Trail, at the Palms picnic site, turn left and head down the paved roadway.

4.2 Reach the junction with the Bay View Trail at the start of the loop. Retrace your steps from here.

4.4 Arrive back at the trailhead and parking area.

28 Rose Hill Cemetery and Chaparral Loop

This former coal-mining district is home to a historic cemetery and dark shafts that yielded the "black diamonds" that fired San Francisco commerce in the early twentieth century. Views of Suisun Bay and a walk on smooth sandstone punctuate the trails.

Start: Signed Nortonville trailhead in upper parking lot
Distance: 2.8 miles, out and back with a loop
Hiking time: About 3 hours for both trails, including time to explore cemetery and mining relics. If you chose to do the trails separately, plan on 1.5 hours for Rose Hill Cemetery and 1.5 hours for the Chaparral Loop.
Difficulty: Moderate due to steep pitches along both the Nortonville and Chaparral Trails. The Chaparral Loop Trail also features a stretch of smooth, potentially slick sandstone.
Trail surface: Dirt service/fire roads, dirt trail, pavement
Best season: Spring and fall. The trails have little shade, so can be miserable on a hot summer day. Winter rain may render the trails muddy and slippery.
Other trail users: Mountain bikers, equestrians
Canine compatibility: Leashed dogs permitted where posted, in parking lots, and in picnic areas. Dogs may be off-leash on trails outside these areas provided they are kept under control.

Land status: Black Diamond Mines Regional Preserve
Fees and permits: Parking fee; dog fee; fee for mine tours
Schedule: Park hours change seasonally. Gates open at 8 a.m. and generally close at about sunset; check park website at www.ebparks .org/parks/black_diamond for exact closing times.
Trailhead amenities: Restrooms, picnic sites, trash cans, water; information at Greathouse Visitor Center
Maps: USGS Antioch South; East Bay Regional Park District map and brochure available at visitor center or online at www.ebparks.org
Special considerations: Remain on trails to avoid contact with poison oak. Historic artifacts in the preserve are protected and should be left in place for future visitors to enjoy.
Trail contact: East Bay Regional Park District, 2950 Peralta Oaks Ct., PO Box 5381, Oakland, CA 94605-0381; (888) EBPARKS (888-327-2757), option 3, ext. 4562; www.ebparks.org

Finding the trailhead: The park is at 5175 Somersville Rd. in Antioch. From CA 4, take the Somersville Road exit. Head south on Somersville Road for 2.4 miles to the Black Diamond Mines Regional Preserve boundary. Continue another mile to the upper parking lot and trailhead. GPS: N37 57.544' / W121 51.800'

The Hike

Mining is a dirty business, no matter the pretty names—black diamonds for coal, quicksilver for mercury. Given the damage done as ores were wrestled from Bay Area mountains in the late nineteenth and early twentieth centuries, some of these sites have been effectively and poignantly reclaimed. Black Diamond Mines Regional

A hiker pauses among the headstones in the Rose Hill Cemetery.

Preserve, which links remnants of its mining history via pleasant trails through recovering habitats, is an example of how this reclamation can be done well.

In the late nineteenth century, these steep hills and canyons were part of the largest coal-mining district in California. The twelve mines yielded more than 4 million tons of black diamonds, according to park literature, with about 150,000 tons alone hauled out of the Eureka Mine over a thirty-five-year period. The Eureka coal was carried from the shaft, which plunged nearly 300 feet into the earth, on counterbalancing rail cars.

The coal played out just after the turn of the twentieth century, but the mining district was revived in the 1920s by the opening of sand mines, including the Hazel Atlas Mine, which can still be toured. About 1.8 million tons of sand were extracted before those operations were shut down in 1949; the sand was used in glassmaking and at a local steelworks.

These two trails showcase some of the shafts from which miners extracted their livelihoods and the cemetery where mine workers and their families, who lived in the five mining camps that grew up around the coal and sand works, were buried.

▶ The Rose Hill Cemetery is said to be haunted by a "white witch," the ghost of Sarah Norton, a midwife killed in a buggy accident in the late 1800s.

Wandering among the gravestones in the cemetery is poignant and provocative. Markers cascade down the hillside, siting the graves of beloved matriarchs, the victims of epidemics, natives of South Wales, and a disheartening number of infants. Take the time to read some of the engravings, like this one for two-year-old Julia Etta:

Looking north through folds in the hills to the sloughs in the Sacramento–San Joaquin Delta

> *Too sweet a flower to bloom on Earth*
> *She is gone to bloom in Heaven.*

Begin on the paved Nortonville Trail. At the top of a rise, you'll pass an interpretive sign that overlooks the site of Somersville on the right (west) and the trail to the Stewartville Townsite on the left (east). At the junction, just beyond a large pile of tailings (the debris left after valuable ore has been extracted from its source), you can either head up to Rose Hill Cemetery, then to the mine shafts along the Chaparral Loop, or vice versa. The route is described beginning with the climb to Rose Hill Cemetery, then with the journey around the Chaparral Loop.

The Nortonville Trail, a dirt road that leads up to the cemetery and beyond, is straightforward and climbs steadily, peppered with some steep pitches. The side trail to the cemetery is at the 0.6-mile mark; turn right on the narrow track, heading up toward the unlikely spires of cypress trees that mark the site. Take your time in this remarkable place; it's too special to hurry through.

To tour the mines, return as you came to the Hazel Atlas Trail intersection at the tailings pile, then head up toward the Greathouse Visitor Center. You can round the Chaparral Loop Trail in either direction; for this hike, turn right at the Greathouse Visitor Center, which was once the entry to the sand mine.

A staircase leads up to the Eureka Slope, a great gated shaft that dives into the earth. The Chaparral Trail switchbacks uphill from the shaft through a gnarly manzanita forest to the Manhattan Canyon Trail junction; stay left on the Lower Chaparral Loop, climbing first through more manzanita, then over smooth sandstone as the trail crests.

The Chaparral Loop passes an archway cut from sandstone.

At the high point of the loop, views open downvalley to Suisun Bay, the confluence of the Sacramento and San Joaquin Rivers as they drain into San Francisco Bay. The trail turns sharply north and drops over more sandstone, then past the cool cave of the powder magazine, to the Hazel Atlas portal, where mine tours begin. From the Hazel Atlas it's a quick descent on a wide track back to the picnic area below the Greathouse Visitor Center, and from there to the parking lot and trailhead.

Miles and Directions

0.0 Start at the parking lot on the paved Nortonville Trail.

0.2 Pass the Stewartville Trail intersection and the Somersville interpretive sign. A large tailings pile marks the intersection of the Nortonville Trail and the trail to the Hazel Atlas portal. Go right on the Nortonville Trail toward Rose Hill Cemetery.

0.3 Pass the first intersection with the Manhattan Canyon Trail on the left; keep climbing on the Nortonville Trail.

0.5 Pass the second Manhattan Canyon Trail intersection.

0.6 Reach the side trail to Rose Hill Cemetery. The cemetery gate is less than 0.1 mile up. Explore the cemetery, exiting at the upper gate. Go left to the Nortonville Trail, and return as you came to the Hazel Atlas trailhead near the tailings pile.

1.5 At the Hazel Atlas trail intersection, turn right onto the Chaparral Loop Trail. The trail splits in the picnic area, where you'll find trash cans, tables, restrooms, and water. Go right (southwest) on the Chaparral Loop Trail, past the Greathouse Visitor Center.

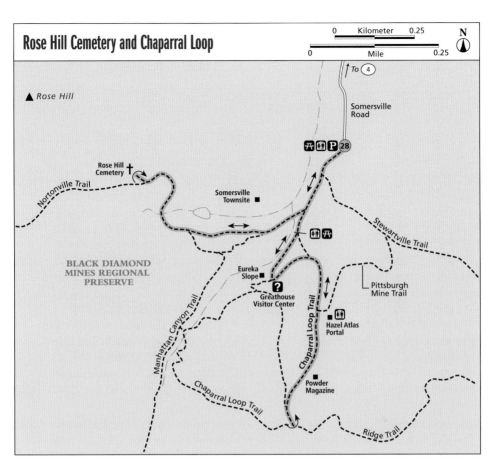

Rose Hill Cemetery and Chaparral Loop

0   Kilometer   0.25

0   Mile   0.25

N

▲ Rose Hill

Somersville Road

To 4

Rose Hill Cemetery

Nortonville Trail

Somersville Townsite

Stewartville Trail

BLACK DIAMOND MINES REGIONAL PRESERVE

Eureka Slope

Greathouse Visitor Center

Pittsburgh Mine Trail

Manhattan Canyon Trail

Chaparral Loop Trail

Hazel Atlas Portal

Chaparral Loop Trail

Powder Magazine

Ridge Trail

1.6 Climb the staircase to the Eureka Slope portal. Go right (west) to the Chaparral Loop Trail, climbing a narrow path that switchbacks up the hillside behind the Eureka shaft.

1.7 Reach the junction of the Chaparral and Lower Chaparral Trails. Go left on the Lower Chaparral Trail.

2.0 Climb through scrub to a traverse that offers views east of Suisun Bay, then rises steeply up over smooth sandstone and past an airshaft on the right to a signed junction. Go sharply left (downhill and north) on the Chaparral Loop.

2.1 The trail descends steeply over a sandstone apron—there is no distinct path, but in dry conditions the footing is good. At the base of the apron, two paths diverge; stay right on the steeper track to a trail marker for the Chaparral Loop. A quick jog to the right takes you to the powder magazine.

1.9 Stay left at another shaft on the main path and drop to a garage and the portal to the Hazel Atlas Mine. Railroad tracks lead out of the mine to a platform overlook in the shade.

2.0 Descend from the mine on a gravel road to the picnic area. Retrace your route to the trailhead and parking lot.

2.2 Arrive back at the trailhead.

29 Wildcat Peak and Laurel Canyon

Climb to the summit of Wildcat Peak, where a lookout offers panoramic Bay Area views. On the descent, a side trail leads into the thought-provoking Rotary Peace Grove.

Start: Paved trail fronting Environmental Education Center

Distance: 4.5 miles (including exploration of Rotary Peace Grove)

Hiking time: 3–4 hours

Difficulty: Strenuous due to elevation changes and length

Trail surface: Pavement, dirt roadway, dirt trail

Best season: Year-round. Trails may be muddy and slick after winter storms. Wildflower blooms on the high ground are best in spring.

Other trail users: Trail runners

Canine compatibility: No dogs allowed

Land status: Tilden Regional Park

Fees and permits: None

Schedule: Park open 5 a.m. to 10 p.m. daily; curfew imposed between 10 p.m. and 5 a.m.

Trailhead amenities: Water, restrooms, picnic facilities, a tot lot, and information, including trail maps, are available in the Tilden Nature Area parking lot and at the Environmental Education Center, just a little way down the trail.

Maps: USGS Richmond; East Bay Regional Park District brochure and map available at trailhead and online at www.ebparks.org

Trail contact: East Bay Regional Park District, 2950 Peralta Oaks Ct., PO Box 5381, Oakland, CA 94605-0381; (888) EBPARKS (888-327-2757), option 3, ext. 4562; www.ebparks.org

Finding the trailhead: From I-80, take the Buchanan Street exit and head east on Buchanan for 0.2 mile to merge onto Marin Avenue. Continue east on Marin Avenue for about 1.8 miles to the roundabout (the Circle). Go around to Marin Avenue (the second exit) and turn right. Go another 0.7 mile up Marin Avenue to Grizzly Peak Boulevard. Turn left (north) on Grizzly Peak Boulevard and go 0.1 mile to Sunset Lane. Turn right onto Sunset Lane and go 0.2 mile to Wildcat Canyon Road. Turn right onto Wildcat Canyon Road and go 0.5 mile to Central Park Drive. Turn left onto Central Park Drive and go about 1.1 miles to its end in the nature area parking lot. GPS: N37 54.540' / W122 15.911'

The Hike

In addition to being in one of the premier parks above one of the premier universities in the world, this loop also dips into the Rotary Peace Grove, where for more than fifty years giant sequoias have been planted to honor the premier peacemakers and thought leaders of our time. At the apex a lookout—another Rotary contribution—presents the hiker with premier 360-degree views.

The University of California at Berkeley, while not directly incorporated into the hike, is located just below Tilden Park. Established in 1868, Cal has long been an educational powerhouse. It consistently ranks among the top 20 universities in the nation, a remarkable feat considering the rankings are stuffed with private and Ivy League

▶ Anglican bishop, philosopher, and poet George Berkeley is the namesake of both the university and the city. The Berkeley Historical Society recounts how the university trustees, contemplating what to call their gestating college, were inspired by a Berkeley poem that celebrates free and original thought fostered in a new and inspiring place.

institutions. Cal is a rebellious school, and the community that surrounds the campus reflects the creative and intellectual stimulation it fosters. From earthquake science to the mitochondrial Eve, the Sierra Club to the atomic bomb, fruit cocktail to no-fault divorce, researchers, students, and faculty have helped shape the world as we know it.

When not occupied with their studies or promoting social change by protesting for free speech or the end to apartheid, many students take to the hills. The magnificent parks that top the ridgeline above the school, and the trails that snake through them, are their playground. Many of the routes lead to the crest, where on clear days you can look west past the Golden Gate to the broad Pacific and east across the Great Valley toward the Sierra Nevada.

This route begins in the park's nature area. Pick up a map and any information you need at the Environmental Education Center, then head down the paved trail toward Jewel Lake. Almost immediately a boardwalk breaks left from the paved route, passing through the dense alder and willow alongside hidden Wildcat Creek. The boardwalk ends at Jewel Lake, a tiny reservoir with benches along the shoreline. This is also where the flats end; from here it's all uphill to the summit, then downhill back to the trailhead.

At the far end of the lake, pick up the Sylvan Trail to Wildcat Peak, climbing into eucalyptus. These trees add a crisp perfume to the air, but in wind the forest is eerie, the trunks and limbs creaking like squeaky doors in a haunted house. A couple of easy switchbacks lead up to the junction where the Peak and Sylvan Trails split; stay left on the Peak Trail and continue to climb.

The route breaks out of the woods within 0.25 mile, forest slowly giving way to chaparral and grassland. The crest of the ridgeline is visible above, and the trail zigzags through the brush, always ascending but never painfully steep. Though there is little shade, maritime breezes and breaking fogbanks moderate temperatures on all but the hottest summer days. A little higher and the westward views start to open, of the city and the Golden Gate and San Pablo Bay to the north.

At the unmarked trail junction at about 2 miles, break left to a pretty overlook shaded by a giant Monterey pine. A livestock fence runs along the right (east) side of the spur. Take in the panoramic views, then return to the main trail and continue climbing.

The Peak Trail ends on Nimitz Way, a broad dirt track. Go left and steeply uphill to the Rotary lookout, a stone platform on the ridgetop. On a clear day the views are outstanding, of Oakland, Berkeley, San Francisco, the Golden Gate, Mount Tamalpais,

Steep steps lead down to the crossing of Laurel Creek.

San Pablo Bay, the rolling hills surrounding the San Pablo Reservoir, Mount Diablo, and finally the rolling crest of the Oakland hills as you scan from west to east and back again.

Tilden's Botanic Gardens and More

Tilden is one of the oldest parks in the East Bay Regional Park District, and one of the best outfitted in the entire Bay Area. Within its boundaries you can take a whirl on a merry-go-round, pet a goat, ride a steam train, explore exotic gardens, dip into Lake Anza, or simply sit in the shade on a hillside with stunning views.

Begin or end your hike with a tour of the Environmental Education Center, which features a walk-through display of the ecology and history of the Wildcat Canyon watershed, including geology, flora and fauna, and human history. From conquest to coyotes, you'll find it here. The center is open Tuesday through Sunday from 10 a.m. to 4:30 p.m. year-round; it is closed Christmas, Thanksgiving, and New Year's Day.

The Little Farm has been a family favorite since it opened in 1955. It is located next to the environmental center and is open daily from 8:30 a.m. to 4 p.m.

Farther afield but well worth the trek is Tilden's Botanic Garden. This stand-alone hike, albeit a short one, immerses visitors in the amazing diversity of California's herbal and floral heritage. Students and faculty from Cal have used the garden for botanical research and conservation of rare species native to the state for more than seventy-five years. Along its historic paths California becomes a small world, where only a few steps separate the floral wonders of the Sierra from those of the seashore.

The botanic garden was established in 1940, under the direction of longtime garden administrator James Roof and with the help of the New Deal's Works Project Administration. The redwood grove, a distinctly California phenomenon, was among the first garden "rooms" planted; this is now surrounded by gardens from the Shasta area, the Channel Islands, and Southern California's deserts. Development of the garden was interrupted by World War II and by fires and floods in the 1950s, but by the time Roof retired in 1975, it was firmly established.

The garden is open from 8:30 a.m. to 5 p.m. (5:30 p.m. in summer) daily, and closed on Thanksgiving, Christmas, and New Year's Day. From the nature area, head back up to Wildcat Canyon Road and turn left. Follow Wildcat Canyon Road for about 0.5 mile to the well-signed parking area on the right. GPS: N37 53.546' / W122 14.572'

Back on Nimitz Way, head steeply downhill to the Rotary Peace Grove. A large plaque lists the dignitaries commemorated within—popes and presidents, scientists and writers and philanthropists, a surprising compilation of names whose achievements have had historic, if sometimes controversial, impacts on humankind. Benches and a small picnic area offer respite. Meander through the grove, reading the small plaques, like gravestones, that mark the bases of each tree; on some the metal has gone green with age, and the stones have been knocked off-kilter as the roots have knuckled up.

From the grove, continue down Nimitz Way to a connector trail that breaks to the right. Though marked, the path is not obvious, but it connects with the Laurel Canyon Fire Road, which in turn connects with the lovely, meandering Laurel Canyon Trail.

True to its name, bay laurels drape much of the Laurel Canyon. The scent is thick and distinct, the smell of home to any Northern Californian. The trail descends swiftly into the Laurel Creek drainage and crosses the perennial creek via a rock hop near a tiny dam. Ferns cloak the steep walls of the ravine; the setting is enchanting. The trail continues to dip through streambeds as it descends; the streams may be dry by late season. It also passes a junction with the Pine Tree Trail. Farther down, metal mesh has been installed on steps and little bridges to keep hikers from slipping when these become slick.

As you near the more-developed nature area, the laurels give way to the nonnative eucalyptus. The final stretch, well marked, crosses the Loop Road and a service road before depositing you on the lawn behind the Environmental Education Center at the trailhead.

Miles and Directions

0.0 Start on the paved trail toward Jewel Lake, passing Little Farm and the Environmental Education Center.

0.2 Veer left onto the boardwalk.

0.4 The boardwalk ends at Jewel Lake.

0.6 At the junction at the far end of the lake, go right onto the Sylvan Trail (also signed for Wildcat Peak). About 200 yards beyond, stay left on the Sylvan Trail; the Jewel Lake Trail goes right and heads back to the Environmental Education Center.

1.0 At the junction, go left onto the signed Peak Trail and continue climbing.

1.6 Now climbing through scrub, views open to the west and north.

2.0 At the unsigned junction, go left to an overlook shaded by a huge pine, then retrace your steps to the main trail.

2.2 Back on the main trail, continue climbing.

2.4 Reach Nimitz Way. Go left and uphill.

2.5 Arrive at the Rotary lookout. Take in the views, then retrace your steps, passing the junction with the Peak Trail as you descend steeply on Nimitz Way.

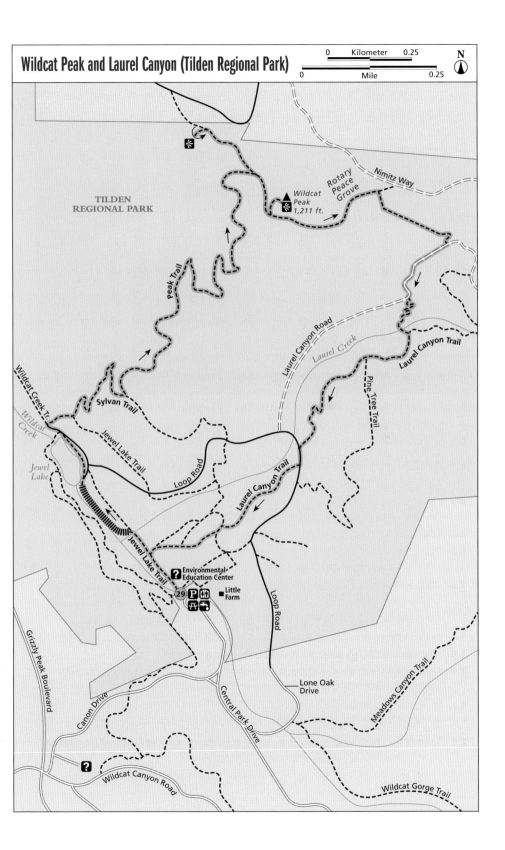

Wildcat Peak and Laurel Canyon (Tilden Regional Park)

0   Kilometer   0.25

0   Mile   0.25

N

Nimitz Way

Rotary
Peace
Grove

▲ Wildcat
Peak
1,211 ft.

TILDEN
REGIONAL PARK

Peak Trail

Laurel Canyon Road

Laurel Creek

Laurel Canyon Trail

Pine Tree Trail

Sylvan Trail

Wildcat Creek Tr.

Wildcat
Creek

Jewel Lake Trail

Loop Road

Laurel Canyon Trail

Jewel
Lake

Jewel Lake Trail

Environmental
Education Center

■ Little
Farm

29 P

Loop Road

Grizzly Peak Boulevard

Canon Drive

Central Park Drive

Lone Oak
Drive

Meadows Canyon Trail

Wildcat Canyon Road

Wildcat Gorge Trail

Looking northwest from the lookout on Wildcat Peak

2.7 Go left into the Rotary Peace Grove. Explore the Who's Who of history commemorated there, then return to Nimitz Way and continue downhill.

3.0 Reach the junction with the signed trail that leads down into Laurel Canyon. If you reach the paved Skyline Trail, you've gone about 50 yards too far.

3.2 Drop onto the broad, dirt Laurel Canyon Road. Continue downhill.

3.4 Reach the junction with the Laurel Canyon Trail. Head left onto the trail, descending steep switchbacks into the Laurel Creek drainage.

3.5 Cross Laurel Creek. The route roller-coasters through several more drainages as it continues downhill.

3.7 At the junction with the Pine Tree Trail, continue downhill on the Laurel Canyon Trail.

4.0 At the junction with the Loop Road, hitch up about 100 feet to the signed Laurel Canyon Trail and continue downhill.

4.3 At the junction with the dirt service road, hitch up about 10 yards to the signed Laurel Canyon Trail. Pass a pond and outbuildings for the Little Farm.

4.4 Reach the lawn behind the Environmental Education Center. Continue around (or through) the center to the paved Jewel Lake Trail.

4.5 Arrive back at the trailhead.

30 Round Top and Volcanic Trails

This ramble around a long-extinct volcano features lovely views of San Francisco Bay and Mount Diablo and offers interesting insights into the Bay Area's volatile geology.

Start: Kiosk at staging area
Distance: 4.2-mile double loop
Difficulty: Moderate
Trail surface: Pavement, dirt trail, dirt roadway
Best season: Spring, summer, and fall. Winter rains may create muddy conditions on unpaved trail sections.
Other trail users: Trail runners, the occasional mountain biker
Canine compatibility: Leashed dogs permitted in parking lot and near staging area. Dogs may be unleashed elsewhere but must be under voice control, and owners must carry a leash.
Land status: Sibley Volcanic Regional Preserve
Fees and permits: None
Schedule: Park open 5 a.m. to 10 p.m. unless otherwise posted; parking lot may close at 6 p.m. Nov through Mar.

Trailhead amenities: Picnic sites, restrooms, trash cans, water, informational signboards and exhibits
Maps: USGS Oakland East; East Bay Regional Park District map and brochure available at the trailhead and online at www.ebparks.org
Special considerations: Interpretive displays have been installed in the shelter at the staging area, including a geologic time line of the Berkeley/Oakland hills. The park brochure and map include a guide to the interpretive stations along the Volcanic Trail.
Trail contact: East Bay Regional Park District, 2950 Peralta Oaks Ct., PO Box 5381, Oakland, CA 94605-0381; (888) EBPARKS; www.ebparks.org

Finding the trailhead: The park is located at 6800 Skyline Blvd. in the Oakland hills. From CA 24 in Oakland, take the CA 13 exit. Follow CA 13 south for 0.4 mile to the Broadway Terrace exit. Go left onto Broadway Terrace, and follow it east/uphill for about 1.7 miles, passing a number of intersections with residential streets as you climb. When you reach Skyline Boulevard, turn right (south), and follow Skyline about 1 mile to the park entrance on the left. Alternatively, follow CA 24 through the Caldecott Tunnel to the Fish Ranch Road exit. Follow Fish Ranch Road to Grizzly Peak Boulevard, and turn left (south) on Grizzly Peak. Follow Grizzly Peak Boulevard and Skyline Boulevard south for 2.4 miles to the park entrance on the left (east). GPS: N37 50.860' / W122 11.963'

The Hike

The gentlest volcano you'll ever hike, Round Top distinguishes itself from neighboring heights in the Oakland and Berkeley hills by virtue of its fascinating geological history.

The volcano was a cauldron of activity about ten million years ago, when it spewed the various lavas (tuffs, basalts, breccias) that underlie the current landscape. Pressure from nearby earthquake faults have lifted and twisted the old volcano over

Hikers walk the labyrinth in the bottom of the old quarry in Sibley Volcanic Regional Preserve.

the eons; Round Top now lies on its side, exposing its innards for the education and enjoyment of scholars and hikers alike.

This double loop takes in both the Round Top Trail, which loops the high point, and the Volcanic Trail, which is keyed to the interpretive guide in the park brochure. A side trip to the labyrinth at the base of the old quarry is also included.

Begin by checking out the exhibits at the staging area, which provide an introduction to the complex geology you'll pass along the route. The Round Top Loop Trail starts on the paved Round Top Road, climbing through a mixed forest of oak, manzanita, and bay laurel as it traverses the upended volcano's south-facing slope, and offering views into the forested canyons of neighboring Huckleberry Botanic Regional Preserve. Just before the 0.4-mile mark, the Round Top Loop Trail breaks off to the right (southeast), leaving the roadway. The singletrack traverses through pines, oaks, and eucalyptus: The understory is thick with poison oak, so be sure to stay on the path.

Rounding the east face of the volcano, climb a short, steep pitch through a meadow (look for wildflowers in spring) and pass through a gate, closing it behind you. Ascending through the grasslands, views open to the east, toward Mount Diablo. The quarries that delved into Round Top are visible as well. Top out at nearly 1,600 feet, where a short side path leads to an overlook, then descend to the trail junction at 1 mile.

From the short railing at the junction, you can peer down over the edge of the cliff into the quarry pit, where a large labyrinth—a stone meditation ring—swirls on the floor. A small satellite labyrinth has been built to the side. The trail into the quarry breaks to the right, a steep but short plunge to the base. Basalt used in area road-building was quarried from the pit, and excavations have exposed the interior of the old volcano, giving researchers an inside look at its makeup. Take a break to walk the careworn and overgrown labyrinth: Try not to overthink it, simply following the circling path, decorated with offerings, around and around to the center, then around and around to the exit.

Back atop the rim of the quarry, follow the dirt Round Top route north to the junction with the Volcanic Trail. This stretches into grassland, passing upheaval and chaos overlain with a blanket of green or gold, depending on the season. The dramatic stories told by the rock are subtle and easily overlooked by the layperson—especially a hiker with far-ranging eyes, given that views along the traversing path reach west across the wooded ridgelines to the sparkling bay and northwest to Mount Tamalpais. The interpretive guide is a great resource, directing you down side paths to view sites such as "bake zones," where heat and steam oxidized the rock, giving it a reddish hue; distinctive formations of mudstone and river gravel; flows of basalt defined by how they formed and cooled; and examples of tuff, breccia, and cinder.

▶ **One of the oldest parks in the East Bay Regional Park system, Sibley Volcanic is named for one of the district's founders, Robert Sibley.**

The Volcanic Trail ends in a flat clearing overlooking summits topped with radio towers. Drop onto the paved Quarry Road and follow it down to the junction with the Quarry Trail, which begins near a corral and makes a gentle climb that roughly parallels the Volcanic Trail back toward the ridge crest. Pick up the Round Top Trail and go right to complete the loop, traversing through grassland and chaparral along the west face of the peak. Pass another cattle gate, and at the four-way intersection, pick up the Sibley Interpretive and Overlook Trail on the right. Meander down through eucalyptus, passing the Backpack Camp, to an interpretive platform, then follow the paved pathway through deep shade back to the staging area and trailhead.

Miles and Directions

0.0 From the staging area, head uphill on the paved Round Top Road.

0.2 At the Y junction, stay right on the paved route.

0.3 Pass the junction with the Bay Area Ridge Trail, remaining on the paved road.

0.4 At the junction, break right onto the dirt Round Top Loop Trail.

0.8 Pass the gate on the hillside meadow.

1.0 Arrive at the trail intersection above the quarry pit. Go right and downhill on the trail into the quarry.

1.1 Reach the floor of the quarry and the labyrinth. Mileage includes walking the maze. When you're done, retrace your steps to the junction above the quarry.

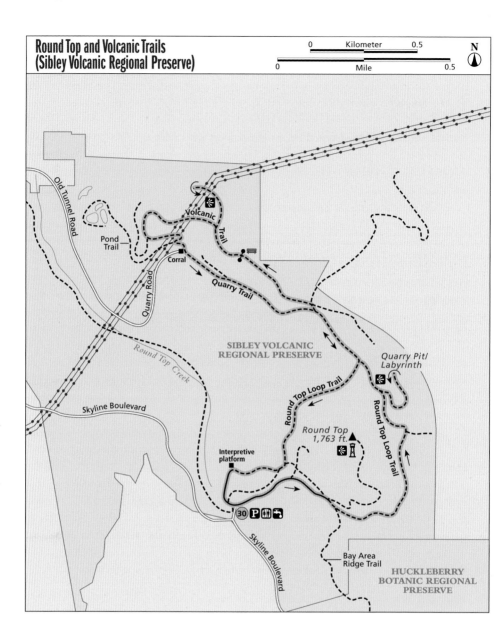

1.5   From the junction at the overlook, continue north on the Round Top Trail.

1.6   Reach the intersection with the Volcanic Trail; the Round Top loop bends sharply left. Stay right on the Volcanic Trail.

1.8   At the junction with the Quarry Trail, which heads left and downhill, stay right on the Volcanic Trail. The wide dirt roadway is easy to follow, with side trails, as indicated on the guide/map, breaking right to interpretive sites.

2.2   Reach marker #7, then a bench with a fleeting view of the Golden Gate. Pass through a cattle gate.

Views open eastward from the Round Top Trail.

2.4 At the junction, go right to check out interpretive markers 9–11. Back on the Volcanic Trail, reach a wide, flat clearing and drop left onto the paved Quarry Road.

2.6 Drop down two quick switchbacks and pass the Pond Trail, which breaks to the right.

2.8 At the corral, go left onto the dirt Quarry Trail.

3.3 Arrive back at the junction of the Quarry and Volcanic Trails. Retrace your steps to the Round Top Loop Trail.

3.5 At the junction, go right onto the Round Top Loop Trail.

3.9 Pass through the gate to the four-way trail junction and the paved Round Top Road. Go right onto the Skyline/Sibley Interpretive and Overlook Trail, then right again after about 50 feet onto the overlook trail.

4.1 Pass a junction with a trail to the Backpack Camp, then drop to an interpretive platform. Continue down the paved path.

4.2 Arrive back at the trailhead and parking lot.

31 West Side Trail and Historical Walk

Trace the shoreline of Lake Chabot to an interpretive area surrounding the dam and spillway built by "Water King" Anthony Chabot.

Start: West Shore Trail at its junction with East Shore Trail

Distance: 4.2 miles out and back

Hiking time: 2–3 hours

Difficulty: Easy

Trail surface: Pavement

Best season: Year-round; spring offers cooler temperatures and wildflower viewing.

Other trail users: Trail runners, cyclists, dog walkers

Canine compatibility: Leashed dogs permitted

Land status: Anthony Chabot Regional Park

Fees and permits: Entrance fee; dog fee

Schedule: Trails accessible sunrise to sunset daily

Trailhead amenities: Restrooms, water, information signboards, and picnic sites surround the parking area near the marina. Camping is available in the park as well.

Maps: USGS Hayward; online at www.ebparks .org/parks/anthony_chabot#trailmap

Special considerations: An online guide to the lake's history walk is available at www .ebparks.org/Assets/files/lake_chabot_ history_walk_1997.pdf.

Trail contact: Anthony Chabot Regional Park, East Bay Regional Park District, 2950 Peralta Oaks Ct., Oakland, CA 94605; 888-EBPARKS (888-327-2757), option 3, ext. 4502; www .ebparks.org/parks/anthony_chabot

Finding the trailhead: To reach the park's marina entrance from I-580 in San Leandro, take the Fairmont Drive/150th Avenue exit. If southbound, head left, over the freeway, then go right for 1 block on Foothill Boulevard to Fairmont Drive. If northbound, follow Foothill Boulevard 1 block north to Fairmont Drive. Head east on Fairmont Drive for 1.8 miles to the marina entrance. Alternatively, from I-580 in Castro Valley, take the Strobridge Avenue exit. Follow Strobridge to the right to Castro Valley Boulevard and turn right. Follow Castro Valley Boulevard to Lake Chabot Road, and follow Lake Chabot Road about 2 miles to the marina entrance. GPS: N37 42.956' / W122 06.165'

The Hike

Water has long been a source of power and prestige in California. To this day, if you have water, you prosper, whether as a rancher, a miner, a farmer, or, on a larger scale, as a developer, a city, or a county.

Anthony Chabot understood the power of water. Chabot, a self-taught engineer, harnessed that power during his days as a forty-niner in the California gold rush, pioneering the use of canvas hoses and water pressure to expose gold. This led to the development of hydraulic mining methods that, when placer and other more conventional deposits began to peter out, would be used to wash away entire mountainsides to expose ore. The damage caused by hydraulic mining in the foothills of the Sierra, as exemplified by the pit preserved in Malakoff Diggins State Historic Park, eventually led to the outlawing of the technique.

Lake Chabot was at one time a primary water source for Oakland and San Leandro. It remains a backup reservoir.

Chabot eventually left the Sierra for San Francisco, where "water works" would remain the mainstay of his life and livelihood. He would go on to establish the Contra Costa Water Company and build a dam on Temescal Creek, forming Lake Temescal, which supplied water for the city of Oakland in the mid-1800s.

But his masterwork was construction of the dam that stems the flows of San Leandro Creek and Grass Valley Creek in the reservoir that now bears his name. Lake Chabot, formerly the San Leandro Reservoir, was contained by an earthwork structure built by hand and horse in 1874–75. The interpretive signs that line a stretch of

Anthony Chabot Regional Park's West Shore Trail describe the dam construction process, from the 800 Chinese laborers who moved thousands of tons of soil to the teams of horses that paced the earthworks to tamp them down.

The route to the dam and its interpretive Historical Walk is straightforward. The paved West Shore Trail traces the edge of the lake, meandering through a lush oak woodland underlain with green grass and wildflowers in spring and early summer and parched by the end of the dry season. Sheltering oaks and bays offer shade; the sun can be brutal on hot summer days. There are a few ups and downs along the route, but none are long or particularly steep. Side trails lead to the shoreline, with picnic sites and beaches at Coot Landing and Alder Point. Benches also line the route.

▶ Anthony Chabot, dubbed the "Water King," is also remembered as a philanthropist. Beneficiaries of his charity included veterans and unemployed women. In 1883 he also donated an 8-inch telescope, called "Leah," to what is now the Chabot Space and Science Center in Oakland.

The Historical Walk, with interpretive signs and markers keyed to an online guide, begins on the south side of the dam. Stops along the trail mark and/or describe Tunnel 1, which diverted San Leandro and Grass Valley Creeks so that the dam could be raised in the gorge; Tunnel 2, which diverted water stored in the reservoir into the pipelines that transported it to the cities of Oakland and San Leandro ("Diana's temple" was built atop this tunnel); and Tunnel 3, which served as an outlet and helped filter the lake water.

The dam itself is not particularly scenic, corralled by chain-link fencing that has clearly been breached, as graffiti mars the temple that sits atop Tunnel 2. While the lake is no longer Oakland's primary water supply—Lake Chabot was designated a "stand-by" source in 1964—the fencing is evidence that both safety and preservation of the integrity of the water and the dam are priorities.

On the far side of the dam, a switchback leads up to the sites of the superintendent's cottage and "Slate House," both no longer standing; the site of "Yema-po," the Chinese workers' camp; the control shaft for Tunnel 1; and the filter and filter ponds that were required because, according to the historical brochure, the remnants of a garden that was submerged left the water with an "unpleasant taste" that meant "[u]nfortunate recipients of the water had to put strainers over their faucets and these soon resembled used tea bags."

When you've completed your explorations, return as you came.

Miles and Directions

0.0 Start on the paved West Shore Trail at the junction with the East Shore Trail, heading left on the West Shore Trail and passing picnic sites, restrooms, a cafe, and the marina.

0.3 As the trail moves lakeside, pass side paths that lead down to small beaches along the shoreline.

0.5 Pass a mile marker and begin a short climb.

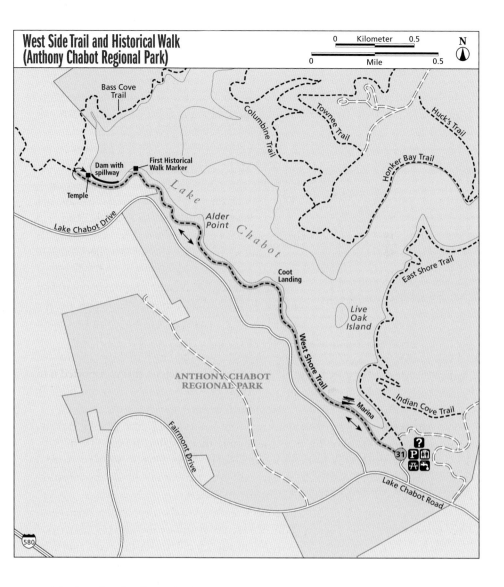

West Side Trail and Historical Walk (Anthony Chabot Regional Park)

0   Kilometer   0.5

0   Mile   0.5

N

Bass Cove Trail

Townee Trail

Columbine Trail

Huck's Trail

Honker Bay Trail

Dam with spillway

First Historical Walk Marker

Temple

Lake Chabot Drive

Lake

Alder Point

Chabot

Coot Landing

East Shore Trail

Live Oak Island

West Shore Trail

ANTHONY CHABOT REGIONAL PARK

Marina

Indian Cove Trail

Fairmont Drive

31

Lake Chabot Road

580

1.0   Pass Coot Landing on the right, then the 1-mile marker. Remain on the paved West Shore Trail.

1.4   Pass Alder Point on the right, at the base of a hill. At the Y at the top of the hill, stay right on the paved route.

1.7   Reach the first marker for the Historical Walk.

1.8   Cross the dam.

2.1   Explore the markers and sites on the far side of the dam. This is the turnaround, though the West Shore and Bass Cove Trails continue around the reservoir. Retrace your steps to the trailhead.

4.2   Arrive back at the trailhead.

32 Mary Bowerman Trail

Encircling the top of the Bay Area's highest peak, on a clear day views from the Mary Bowerman Trail stretch west to the Pacific Ocean and the curve of the earth and east across the Central Valley to the distant peaks of the Sierra Nevada.

Start: Lower parking lot at the summit of Mount Diablo
Distance: 0.7-mile loop
Hiking time: Less than 1 hour
Difficulty: Easy
Trail surface: Pavement, dirt trail
Best season: Year-round, though your best chance for a clear day with panoramic views is in fall, particularly after a rain.
Other trail users: None
Canine compatibility: No dogs allowed
Land status: Mount Diablo State Park
Fees and permits: Entrance fee
Schedule: Gates open at 8 a.m. and close at sunset. Watch the time so you don't get locked in.
Trailhead amenities: Restrooms, picnic sites, trash cans, information signboard. More information is available at the nearby Summit Visitor Center. An interpretive guide to the trail, published by the Mount Diablo Interpretive

Association, is available at www.mdia.org/site/docs/Franks-Favorite-Hikes/Mary-Bowerman-Trail.pdf.
Maps: USGS Clayton; Mount Diablo State Park trail map available at park entrance stations, Summit Visitor Center, and online at www.parks.ca.gov/pages/517/files/mtdiablo brochure.pdf
Special considerations: Weather is changeable on the summit and may be very different from what you left behind in the valley. Wind is common. If hiking in winter, dress in layers and bring extra clothing. If snow is going to fall in the Bay Area, it'll lie thickest on the summit of Diablo.
Trail contact: Mount Diablo State Park, 96 Mitchell Canyon Rd., Clayton, CA 94517; (925) 837-2525; www.parks.ca.gov. Mount Diablo Interpretive Association, PO Box 346, Walnut Creek, CA 94597-0346; (925) 927-7222; www.mdia.org.

Finding the trailhead: From I-680 in Danville, take the Diablo Road/Danville exit. Go left (east) on Diablo Road for 0.8 mile to the intersection with El Cerro Boulevard. Turn right on Diablo Road, and follow it another 2.2 miles. At the 3-mile mark, go left (east) on the steep, winding Mount Diablo Scenic Boulevard, which becomes South Gate Road once you enter the park at 4 miles. The entrance station is at 5.7 miles. At 8.8 miles, arrive at the intersection with North Gate Road, which leads down into Walnut Creek. Go right (up and generally northeast) on Summit Road for another 4.6 miles to the summit parking lots. The trail begins in the lower parking lot (13.4 miles total). GPS: N37 52.848' / W121 55.033'

The Hike

At 3,849 feet, the summit of Mount Diablo is more than 1,000 feet higher than its nearest neighbor. So it should come as no surprise that the views from the top—especially on a clear day—are superlative.

It should also come as no surprise that history lies thick on this iconic peak. Scholars of the mountain, including park interpreters, local historical societies, and the Mount Diablo Interpretive Association, have documented and archived its many stories.

Tales of the local Bay Miwok people, who lived and prospered around the base of the mountain before the arrival of colonists, are thin. Their histories were not written but oral, and many were lost when the tribes were decimated by disease and hardship in the wake of Spanish colonization. One story has survived: Mount Diablo's twin summits were the birthplace of the First People, from whom the Miwok are descended.

For the early Spanish explorers, finding their way in an unknown place, the peak was a significant landmark. The Spanish were also the first to call the mountain "Diablo": The name reportedly originated after an attempt to capture a band of natives and move them to the Mission San Jose failed. It was said that the Indians escaped from the thicket where they'd been corralled with the help of the devil. "Monte del Diablo" was first applied to the thicket but in time was misconstrued as the name of the mountain. Over the years there have been several campaigns to change the name to something less diabolical, but nothing has stuck. Perhaps that's because anyone who's hiked on the mountain in summer knows how hellishly hot it can be.

After the gold rush, the mountain would be mined, at various times and in various locations, for coal, copper, lime, and mercury. Its slopes would be incorporated into cattle ranches and its ground tilled for farms and orchards. A wagon road would be built to its summit, and a Mountain House would be built to accommodate sightseers. The mountain's summit would become ground zero for establishing property boundaries in Northern California and Nevada: The Mount Diablo Meridian is an "initial point," established by surveyor Leander Ransom in 1851.

One of the first in the state, Mount Diablo State Park was established in 1921. That didn't prevent other development on the mountain: Among other things, Standard Oil erected an aviation beacon on the summit, and in the 1930s the Civilian Conservation Corps, the workhorse of the New Deal, set about building campgrounds, shelters, trails, and the structure that houses the Summit Visitor Center. When threats of development encroached on the park, local conservationists, including Mary Bowerman, would battle, successfully, to preserve its integrity.

▶ The trail's namesake, Mary Bowerman, was a botanist who trained at UC Berkeley and documented the flora of Mount Diablo for her doctorate. Her work was later published in *The Flowering Plants and Ferns of Mount Diablo, California*. She was a founding member of Save Mount Diablo, an organization dedicated to the preservation of the mountain and its environs, and a member of the Mount Diablo Interpretive Association.

The Mary Bowerman Trail (aka the Fire Interpretive Trail) circumnavigates the summit and offers up the same views as from the peak's apex, with the added benefit of a lesson in the mountain's natural history.

Begin the hike in the lower summit parking lot, which is about 0.1 mile downhill from the Summit Visitor Center. The trailhead is about 30 yards above and left (northeast) of the parking lot entrance, across the road and adjacent to a small picnic area. You can see the trail's end from the parking area to the right (southeast).

▶ Stop in at the picturesque Summit Visitor Center, which houses interpretive displays describing the mountain's human history and ecology. The must-visit observation deck caps the center. Hours are 10 a.m. to 4 p.m. daily.

Pick up a guide at the trailhead if available, and head off into the oak scrubland that encompasses the first section of the route. Pass the first interpretive marker almost immediately; this describes the habitat you are traveling through. The markers are wooden posts with white tops, and can't be missed.

Beyond marker 2 (beware the poison oak) views open of the quarry on Mount Zion. You can also see Suisun Bay, where the Sacramento and San Joaquin Rivers meet before flooding into San Francisco Bay, blue veins on a skin of gold or green, depending on the season. The interpretive markers will draw your attention—at least momentarily—away from the views and to the stone bed that underlies the paved path or to the foliage that crowds it.

At the 0.1-mile mark reach an overlook with more views. A larger overlook, outfitted with decking, fencing, and benches, offers fabulous views north and east, across the expanse of the Central Valley toward the Sierra Nevada. A few yards beyond the overlook the trail turns to dirt and swings onto the east face of the peak. The summit observation deck is above and to the right, and oak scrub provides pockets of welcome shade on a hot summer day. Signs of the 1977 fire that charred this face are slowly being replaced by brushy, fragrant chaparral.

At the trail's halfway point, where the path arcs onto the mountain's southeast face and offers views of the Oakland hills, the Golden Gate, and the distant Pacific, you'll pass the impressive Devil's Pulpit. Resist the temptation to climb the pulpit, as the rock is crumbly and unstable.

Pass the final interpretive markers and enter the grassland plant community as you traverse the southwest face. The trail is exposed in places and might give pause to hikers with vertigo. A gentle ascent leads to trail's end at 0.7 mile. Drop quickly from the trail into the parking lot.

Miles and Directions

0.0 Start from the small picnic area in the lower summit parking area.

0.1 Pass the first few interpretive markers to a viewpoint on the paved path.

0.3 Reach the second larger outlook. The trail turns to dirt and views open onto the Sacramento–San Joaquin Delta.

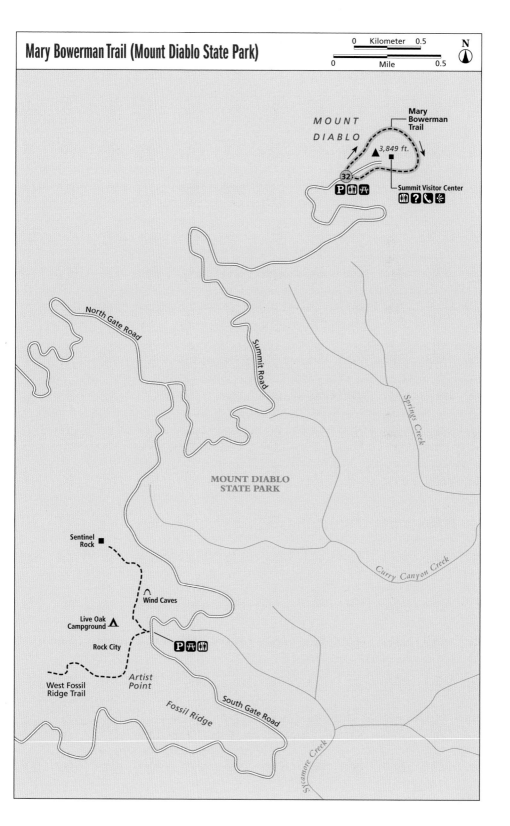

Mary Bowerman Trail (Mount Diablo State Park)

0   Kilometer   0.5

0   Mile   0.5

N

MOUNT
DIABLO

Mary
Bowerman
Trail

▲ 3,849 ft.

32

Summit Visitor Center

North Gate Road

Summit Road

Springs Creek

MOUNT DIABLO
STATE PARK

Curry Canyon Creek

Sentinel
Rock

Wind Caves

Live Oak
Campground

Rock City

West Fossil
Ridge Trail

Artist
Point

Fossil Ridge

South Gate Road

Sycamore Creek

0.4 Round onto the southeast face, passing the Devil's Pulpit. Lower rock outcrops make great viewing platforms. Social trails lead to various outcrops, but the route proper is well marked with an arrow and trail sign.

0.5 Traverse across the southwest face. The trail begins an easy ascent past the last interpretive markers.

0.7 Arrive at the end of the trail.

Option: The Trail Through Time, located lower down on Diablo's east slope, explores Rock City's Wind Caves, sandstone rock outcrops that have been sculpted by wind, water, and time. Lots of social trails intermingle in this area; if you head left (west) toward the first obvious rock formations, you can scramble down to the Elephant Rock picnic area and its huge cave-like alcove with sandstone "tusks" overhanging the entrance. The Wind Caves are above the Big Rock picnic area, along with an interpretive billboard marking the Trail Through Time. Walk left on the trail alongside a 100-foot sandstone wall, where wind and water have carved nearly perfectly circular alcoves, some standing alone, some linked by threads of rock. These hollows freckle the sandstone, making perfect perches for children. At the end of the wall, follow a narrow dirt track through oak woodlands to a trail fork; stay left (north) and head uphill to the trail's end at Sentinel Rock. Pull up a flat section of rock and enjoy views north across the slopes of Mount Diablo, which are pocked with similar outcrops. Return as you came, arriving back at the trailhead at 0.6 mile.

The Rock City parking lots and picnic areas, along with the Live Oak Campground and trailheads, are 1 mile from the Diablo entrance kiosk, about 6.7 miles from the start of the Mount Diablo Scenic Highway/South Gate Road. There are several parking lots at Rock City; park in the lot serving the Big Rock picnic area, at the top of the access road to Live Oak Campground. GPS: N37 50.934' / W121 56.000'

33 Dry Creek Trail Loop

This route loops through a family park outfitted with a playing green, sycamore-shaded picnic areas, a pond that provides habitat for ducks and other waterfowl, and the historic Dry Creek Cottage and gardens.

Start: Trailhead near the Garin Barn Visitor Center
Distance: 3.5-mile loop
Hiking time: About 3 hours
Difficulty: Moderate due to elevation changes
Trail surface: Dirt trail, dirt farm road, paved pathway
Best season: Spring and fall. The loop can be hiked year-round, but winter rains may render trail surfaces muddy.
Other trail users: Equestrians, trail runners, cyclists on portions of trail around Jordan Pond and on ranch roads
Canine compatibility: Leashed dogs permitted
Land status: Garin/Dry Creek Pioneer Regional Parks
Fees and permits: Entrance fee; dog fee
Schedule: Park opens at 8 a.m. Specific closing times are posted at entry kiosk; they correspond to seasonal sunsets. A curfew is imposed between 10 p.m. and 5 a.m. Garin Barn Visitor Center open weekends and holidays between Memorial Day and Labor Day 11:30 a.m. to 6 p.m. Dry Creek Garden open Thurs through Sat 10 a.m. to 4 p.m.
Trailhead amenities: Restrooms, water, trash cans, information when Garin Barn Visitor Center is open
Maps: USGS Niles and Newark; East Bay Regional Park District brochure and map available at trailhead and online at www.ebparks.org
Special considerations: Fishing is permitted at Jordan Pond, but no swimming is allowed. Carry a map; it can clarify any confusion about route-finding in the Dry Creek drainage.
Trail contact: East Bay Regional Park District, 2950 Peralta Oaks Ct., Oakland, CA 94605; 888-EBPARKS (888-327-2757), option 3, ext. 4502; www.ebparks.org/parks/garin

Finding the trailhead: From I-880 in Hayward, take the Whipple Road/Industrial Parkway exit. Head northeast on Industrial Parkway for 2 miles to Mission Boulevard (CA 238). Go right (south) on Mission Boulevard for 0.1 mile to Garin Avenue. Turn left onto Garin Avenue and follow it 0.8 mile east to the park entry kiosk. Park in any of the lots, and cross a bridge to the picnic area. Go south on the paved path to the trailhead at the south end of the picnic green. GPS: N37 37.604' / W122 01.681'

The Hike

As quoted in the park brochure, Edith Meyers extended an invitation to the ranch that flourished along Dry Creek in the twentieth century: "Leave care and worry behind you; enjoy the beauties of nature here in your midst; and pause for a moment in your rush through life to give thanks to the great artist who painted this ever-changing picture of the hills and fields and streams."

If you are lucky, you will get a bit lost on the Dry Creek Trail . . . but not really. The signs of civilization that orient us in the modern world are lacking here, lending the trail an air of seclusion.

The trail begins at the Garin Barn, where rusting farm machinery is displayed on the grounds, scattered between the barn, the historic blacksmith shop, and the tool shed. Once a working ranch, artifacts illuminating the ranching history of the region are on display inside the visitor center. The property's old apple orchard, which boasts about 200 trees and nearly that many varieties of "antique" apples, hosts an annual Apple Festival in late fall; the apples can be sampled both raw and as juice. An extension of the property's long history of hosting festive gatherings of family and friends, more information about the festival is available on the park website.

At the far end of this loop lies the Dry Creek Cottage and gardens. Once the home of the three philanthropic Meyers sisters, including Edith, the property was donated to the East Bay Regional Park District upon the last sister's death. The district has since restored the cottage (which may one day host weddings and other events) and preserved the 2 acres of gardens that surround the building.

The loop begins at the southern edge of the large picnic green. The trail drops down along Dry Creek (true to its name, running dry in summer and fall) to Jordan Pond. Families cluster around picnic tables shaded by willow and sycamore on the pond's shoreline and fish off the small pier. The pond is stocked with catfish and also supports a breeding population of bluegill and bass.

At the pond's earthen dam, a trail marker points the way down the Dry Creek Trail. Posts along the trail are keyed to a guide available at the Garin Barn Visitor Center. It's insta-nature at the dam's base: The track turns to dirt, birdcall rings in the riparian brush bordering the banks, and old oaks and sycamores tangle overhead. The trail roughly follows the streambed, with spurs leading creek-side, to one of several scenic bridges spanning the creek bed—the wooden structure is wide enough for a single person to pass.

Ignoring social trails that drop from the main track to the creek, proceed through a woodland so quiet you can hear lizards scrabbling in the leaf litter on the forest floor. Occasionally the distant holler of a train wafts into the canyon. Reach an interpretive post and an unmarked trail intersection at 0.6 mile and go right (south) to cross a second narrow wooden bridge. The path then climbs onto a hillside above the creek and traverses grassy slopes that host wildflowers in spring.

Take the right-hand track when the trail splits into three fingers, and drop through the creek bed. Climb to a trail intersection; a left turn takes you to the first sign

▶ Property in the Garin/Dry Creek parks was once part of the refuge of Father Agapius Honcharenko and his wife, Albinia, according to park literature. A writer as well as a man of the church, Father Honcharenko's socialist views resulted in his exile from Russia in the late nineteenth century. The Ukraine refugees found sanctuary farming in the hills east of San Francisco.

Narrow bridges like this span Dry Creek.

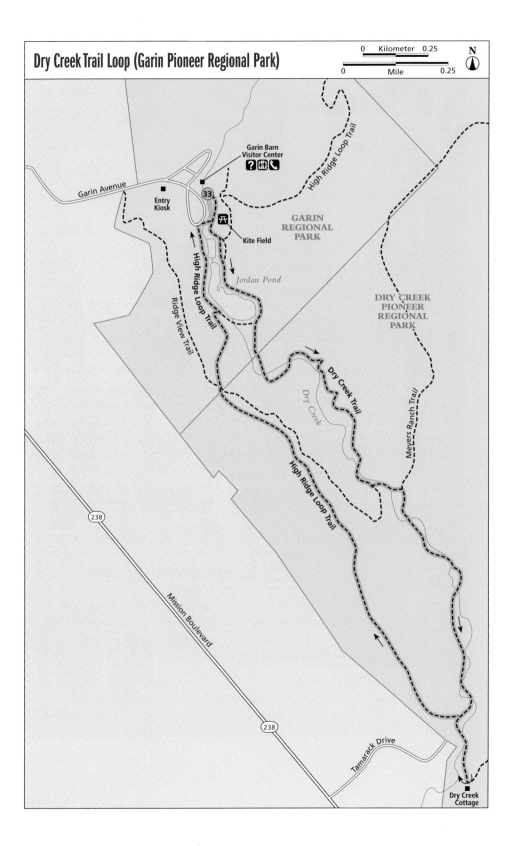

Dry Creek Trail Loop (Garin Pioneer Regional Park)

0   Kilometer   0.25

0   Mile   0.25

N

Garin Avenue

Garin Barn
Visitor Center

Entry
Kiosk

33

High Ridge Loop Trail

GARIN
REGIONAL
PARK

Kite Field

Jordan Pond

Ridge View Trail

High Ridge Loop Trail

DRY CREEK
PIONEER
REGIONAL
PARK

Dry Creek Trail

Dry Creek

Meyers Ranch Trail

238

High Ridge Loop Trail

Mission Boulevard

238

Tamarack Drive

Dry Creek
Cottage

of civilization since the bridge crossings—the marked junction of the Dry Creek, Meyers Ranch, and High Ridge Trails. Continue on the Meyers Ranch Trail, which crosses the streambed several more times before reaching the junction with the High Ridge Loop Trail. Continue down the Meyers Ranch Trail to the Dry Creek Cottage and gardens; the High Ridge Loop Trail is part of the return route.

After touring the gardens, retrace your steps to the High Ridge Loop Trail and climb onto the ridgeline, where views open across the Dry Creek valley to the eastern hills. At the junction with the Ridge View Trail, the track tops the ridge crest. Take a break on the bench at the trail junction and enjoy the views across the sprawling East Bay. A short descent drops you on the western shoreline of Jordan Pond. The picnic areas and parking lots are just north of the pond.

Miles and Directions

0.0 Start at the far end of the playing green.

0.2 Circle Jordan Pond to the Dry Creek Trail sign and head down the paved path to the base of the dam, where the trail surface changes to dirt.

0.5 Cross the one-person bridge that spans the creek. At the intersection that follows, stay right.

0.7 Cross another narrow bridge. At the junction on the far side, go right; the left-hand trail circles back to meet the main trail in a little loop.

1.0 After traversing a hillside above the creek, the trail splits; take the right track, and drop down across the dry creek bed. Climb past a trail marker to an unmarked trail intersection and go left (south).

1.1 Arrive at the signed intersection of the Dry Creek Trail and the Meyers Ranch Trail. Continue left on the Meyers Ranch Trail.

1.8 Cross the creek several times before reaching the junction with the High Ridge Loop Trail (part of the return route). Stay left on the Meyers Ranch Trail. At the junction with the May Trail, go right toward the Dry Creek Cottage.

1.9 Arrive at the Dry Creek Cottage and gardens. Tour the gardens, then retrace your steps to the junction with the High Ridge Loop Trail.

2.1 Go left onto the High Ridge Loop Trail, climbing toward the crest of the ridge.

2.4 Crest the ridgetop and enjoy the views as you hike northward.

3.1 At the junction with the Ridge View Trail, stay right on the High Ridge Loop Trail, which drops quickly to the west shore of Jordan Pond. Turn left (north) and follow the pond road toward the picnic green and visitor center.

3.5 Arrive back at the trailhead on the picnic green.

Midpeninsula and the
South Bay

The April trestle in Almaden Quicksilver County Park

34 Filoli and Pulgas Water Temple

While the spectacular home and gardens of the Bourn family are the main attractions, docent-led nature hikes into the backcountry of this expansive estate add nuance to the story. The nearby Pulgas Water Temple is a testament to the power of San Francisco's political titans, who won a long battle to bring water from Yosemite to the City by the Bay.

Start: Signed nature walk trailhead on grounds of Filoli

Distance: Variable; 2.0- to 3.0-mile loops, depending on the docent and fellow hikers

Hiking time: About 2 hours

Difficulty: Easy, though some routes involve short, steep climbs.

Trail surface: Dirt trail, historic carriage roads, pavement and brick walkways

Best season: Late spring and early summer, when the Filoli gardens are in full flush

Other trail users: None at Filoli; cyclists at Pulgas Water Temple

Canine compatibility: No dogs allowed

Land status: Filoli is a National Trust for Historic Preservation site. The Pulgas Water Temple is overseen by the San Francisco Public Utilities Commission.

Fees and permits: Fee for docent-led tours at Filoli, which also includes admission to house and garden. No fees are levied at Pulgas Water Temple. Free to Filoli members.

Schedule: Docent-led tours of the Filoli property are scheduled for Sat mornings during spring, summer, and fall, with schedules, sign-ups, and additional hiking dates posted at www.filoli.org/plan-your-visit/tours.html. Filoli

is open for tours Tues through Sun from Feb through Oct; check website for exact dates. The Pulgas Water Temple is open to the public Mon through Fri from 9 a.m. to 4 p.m.

Trailhead amenities: Restrooms, water, information, cafe, gift shops, and guided tours of mansion and gardens at Filoli. Restrooms, water, and information signboards at Pulgas Water Temple.

Maps: USGS Woodside (no map is needed)

Special considerations: There is a 30-minute parking limit in the Pulgas Water Temple lot. Exploring the temple can be done well within that time. But if you want to make it more of a "hike," you can follow the dirt path that traces the west side of Cañada Road from its junction with Edgewood Road out and back (a total of 3.2 miles), or you can tie the temple into an exploration of Filoli by walking the access road out to Cañada Road, then following the roadside path to the temple grounds.

Trail contact: Filoli, 86 Cañada Rd., Woodside, CA 94062; (650) 364-8300; www.filoli.org. Pulgas Water Temple, San Francisco Public Utilities Commission, 525 Golden Gate Ave., San Francisco, CA 94102; (415) 551-3000; www.sfwater.org/index.aspx?page=93.

Finding the trailhead: From I-280 in Woodside, take the Edgewood Road exit. Head west, toward the valley floor, to Cañada Road. Go right onto Cañada Road, and drive for 1.3 miles to the gated entry for Filoli. To reach the Pulgas Water Temple, continue on Cañada Road for another 0.3 mile (1.6 miles total from the junction of Edgewood Road). GPS for Filoli: N37 28.283' / W122 18.587'; GPS for Pulgas Water Temple: N37 28.968' / W122 18.918'

The Hike

The terrain covered on a nature walk on the grounds of Filoli will be familiar to any Bay Area hiker: Trails wander through meadows that bust out green when fed by rain and burn to gold under the long summer's sun, through oak woodlands, up streams lined with redwoods, across slopes where hardy chaparral plants grow in thickets. But the paths on Filoli are underlain by an extraordinary story, and the gateway is the magnificent country house of one of San Francisco's turn-of-the-twentieth-century financial titans.

California's gold rush gave rise to railroad barons, banking barons, retail barons, water barons, and others that never actually worked a mine but profited off those who did. William Bourn Sr. was one of the rare exceptions: His fortune was generated in the gold fields of the Sierra Nevada, at Grass Valley's Empire Mine. He also prospered from his interests in the Comstock Lode, which spurred a silver boom on the far side of the Sierra, in Nevada.

His son, William Bourn II, took over the Empire in 1878 and advanced the family fortune. But the younger Bourn had other interests, including serving as president of the San Francisco Gas Company (predecessor to today's Pacific Gas & Electric Company, primary provider of energy to much of Northern California) and president of the Spring Valley Water Company, a monopoly that would propel San Francisco into the controversial Hetch Hetchy water project. Bourn II was also fond of grand housing: His Empire Cottage in Grass Valley is hardly a cottage, and the family also had mansions in San Francisco, St. Helena, Pebble Beach, and County Kerry, Ireland. Filoli, completed in 1917, boasts a ballroom where more than 200 ounces of gold leaf from the Empire Mine was used as decoration, according to one source.

The location of the estate was intended to put some distance between the family and temblors like the one that leveled much of San Francisco in 1906. Ironically, the property lies smack in the middle of the San Andreas Rift Zone; at one point on one of the trails, hikers can stand with a foot on the Pacific tectonic plate and the other on the North American tectonic plate.

The Bourns lived at Filoli for about twenty years before selling the estate to the Roth family in 1937. William Roth was president of the Matson Navigation Company, a shipping empire started by his wife's father that would eventually include luxury liners and upscale hotels. Lurline Matson Roth fostered and expanded the amazing Filoli Gardens.

You can only explore the trails of Filoli on a docent-led nature walk. Since routes will vary, only a cursory description is provided here. Getting lost is not an issue, since the docents are both knowledgeable and experienced. Among the sights on the 650-acre property are the Old Cañada Road (William Bourn had the road moved to its present location so traffic didn't run through his land); the Sally McBride Nature Center, in which taxidermied specimens of wildlife found on Filoli are kept; and a pond and flume that provides water for the estate. California newts can be seen near

Members of the Bourn family are buried above their spectacular estate in Woodside.

or in the pond in season. At the Bourn family cemetery, on a hilltop overlooking the rift valley, a monument has been erected: *Filoli* is derived from the motto "Fight, Love, Live," but the masons made a mistake on the stone, which reads "Fight, Live, Live."

The Pulgas Water Temple on San Francisco's Crystal Springs Reservoir marks where water from the Tuolumne River ends its long journey from Hetch Hetchy in Yosemite National Park.

All roads lead back to the house and garden; any hike on the property should culminate with a tour of both. The garden is composed of "rooms"—a cutting garden, a knot garden, a rose garden, a hydrangea garden, a sunken garden—each distinct and impeccably maintained. The house is stunning as well: Tour its muraled ballroom, paneled library, expansive dining room, and massive kitchen to get a sense of how the moguls lived.

Due to proximity, it makes good sense to link a hike at Filoli with a quick walk around the grounds of the Pulgas Water Temple.

That a temple would be erected to commemorate the outlet of a water source is testament to the power of water in the state of California. On the far side of the

Building the Empire

William Bourn's empire has its roots in 1850, when enterprising gold-seekers sunk relative shallow "coyote holes" to reach the gold-bearing quartz that had been discovered in what is now Grass Valley. By the time the Bourn family's Empire Mine was retired, more than a century later, the deepest point in the complex was 11,000 feet belowground. Miners at the Empire went nearly as deep as the Sierra Nevada are high.

In the end, the underground workings of the Empire and its forty-eight companion mines encompassed 5 square miles and 367 miles of tunnel and shaft. In addition to this subterranean maze, reconstructed in scale in the museum at the Empire Mine State Historic Park, a dam was built to prevent water from flowing into the Empire from the neighboring Bullion Mine.

The mine complex encompassed all aspects of ore processing, from blasting it out of the ground to crushing it and running it through the stamp mill, where it was washed with water and quicksilver. The quicksilver bonded to the gold and made it sink into sand, from which it could be more easily extracted. Cyanide was also used in the refining process, hence the toxicity of the waste products from the mine. Retort was the last step, where the mercury was removed and the gold "sponge" that remained melted into ingots.

The production record of the mine is astounding: About 5.6 million ounces of gold, worth an estimated $40 million, was extracted over the one-hundred-year life of the mine. The mine ceased operation in 1956, and the shafts and tunnels are now filled with water. For more information, contact Empire Mine State Historic Park, 10791 E. Empire St., Grass Valley, CA 95945; (530) 273-8522; www.empiremine.org.

temple, out of sight of the reflecting pool, the Tuolumne River empties into Crystal Springs Reservoir and flows from there through the faucets of San Franciscans. The temple is a little jewel in the Beaux Arts style that hides the nuts and bolts of a water project that remains controversial to this day.

In some ways the Pulgas Water Temple is as completely out of place in the otherwise undeveloped Crystal Springs watershed as the O'Shaughnessy Dam is in Yosemite National Park. Still, the setting is lovely, with the reflecting pool shimmering blue on a verdant lawn and the forested folds of the Coast Ranges rising to the west. A

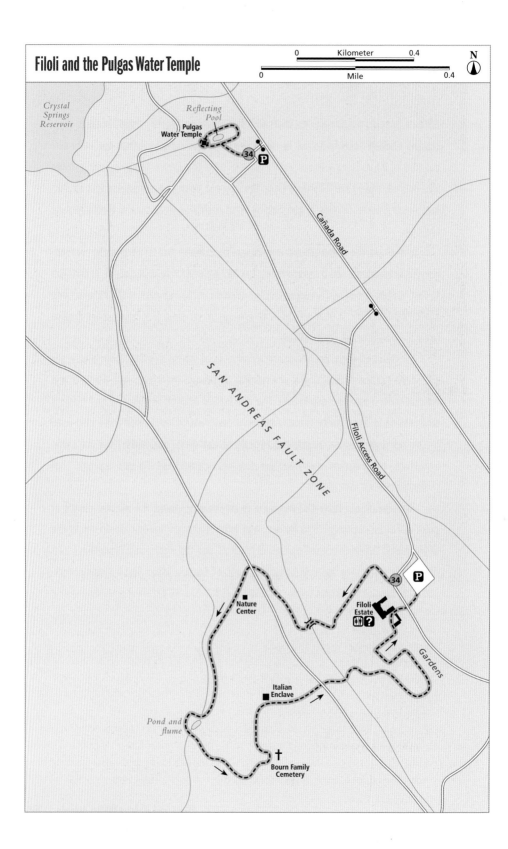

Filoli and the Pulgas Water Temple

Crystal
Springs
Reservoir

Reflecting
Pool

Pulgas
Water Temple

34
P

Cañada Road

SAN ANDREAS FAULT ZONE

Filoli Access Road

Nature
Center

34
P

Filoli
Estate

Gardens

Italian
Enclave

Pond and
flume

Bourn Family
Cemetery

0   Kilometer   0.4

0   Mile   0.4

N

The sunken garden is one of many garden rooms you can tour while on the grounds of Filoli.

0.4-mile lollipop leads to the temple and circles around it, with interpretive signs lending insight into the Hetch Hetchy water project it commemorates.

Miles and Directions

Note: Because all hikes on Filoli are docent-led, your route may vary. These key points represent only one possible loop.

0.0 Start at the Nature Hike trailhead, located just north of the house.

0.4 Cross Fault Creek, where you can straddle the San Andreas. The Scarp Trail climbs up and along a small hill, passing through oak woodland.

0.6 Reach a junction with the Old Cañada Road.

0.7 Arrive at the Sally McBride Nature Center.

1.1 After climbing alongside Spring Creek, pass through a redwood grove with an overlook of the bottom of a flume.

1.2 Cross the dam that contains a pond. A walkway leads out over the water, the perfect spot to look for newts.

1.5 Climb to the Bourn family cemetery.

1.8 Pass the Italian enclave, where the immigrant garden staff, who built and cared for the garden and property, lived.

2.0 Arrive back on the formal grounds of the property at the High Place. Wander through the garden rooms back to the house and trailhead.

35 Jean Lauer Trail at Pillar Point

This scenic trail along the bluffs overlooking the Pacific traces the terrestrial boundary of a marine reserve and overlooks the famed Mavericks surf break.

Start: Jean Lauer trailhead off Airport Road
Distance: 4.5 miles out and back incorporating loops
Hiking time: 2–3 hours
Difficulty: Easy
Trail surface: Dirt trail, dirt roadway, paved roadway
Best season: Spring, summer, and fall. The best chance for a fog-free day is in fall.
Other trail users: Trail runners
Canine compatibility: Leashed dogs permitted outside boundaries of Fitzgerald Marine Reserve. No dogs allowed on reserve property.
Land status: San Mateo County Park
Fees and permits: None
Schedule: Sunrise to sunset daily
Trailhead amenities: Restrooms, trash cans, information signboard

Maps: USGS Montara Mountain OE W; online at parks.smcgov.org/jean-lauer-trail. A map for the Fitzgerald Marine Reserve is at parks .smcgov.org/sites/parks.smcgov.org/files/ Map_from_FitzgeraldBrochureDec2014.pdf.
Special considerations: The Fitzgerald Marine Reserve hosts educational programs for adults and school groups. For information on tours or events, visit the Friends of Fitzgerald Marine Reserve website at www.fitzgeraldreserve.org.
Trail contact: San Mateo County Department of Parks, 455 County Center, 4th Floor, Redwood City, CA 94063; (650) 355-8289; parks.smcgov.org/pillar-point-bluff. Friends of Fitzgerald Marine Reserve, PO Box 669, Moss Beach, CA 94038; (650) 728-3584; www .fitzgeraldreserve.org/newffmrsite.

Finding the trailhead: To reach the Jean Lauer trailhead from CA 1 in Moss Beach, about 5 miles south of Pacifica and just north of Half Moon Bay, turn west onto Cypress Avenue. Follow Cypress Avenue for 0.2 mile to Airport Street and turn left. Follow Airport Street for 0.8 mile to the trailhead and parking lot on the right. GPS: N37 30.690' / W122 30.063'

To go directly to the Fitzgerald Marine Reserve in Moss Beach, turn right (west) from CA 1 onto California Avenue. Follow California Avenue 0.3 mile to the reserve parking lot at the end of the road at North Lake Street. The parking lot is on the right (north), with a small visitor center, restrooms, picnic tables, and trash and recycle bins. The trailhead is at the corner of North Lake Street and California Avenue. GPS: N37 31.412' / W122 30.949'

The Hike

No natural interface is as dramatic as that between the land and the sea. The boundary's dynamics add an element of danger to its exploration, for though tides are predictable, waves are not. Even the trails overlooking the meeting place of earth and water on Pillar Point Bluff and in the Fitzgerald Marine Reserve bear signs of how volatile the zone is, running close to the ragged, dynamic edge above the churning surf below.

▶ Tide-pooling is a major activity at Fitzgerald Marine Reserve. Tide pools on the reserve contain many fragile and exotic creatures, including sea stars, mussels, limpets, anemones, and sea urchins. Sea mammals can also be spotted in the water. Consult a tide chart (published online and in many Bay Area newspapers) if you want to add this activity to your visit. Please observe proper etiquette when exploring: Tread lightly and carefully to avoid crushing tidal residents. Leave all sea life undisturbed—collecting, turning, or moving tidal animals threatens their survival.

While rich tide pools and a craggy shoreline are the reserve's main attractions, the trail on Pillar Point Bluff offers expansive views in all directions, fragrant and colorful coastal scrub, and benches for relaxation and contemplation. Interpretive signs describe the geography of the ocean floor just offshore, which, under the right conditions, gives rise to the walls of water that fuel the legendary Mavericks surf competition.

On the bluff top, you'll share the trail with cyclists and dogs, some off-leash despite the leash law. The great white ball on Pillar Point, part of a US Air Force installation, is the dominant landmark, though one that can't be accessed by trail. Paths on the bluff are braided and there are no signs, but two routes get the bulk of use: a broad pounded track just inland from the cliff, and a broader dirt road farther inland. As a ranger at the reserve advised, if you keep the ocean on one side and CA 1 on the other, you can't lose your way.

The trail begins on the flats, passing through a small marshland before reaching a trail junction. You can go either way, but this loop heads left and is described in a clockwise direction. As you ascend the scrubby east side of the bluff, you'll be looking down on an interesting mix: The Half Moon Bay Airport, built by the US Navy during World War II and now used by private planes, ranges along CA 1, with a trailer park next door. Across the highway stretch farm fields, with the coastal hills rising behind.

Once on top of the bluff, stay left, following the broad path as it loops westward toward the sea. A web of trails fans to overlooks at the cliff's edge. Pick one and check out the views: the golf ball on the point, the crescent beach below, the rocky shallows where you might spy seals, and the vast blue Pacific.

When ready, return to the main path and head north along the bluff top, passing a pair of benches before the route curls inland. Stay left to follow the path northward along the seaside; the path is wide enough to walk and talk with a fellow hiker. Staying left at junctions as you head toward Seal Cove, its cottages visible to the north, leads to the Bernal Avenue trailhead.

You can loop back to the Airport Road trailhead from Bernal Avenue, but this trail links Pillar Point Bluff with the short trail in the Fitzgerald Reserve and a stretch through the charming neighborhood of Seal Cove. The buckling pavement of Ocean Boulevard leads to the historic Moss Beach Distillery, then passes along seafront

Looking south from the bluff's edge toward the tip of Pillar Point

streets lined with homes guaranteed to inspire coast-living envy in the staunchest mountaineer.

Enter the Fitzgerald Reserve property and follow the short bluff-top trail, which is lined with a fence along the crumbling cliff edge, to an overlook of the tide-pooling area and beach. Drop down through the cypress forest that shades much of the reserve and cross San Vicente Creek to reach the main staging area for the reserve.

The extremely short trail to the tide-pooling area begins at the intersection of North Lake and Nevada Avenues, on the northwest edge of the parking lot. The trail is lined with interpretive signs and drops directly to the rocky shore, where you can check out the starfish, anemones, limpets, and barnacles until the tide washes over them once again.

Return as you came to the Bernal trailhead for Pillar Point Bluff, and stay left again at all the junctions, following the wide dirt road. Close the loop at the trail that climbs up from the Airport Road trailhead, retracing your steps to the trailhead.

Mavericks

Forget board shorts and bikinis and gentle curling waves folding onto smooth white-sand beaches. Surfing in Northern California requires wetsuits and the ability to read waves and currents so as to avoid smashing onto rocky shorelines. It's the extreme side of laid back.

The gnarliest incarnation of NorCal surfing is at the legendary Mavericks surf break. When conditions are right, the waves that form off Pillar Point can surge to more than 50 feet in height, perfect for testing the skills and nerve of the world's most accomplished surfers.

According to the Titans of Mavericks website, area surfers first noticed the swell that would become Mavericks (named for one of those locals' dog) in the early 1960s. But it would be years before one of them, Jeff Clark, would finally surf the giant swell. And it would be another fifteen years before Clark would convince fellow surfers to join him—for good reason. These dangerous waves can be killers, and only the most skilled and best-educated big-wave surfers could take them on.

The Titans of Mavericks competition, established in 1999, is exclusive: Only twenty-four surfers are invited to compete. And it's elusive: The waves are only generated under certain conditions, fired by storms off Japan and amped up by the structure of the sea floor, which has been sculpted by faulting to create the perfect funnel for monster waves. If those conditions don't jibe, Mavericks doesn't happen; it's been canceled four times for want of waves. The window for the competition is months' long, typically from November to March. Competitors are given just forty-eight hours' notice before the event. And when the word goes out, thousands of fans descend on tiny Half Moon Bay to watch.

Visit the Titans of Mavericks website, titansofmavericks.com, for the most thorough information on the event.

Jean Lauer Trail at Pillar Point

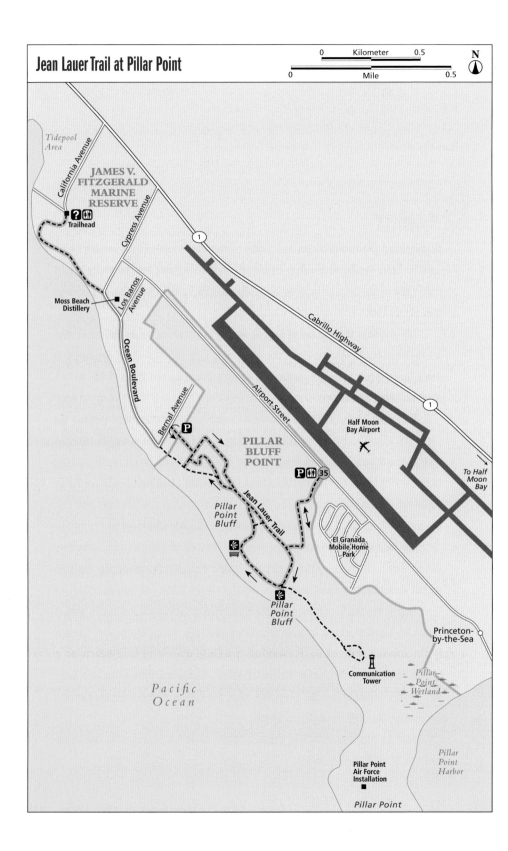

Miles and Directions

0.0 Start by walking into the small marsh; a boardwalk protects habitat and boots.

0.1 At the Y junction, go left, traversing up toward the bluff top.

0.3 A spur trail breaks to the left; stay right on the obvious main path, still climbing.

0.4 On the bluff top, stay left at the junction.

0.5 Reach the overlook, with trails scattering to points overlooking the sea.

0.7 Pass an interpretive sign and a bench.

0.8 Pass a second bench and overlook, this one oriented northward. The trail curls left, away from the sea.

0.9 At the junction, stay left. Several more trail intersections follow; stay left at each, headed toward the homes of Seal Cove.

1.3 At the junction, stay left, dropping to an interpretive sign. Then follow the wide gravel path that leads left to the signed trailhead on Bernal Avenue. *Option:* You can loop back to the Airport Road trailhead by staying right at the junction with the Bernal trail, following the broad dirt path on the east side of the bluff.

1.5 Turn left onto Bernal Avenue, walk a block to Ocean Boulevard, and go right on Ocean Boulevard.

1.8 At the junction with Los Banos Avenue, continue on Ocean Boulevard to the Moss Beach Distillery. Cross the parking lot and continue on Beach Way.

2.1 Reach the entrance to the Fitzgerald Marine Reserve at the junction with Cypress Avenue. Follow the Bluff Trail into the reserve, passing into a cypress forest.

2.4 Arrive at the tide pool overlook. Continue down through the trees to cross San Vicente Creek.

2.5 Reach the reserve parking area. Take time to visit the tide pools, then retrace your steps to the Bernal Avenue trailhead.

3.5 Climb from the Bernal Avenue trailhead back onto the Jean Lauer Trail, staying left at the junction to loop back to the trailhead via the broad dirt track atop the bluff. Stay left at the next few junctions, though you can't really lose your way.

4.1 Reach the unsigned but obvious trail back down to the trailhead. Go left and downhill, retracing your steps.

4.5 Arrive back at the trailhead.

Option: An unmarked trail that breaks south from the Jean Lauer Trail leads to the Pillar Point Wetland. Sloping down along the crest of the bluff, the sparkling waters of Pillar Point Harbor come into view. The trail descends to the harbor, dropping fairly steeply for the 0.1 mile or so. Restrooms, parking, trash cans, and beach access are available at the Pillar Point Harbor trailhead, which borders the pretty wetland: More than 150 different plant and animal species call the marsh home or visit on annual migrations.

36 Salamander Flat Loop

An easy climb through redwoods and eucalyptus leads to Salamander Pond, once a reservoir for the Folger Estate and now the stomping grounds of the rough-skinned newt.

Start: Bear Gulch Trail on south side of stable
Distance: 2.6-mile loop
Hiking time: 1–2 hours
Difficulty: Easy, though there is some climbing.
Trail surface: Dirt trail, dirt farm and carriage roads
Best season: Late spring, summer, and fall
Other trail users: Equestrians, trail runners
Canine compatibility: No dogs allowed
Land status: Wunderlich County Park
Fees and permits: None
Schedule: Park opens at 8 a.m. and closes at approximately sunset; check parks.smcgov.org/ locations/wunderlich-park for exact times.

Trailhead amenities: Informational signboard, restrooms, water
Maps: USGS Woodside; Wunderlich County Park map and brochure available at trailhead and online at parks.smcgov.org/sites/parks .smcgov.org/files/Map_from_Wunderlich BrochureMay2014.pdf
Trail contact: San Mateo County Parks, 455 County Center, 4th Floor, Redwood City, CA 94063-1646; (650) 363-4020; parks.smcgov .org/wunderlich-park. To contact the park directly, call (650) 851-1210.

Finding the trailhead: From I-280, take the Sand Hill Road exit. Head west on Sand Hill Road for 2.1 miles to Portola Road. Turn right (north) on Portola Road, which becomes Woodside Road, and drive 1.1 miles to the park entrance, which is on the left (west). The park's address is 4040 Woodside Rd. GPS: N37 24.668' / W122 15.663'

The Hike

The estates of San Francisco's bygone titans of industry, transportation, water, and agriculture are scattered around the Bay Area. Their names endure on the landscape as well, on monuments, boulevards, and parklands: Stanford, Crocker, Spreckles, Huntington, Hearst, Sutro, Hopkins. The pastoral peninsula south of the city was a favored country sanctuary of these moguls and their families, who acquired vast tracts of former Spanish ranchos sheltered from the fog by the coastal mountains. Some, like William Bourn of Filoli, would move to the peninsula permanently following the devastation of the 1906 earthquake.

The Folger fortune was made in coffee, and the estate of James Folger II, son of a fortune seeker who arrived with the gold rush and found more money in ground coffee than in hard rock, sprawled along the foothills of the Santa Cruz Mountains in Woodside. Before Folger acquired it, the land had been logged by one owner and then planted with vineyards and orchards by another, who dubbed the property Hazel Wood Farm. A portion of those land holdings would eventually become parkland,

Historic buildings, including the carriage house and the Folger Stable, highlight a hike in Wunderlich County Park.

and the spectacular Folger Stable, called a "horse palace" and on the National Register of Historic Places, is one of several structures preserved in Wunderlich Park. Other buildings, which date back to what park literature calls the "Great Estates" period at the turn of the twentieth century, include a carriage house, the stone walls that line trails and roads in the park, a blacksmith barn, and a dairy, or "cold" house, down by the creek near the park's entrance.

The rambling Folger Stable was renovated in 2010 and is still in service, so hikers should expect to encounter equestrians on the trails that wind through the surrounding redwood groves and eucalyptus stands. The stable's carriage room has been converted into a museum, open Saturday from 10 a.m. to 4 p.m.

While Folger's legacy is impressive, his estate wouldn't have been as well preserved if it weren't for the contribution of Martin Wunderlich. In 1974 Wunderlich gave 942 acres to San Mateo County as a park, ensuring generations to come would be able to enjoy both the man-made works preserved there and the natural beauty that surrounds them.

▶ The Folger Stable was designed by architect Arthur Brown Jr., a graduate of the University of California at Berkeley, who would go on to build, among other structures, San Francisco's City Hall, the War Memorial Opera House, Bancroft Library on the Berkeley campus, Hoover Tower on the Stanford University campus, and Coit Tower on Telegraph Hill.

The loop to Salamander Flat follows wide trails that were once carriage roads, farm roads (dating back to the ranching days), and haul roads (built when the hillsides were being logged; the property was also the site of a sawmill in the mid-1800s, and redwood harvested from the property was used to build the stable). The inclines and declines are never too steep, and the width allows hikers to walk side by side, making this a great option for families and friends.

Salamander Flat is dominated by Salamander Pond, a former estate reservoir that serves as habitat for rough-skinned newts. About the cutest creepy-crawly you'll ever see, the orange-bellied newts emerge in wet weather and meander across hillside and trail to the pool. They can, at times, be a plague on the trail: Once you spot one, you'll see them everywhere, causing any conscientious hiker to dance and leap along the path to avoid squishing them.

The route also swings in and out of stands of native redwoods with a vibrant understory of fern and toyon, patches of oak woodland (watch the poison oak!), and groves of nonnative eucalyptus. All impart their unique light and scent to the loop.

All trails are well signed and maintained, making route-finding a breeze. After climbing past the stable on the Bear Gulch Trail, swing onto the Loop Trail, a broad, easy, gently ascending trail wide enough for hikers to walk side by side and for equestrians to pass comfortably. The trail passes through alternating eucalyptus and redwood glades, with views opening occasionally over the treetops to the hills on the other side of the San Andreas Fault rift valley and the bay beyond.

After climbing for about a mile, two quick trail junctions deposit you on the Meadow Trail, which proceeds toward Salamander Flat. The path is well graded and wide—hikers could march up through the eucalyptus four abreast. At the next junction, turn onto the Redwood Trail, entering a grove of stately sequoias. Swing through several gullies as you continue, one with a stair-step cascade that runs in the rainy season. A ramshackle pipe traces the latter portion of this trail section.

The Madrone Trail leads down to Salamander Pond, where you can look for newts. In late season the pond may be covered with a brilliantly green algae. Another late-season eyeful is offered by poison oak that has turned a glowing red, which helps illustrate how versatile the plant is, growing in vines up the oaks and in hedges along the trail.

Beyond the pond, pick up the Bear Gulch Trail, which circles via switchbacks down to the junction with the Loop Trail. From here, retrace your steps to the trailhead.

▶ Two familiar, seemingly peaceful denizens of the Bay Area's oak woodlands are locked in what has been dubbed by some scientists an "evolutionary arms race." The newt produces a toxin that makes it inedible, but garter snakes have developed an ability to digest the poison and, with it, the newt. Each species balances its ability to produce or survive the toxin based on principles of "coevolution," which allows both the snake and the newt to adapt and thrive.

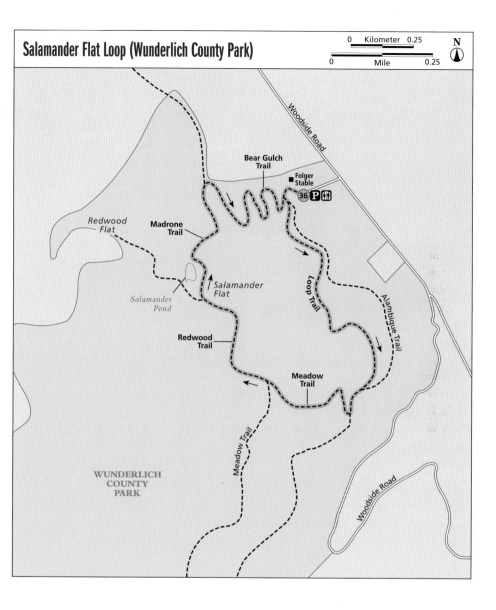

0   Kilometer   0.25
0   Mile   0.25
N

Bear Gulch
Trail

Folger
Stable

36 P

Redwood
Flat

Madrone
Trail

Salamander
Pond

Salamander
Flat

Loop Trail

Alambique Trail

Redwood
Trail

Meadow
Trail

Meadow Trail

WUNDERLICH
COUNTY
PARK

Woodside Road

Woodside Road

Miles and Directions

0.0   Start on the Bear Gulch Trail on the south side of the stable.

0.2   After climbing behind the stable, then through a redwood grove and around a switchback, arrive at the intersection of the service road and Loop Trail. Go left (southwest) on the Loop Trail.

0.5   Curve through another redwood grove in a gully.

1.0   Meet the Alambique Trail, which has been visible below the Loop Trail for the last 0.1 mile or so. Stay straight (right/southwest) on the Alambique Trail.

1.1   At the intersection, go right onto the Meadow Trail toward Salamander Flat.

Salamander Flats—or rather, pond—is at the midpoint of this route through Wunderlich County Park.

1.3 Reach the junction with the Redwood Trail. Turn right (north) on the Redwood Trail.

1.5 At the junction, turn right (downhill) on the Madrone Trail. Salamander Flat and pool are about 75 yards down the Madrone Trail on the left.

2.1 At the intersection of the Bear Gulch and Madrone Trails, make a sharp right turn onto the Bear Gulch Trail.

2.4 Descend a series of switchbacks back to the service road/Loop Trail intersection. Retrace your steps along the Bear Gulch Trail back to the Folger Stable and trailhead.

2.6 Arrive back at the trailhead.

Options: Take some time to tour the Folger estate buildings. The Folger Estate Stable Historic District brochure, compiled by the Friends of Huddart and Wunderlich County Parks, outlines a short interpretive walking tour of the structures on the Wunderlich Park property and is available online at www.huddartwunder lichfriends.org/images/forms/WalkingTour.pdf. To extend an exploration of the park's wildlands, you can create longer loops by continuing on the Alambique Trail to Alambique Flat and beyond, the Meadow Trail to the Meadows, and the Redwood Trail to Redwood Flat.

37 Stanford Dish

Long a favorite escape for students and faculty of nearby Stanford University, this paved loop features great views and its namesake radio telescope.

Start: Stanford Gate off Junipero Serra Boulevard
Distance: 3.7-mile loop
Hiking time: 2–3 hours
Difficulty: Moderate due to steady climbing at outset
Trail surface: Pavement
Best season: Year-round; spring for wildflower blooms
Other trail users: Trail runners
Canine compatibility: No dogs allowed

Land status: Stanford University
Fees and permits: None
Schedule: Sunrise to sunset daily. Specific hours change monthly and are detailed at dish .stanford.edu.
Trailhead amenities: Information signboard, entrance kiosk, trash cans
Maps: USGS Palo Alto (no map is needed)
Trail contact: Stanford University; (650) 723-2560; dish.stanford.edu

Finding the trailhead: From I-280 in Palo Alto, take the Page Mill Road exit. Go east on Page Mill Road for 1.5 miles to Junipero Serra Boulevard. Turn left and follow Junipero Serra Boulevard for about 0.5 mile to Stanford Avenue. Parking is available alongside Stanford Avenue but fills up quickly. GPS: N37 24.609' / W122 09.689'

The Hike

An urban hike with stunning views, the Dish also offers escape. The adjacent campus of Stanford University is lovely and crisscrossed with walking paths, but it's still the campus. To get away, students have been heading to the 2,500-acre open space at the Dish for decades.

The Dish went up long before storied Stanford University became a player in the silicon revolution. The massive radio telescope was built in the mid-1960s, at the height of the Cold War, to detect "atmospheric nuclear bomb blasts," according to a brief history published by the Stanford Historical Society. It was also used to communicate with "satellites and spacecraft," and in both the Apollo and Voyager missions. The structure is massive, measuring 150 feet in diameter, and is still in use, as are the wildlands that surround it, for botanical research and the study of habitat conservation.

▶ Artist Nathan Oliveira, Stanford instructor and creator of the spectacular Windhover Series, nurtured his creativity on walks he took at the Dish with his wife in the 1970s. The birds of the open space were his inspiration; eventually the wing became his focus. Among other things, Oliviera's art plays on, in the artist's words, "the concept of wings as a metaphor for the soaring of one's mind."

The Stanford Dish points heavenward.

These days, the Dish open space is a beacon for hikers and trail runners. The long loop is perfect for a workout, an afternoon escape, or a leisurely weekend walk with family or friends. The views from the crest of the hills spread in all directions, with the dark coastal mountains to the west and midpeninsula development—the Stanford campus surrounding Hoover Tower, the sprawling wooded neighborhoods, and the silver and gray of more congested development—spreading toward the blue of the bay, with the hills of the East Bay behind.

For all that the trail is paved, it is not easy. The climb at the outset is a primer: No matter which way you travel on the loop part of the route, you'll be headed uphill

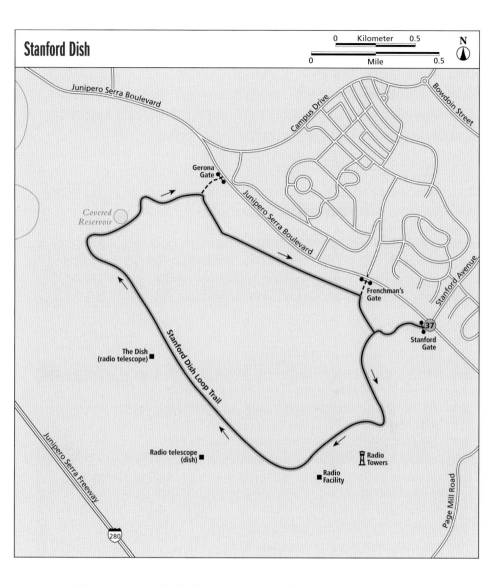

0   Kilometer   0.5

0   Mile   0.5

N

Junipero Serra Boulevard

Campus Drive

Bowdoin Street

Gerona Gate

Junipero Serra Boulevard

Covered Reservoir

Frenchman's Gate

Stanford Avenue

37

Stanford Gate

The Dish (radio telescope)

Stanford Dish Loop Trail

Radio telescope (dish)

Radio Towers

Radio Facility

Junipero Serra Freeway

Page Mill Road

280

toward the crest. Though the loop can be traveled in either direction, it's described here clockwise, with the steepest climbing accomplished first.

A series of service roads intersect the obvious paved route on the ascent. Identified with numbered signs, these spurs of the Reservoir Road lead to facilities or former facilities on the property. The views open as you approach the rolling hilltops, first to the east and south, of the San Mateo Bridge and down into the Santa Clara Valley. As the loop arcs north toward the Dish, vistas open to the mountainous west and the developed east and finally to the north, where the blue waters of the bay spread across the horizon.

The first dish you see is not "the Dish"; that monster becomes apparent as you tuck through a gully on the crest. Pass the smaller dish and other side roads, then

▶ Established in 1891 by railroad magnate and onetime California governor Leland Stanford and his wife, Jane, Stanford University has gone on to become one of the most celebrated private institutions of higher learning in the world. The founders of Google, Larry Page and Sergey Brin, started the groundbreaking Internet company while graduate students at Stanford; a quick Google search shows the university ranks among the top 10 institutions worldwide.

climb to the trail junction at the Dish proper. A side trail leads up to the structure, then down into the neighborhood behind.

Beyond the Dish, now on a mostly downhill run, pass a covered reservoir before dropping alongside Junipero Serra Boulevard, where the spacious, manicured yards of spectacular homes form a buffer between trail and roadway. The last stretch, past the Gerona and Frenchman's Gates, is a roller coaster, finally climbing to close the loop. Unless you are doing laps, retrace your steps to the trailhead.

Miles and Directions

0.0   Start by climbing the steep paved trail.

0.2   At the signed junction, go left and uphill on the pavement.

0.3   Views open to the south and east, of the bay and the San Mateo Bridge.

0.6   Crest the hill at the crossing of a service road. Vistas of the Santa Cruz Mountains and the first dish open to the west.

0.9   Crest a second hilltop and pass another service road on the left.

1.2   Pass 540 Reservoir Road (service road) to the smaller dish.

1.6   Arrive at the Dish and the junction with the trail down to the Piers Gate. Stay straight on the paved loop trail.

2.3   Pass the covered reservoir.

2.7   Pass the junction with the trail to the Gerona Gate.

2.9   Pass a side trail that leads down to a water fountain.

3.4   Pass the side trail that leads down to the Frenchman's Gate.

3.5   Close the loop. Turn left to retrace your steps to the trailhead.

3.7   Arrive back at the trailhead.

38 Mineral Springs and Penitencia Creek Trails

Follow an easy trail past grottos of oozing and burbling springs, then Penitencia Creek up to its confluence with Aguague Creek, where a wintertime waterfall may be seen.

Start: Trailhead near Alum Rock bridge
Distance: 2.0 miles out and back
Hiking time: About 1 hour
Difficulty: Easy
Trail surface: Pavement, dirt trail
Best season: Year-round
Other trail users: Cyclists
Canine compatibility: No dogs allowed
Land status: San Jose Regional Parks
Fees and permits: Entrance/parking fee
Schedule: Sunrise to a half hour after sunset daily
Trailhead amenities: Information board at trailhead. Visitor center amenities include restrooms, water, information, picnic sites, playing greens, a volleyball court, and tot lots. Should you choose to start your hike at the visitor center, add 0.4 mile to your total hiking distance.
Maps: USGS Calaveras Reservoir; Alum Rock park map and brochure available at park visitor center and online at ca-sanjose.civicplus.com/DocumentCenter/View/30229
Trail contact: City of San Jose, 200 E. Santa Clara St., San Jose, CA 95113; (408) 535-3500; www.sanjoseca.gov/Facilities/Facility/Details/Alum-Rock-Park-176

Finding the trailhead: From I-680 in San Jose, take the McKee Road exit. Go west on McKee Road for 0.2 mile to Capital Avenue. Turn left onto Capital and go 1.1 miles to Penitencia Creek Road. Turn right (west) on Penitencia Creek Road and go 1.9 miles to the park's entrance station. The trailhead is at the end of the last parking lot, at the historic Alum Rock Bridge, 1.9 miles from the entrance station. GPS: N37 23.827' / W121 47.878'

The Hike

Tucked in a steep canyon, Alum Rock Park has been a retreat for the bone-weary since 1872. Its mineral springs, captured in grottos and fonts along Penitencia Creek, were incorporated into a world-famous spa at the turn of the twentieth century. More than twenty-five springs spouting seven different minerals, including soda, "magnesia," iron, and odiferous sulphur, collected in pools and baths for visitors' enjoyment. The pools have long since been removed, and the grottos have fallen into charming disrepair, with thick mineral stains surrounding the springs within. But they make for fascinating diversions on a hike along Penitencia Creek.

▶ From a trailside interpretive sign: Eleven doctors recommended taking the waters at Alum Rock to treat "kidney and stomach troubles, rheumatism, and malarial afflictions."

The park's resort days ran from 1890 to the early 1930s. Two bits bought travelers a ticket on the steam train operated by the San Jose and Alum Rock Railroad that ran to the spa, which at one time included a grand indoor pool called the

Springwater pools below one of the historic grottos along Penitencia Creek.

"natatorium," a dance pavilion, a tearoom, and other amenities. Apparently, riding up to the resort wasn't too bad, but the open cars behind the "steam dummies," or engines, frequently jumped the tracks on the ride back down into town. For those with delicate constitutions, the ride no doubt jangled nerves that had been soothed

▶ According to Judy Thompson's *Alum Rock Park: East San Jose's Heart (A Very Brief History)*, the canyon was named by an area farmer not for alum, but for the powdery substance known as thenardite, which could be mistaken for alum, that had been deposited on rocks by the mineral springs.

previously in the baths. Remnants of the railroad (later an electric line) include concrete abutments that once supported the tracks.

The trail that explores the springs also penetrates farther into the Penitencia Creek canyon, where the crowds thin and the canyon grows narrower. At trail's end a bridge crosses the creek to an overlook of a seasonal waterfall above the confluence of Penitencia and Aguague Creeks.

From the trailhead at the Alum Rock Bridge, follow the paved Penitencia Creek Trail to the first bridge. Cross the creek to pick up the Mineral Springs Trail, a narrow dirt track that hugs the canyon wall and passes several of the mineral spring grottos. The creek runs alongside, with little cascades pouring from pool to mossy pool. Pass the second bridge to visit the last of these grottos, then retrace your steps to the bridge and cross to the paved route.

Picnic areas line the Penitencia Creek Trail as it heads farther into the canyon. A forest of buckeye, maple, walnut, oak, and alder, all nurtured by the year-round flow of Penitencia Creek, shade these sites.

Pass the last picnic area and the pavement ends, the trail becoming more natural and rustic. Sycamores and maples provide ample shade in summer, drop orange and yellow leaves in fall, and harbor noisy colonies of jays. The rocky creek bed harbors trickling pools, even at the end of the dry season. The pretty No Horse Bridge spans Penitencia Creek near the turnaround point; the abutment at the far end passing through the split trunk (or trunks) of an old sycamore. The route ends at the overlook at the confluence of Penitencia and Aguague Creeks, immersed in a thick forest that harbors no hint of the storied pools that lie just downstream.

To return to the trailhead, retrace your steps to the junction of the Mineral Springs and Penitencia Creek Trails at the footbridge. Stay left on the paved trail, passing another series of fonts and grottos as you return to the trailhead.

Miles and Directions

0.0 Start by passing the Alum Rock Bridge and picking up the dirt Mineral Springs Trail on the left side of the paved Penitencia Creek Trail. You'll return via the paved route.

0.2 Pass the second bridge, check out the last grotto, then return to the bridge and cross to the Penitencia Creek Trail. Go left to continue upstream.

0.4 Pass the Sycamore Grove picnic area, with a phone, barbecues, trash cans, and a horseshoe pit. The Sycamore Switchbacks to the South Rim Trail depart to the right. Stay straight on the paved Penitencia Creek Trail.

0.5 Pass the Creekside and Live Oak picnic areas.

Mineral Springs and Penitencia Creek Trails (Alum Rock Park)

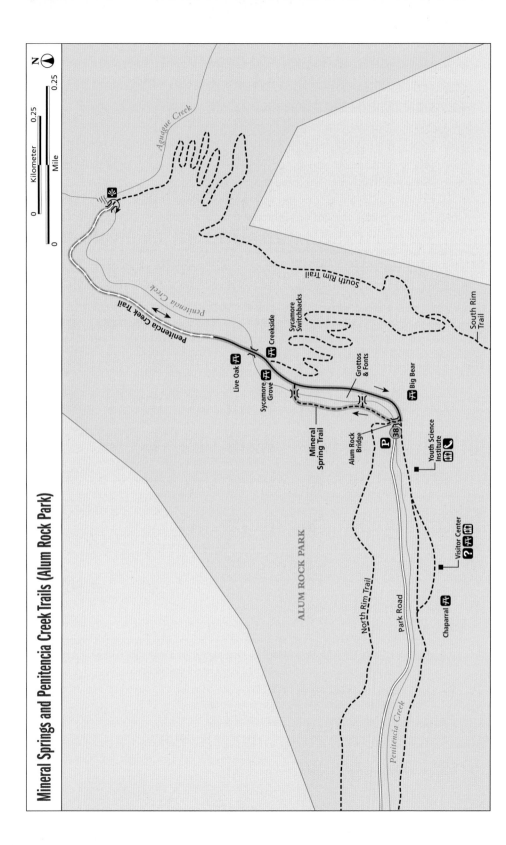

The No Horse Bridge spans Penitencia Creek at its confluence at Aguague Creek.

0.6 The pavement ends.

0.7 Pass Sachi's Rest picnic area.

1.0 Cross the No Horse Bridge, which spans Penitencia Creek, passing through the crotch of a huge old sycamore on the far side. The turnaround is at the overlook at the confluence of Penitencia and Aguague Creeks. If there's enough water, Penitencia Creek tumbles in cascades to meet the Aguague. Retrace your steps toward the trailhead.

1.6 At the junction with the Mineral Springs Trail at the bridge, stay left on the paved Penitencia Creek Trail, passing more grottos and several interpretive signs.

2.0 Arrive back at the trailhead.

Options: The paved Penitencia Creek Trail extends west through the more-developed sections of the park, following a rail-trail that lies on the bed of the former steam and electric rail line. The trail offers access to the Youth Science Institute and the park's visitor center, which is surrounded by playing greens, two tot lots, picnic areas with barbecues, and a sand volleyball court. Beyond this hub, the trail follows the creek west to the trestle over Alum Rock Road and into the Rustic Lands and Quail Hollow picnic areas (about 1.1 miles from the Alum Rock Bridge trailhead). The trail continues to the park's Penitencia Creek Road entrance.

You can also continue east from the overlook at the confluence of Penitencia and Aguague Creeks, climbing steeply onto the rim of the canyon via switchbacks on the South Rim Trail. Descend from the rim via the Sycamore Switchbacks, which drop into the grotto area on the Penitencia Creek Trail, or follow the South Rim route farther west to where it descends the canyon wall near the visitor center. Both options will add about 2.5 miles to the total distance.

39 Wildcat Canyon Loop

Walk through a lovely riparian corridor along Wildcat Creek, climb to an exposed vista point, and visit charming Deer Hollow Farm on this long loop through a popular park.

Start: Main staging area near North Meadow
Distance: 5.7-mile loop
Hiking time: 3–4 hours
Difficulty: Moderate due to length and a couple of steep climbs and descents
Trail surface: Pavement, dirt ranch roads, dirt trails
Best season: Spring and fall. Summer days can be hot, and trails can disintegrate to sticky mud after winter rains.
Other trail users: Trail runners; cyclists
Canine compatibility: No dogs allowed
Land status: Rancho San Antonio County Park and Open Space Preserve
Fees and permits: None
Schedule: Sunrise to a half-hour after sunset daily

Trailhead amenities: Restrooms, water, picnic sites, trash cans, information signboard. Additional picnic facilities are found throughout the developed areas of the county park.
Maps: USGS Cupertino; trail maps in park brochure in information kiosk at trailhead, online at www.openspace.org/sites/default/files/pr_rancho_san_antonio.pdf
Special considerations: The route includes trails in both a regional open space preserve and a Santa Clara County park. The melding of the two is seamless on these impeccably maintained trails.
Trail contact: Midpeninsula Regional Open Space District, 330 Distel Circle, Los Altos, CA 94022-1404; (650) 691-1200; www.openspace.org

Finding the trailhead: From I-280 north of Cupertino, take the Foothill Expressway exit. Head west on the Foothill Expressway (Foothill Boulevard) for 0.1 mile to Cristo Rey Drive. Turn right (north) on Cristo Rey Drive and travel 0.6 mile to the roundabout. Take the second roundabout exit, signed for the park. Continue to the park entrance on the left (west). The trailhead is in the lower parking lot adjacent to the restrooms; begin on the paved road behind the gate. GPS: N37 19.935' / W122 05.246'

The Hike

The story of Rancho San Antonio mirrors that of parklands throughout the San Francisco Bay Area. It starts with the Ohlone, who thrived here for thousands of years before the arrival of the Spanish. The oaks were harvested for acorns (a staple food), and other native plants, including the berries of the bay laurel, buckeye nuts, and willow boughs, were incorporated into foodstuffs, medicine, basketry, and weaponry. Hunters brought home tule elk, deer, bear, and fish. The permanent village near what would become this open-space park was called Partacsi; elements of that village have been replicated at the park.

The end of the dry season brings a golden glow to the canopy shading the trail along Wildcat Canyon.

Enter the Spaniards, who set about colonizing California in the late eighteenth century. Mission Santa Clara de Asís, the first mission in California named for a female saint, was established not far south of Rancho San Antonio in 1777, a lonely outpost in a broad valley at the southern end of San Francisco Bay. For the natives what followed was tragic: Many were killed by disease, and others became neophytes, "saved" by the Franciscan missionaries and put to work on the mission compound.

▶ Since it was established, Mission Santa Clara de Asís has been destroyed and rebuilt six times on three different sites. Fire, flood, and earthquake leveled the various incarnations. Today's mission, a replica of the predecessor erected on the same site in 1825, was constructed following that church's demise by fire in 1926. The mission is on the campus of Santa Clara University.

The park derives its name from its identity during California's long Spanish and Mexican eras. Rancho San Antonio was granted to Juan Prado Mesa who, according to park literature, was a soldier at the San Francisco Presidio and an Indian fighter of some renown. The rancho, like others throughout Alta California, was used to raise cattle for hides and tallow.

After California's incorporation into the United States, the Mexican ranchos became American ranches. One of the landowners was William Dana; another part of the rancho was sold to the Snyder family, who maintained a farm, vineyard, and orchard on the land. Structures dating back to this era—Dana and the Snyders acquired the former rancho land in the mid-nineteenth century—still stand, preserved within Deer Hollow Farm. The county park department and open space district began acquiring the property in 1977; the contiguous parks now encompass more than 4,000 acres and comprise one of the most popular public parklands in the South Bay.

The route described here links trails in both the county park and open-space preserve. The park complex is extremely popular with cyclists, hikers, and trail runners, so be prepared to share the trails with plenty of like-minded visitors. Trail etiquette is important given the high volume of foot and cycling traffic.

Begin by climbing the exposed Hill Trail, from which you can enjoy views east toward the bay. The Coyote Trail, which rolls west to Wildcat Canyon, is well built and shady, traversing through oak woodlands to the stream corridor. Check out the buckeye trees along the well-graded track, which bear fragrant blooms in spring when they leaf out; in fall the heavy nuts dangle like holiday ornaments from the bare branches.

Wildcat Creek is the star of the Wildcat Canyon stretch of trail, flowing beneath a dense canopy of bay and oak. A series of bridges span the flow, which is vigorous in winter and slows to a trickle by the end of the dry season.

To reach the vista point, the Wildcat Canyon Loop trail climbs out of the canyon with the help of switchbacks, topping out at a major trail junction on an open ridge. A short hitch uphill leads to a stunning overlook, where views sprawl across the Santa Clara Valley from the bay to Mount Diablo to Mount Hamilton and points south. Take a seat on the bench to take it all in, then return to the junction to begin the downhill run.

And downhill it is. A series of switchbacks has been carved into the steep hillside above the Rogue Valley. The slopes are shockingly steep, but still support a shady oak woodland. Breaks in the canopy permit glimpses of monster homes bordering the park.

Down in the Rogue Valley, the trail broadens into dirt ranch road and is flat for the duration. The return leg swings past Deer Hollow Farm, a working farm and educational center with livestock, old farm equipment including a wagon seeder, an organic garden, and a historic cabin dating back to the ranching days. The loop concludes in the expansive North Meadow, where an enormous heritage bay laurel rises

Deer Hollow Farm

Deer Hollow Farm is a working farm, educational facility, and historic site. The Grant family lived on the land for seventy-seven years starting in the mid-nineteenth century, raising dairy cows, harvesting lumber for use on the railroad, and finally growing wheat and hay on their 360-acre parcel. The two-room Grant Cabin, used by the farm foreman, dates back to the 1850s; it has been restored and furnished with furniture from the period. The blacksmith shop, now used as a classroom for school groups, is across the way, and a display case outside holds old farm tools that were recovered on the ranch. The apple barn serves as a nature center. Surrounded by gardens and livestock pens, the old buildings evoke times gone by and, at the same time, ring with the delighted voices of young visitors.

School and community groups, as well as the public, are able to tour the Deer Hollow facilities and participate in farming activities. The farm is open from 8 a.m. to 4 p.m. Tuesday through Sunday. It closes at 1 p.m. on Wednesday and is closed on Monday. For more information, contact the City of Mountain View Recreation Department, PO Box 7540, Mountain View, CA 94039; (650) 903-6430; www.openspace .org/what-to-do/education/deer-hollow-farm.

near the monument commemorating St. Joseph's Seminary, which was damaged in the 1989 Loma Prieta earthquake.

Miles and Directions

0.0 Start by crossing the bridge over Permanente Creek and following the paved road uphill above North Meadow.

0.2 Go left through the fence line onto the Hill Trail, climbing up and southwest with views of the bay behind you.

0.5 Pass the junction with the trail to the water tanks on the left (east). Stay right (south) on the Hill Trail.

0.7 Arrive at the four-way junction with the Coyote Trail and the PG&E Trail. Turn right (west) onto the Coyote Trail.

1.4 Reach the junction with the Farm Bypass Trail. Stay left (west) on the Coyote Trail, which continues toward Wildcat Canyon.

1.6 Pass the second junction with the Farm Bypass Trail, which drops right toward Deer Hollow Farm. Stay left (west) toward the junction with the Wildcat Loop Trail.

Wildcat Canyon Loop (Rancho San Antonio County Park and Open Space Preserve)

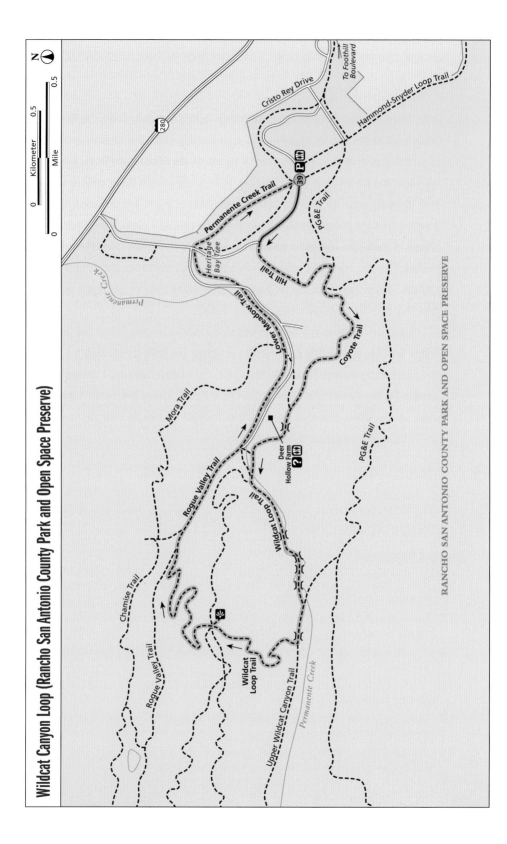

RANCHO SAN ANTONIO COUNTY PARK AND OPEN SPACE PRESERVE

1.7 Arrive at the start of the Wildcat Loop Trail. Go left, walking up the lovely, fragrant canyon. Cross the first of a series of bridges that ford the stream.

2.1 Cross a culvert; a small fall tumbles below.

2.2 Pass the junction with the PG&E Trail. Stay right (straight) on the Wildcat Loop Trail.

2.4 Cross the last bridge and reach the junction with the Upper Wildcat Canyon Trail. Go right on the Wildcat Loop Trail, climbing out of the canyon via switchbacks.

3.1 Arrive at the six-way trail junction on the ridge. Go right onto the grassy summit to the vista point and take in the views, then head back down to the junction.

3.2 Pick up the signed Wildcat Loop Trail, which drops to the north. A series of sweeping switchbacks winds down the wall of the ravine.

4.2 Meet the Rogue Valley Trail. Turn right onto the broad, flat ranch road.

4.5 Arrive at Deer Hollow Farm and the junction with the Lower Meadow Trail. Proceed through the farm on the roadway/trail, checking out the garden, livestock, and historic buildings.

4.8 Cross a bridge on the farm's east border and take the log-lined dirt track signed Lower Meadow Trail, which parallels the paved road. The dirt trail rejoins the roadway 0.1 mile ahead.

4.9 Pass the paved access road to the ranger's office, staying on the Lower Meadow Trail. The Lower Meadow briefly separates from the roadside, then crosses a bridge and climbs to the road. Use the crosswalk to pick up the dirt trail on the other side.

5.4 Pass the boundary between the open space preserve and the county park at a large informational kiosk (with maps). Cross the bike path and roadway onto the gravel, wheelchair-accessible Permanente Creek Trail through North Meadow. Stay right at the next junction, following signs for the parking lots (St. Joseph's Seminary is to the left). Pass tennis courts and then the impressive heritage bay.

5.7 Arrive back at the trailhead.

40 Zinfandel and Orchard Loop Trails

This short, easy trail above the Stevens Creek Reservoir begins and ends at a historic winery.

Start: Signed trailhead adjacent to winery picnic area
Distance: 1.6-mile lollipop
Hiking time: About 1 hour
Difficulty: Easy
Trail surface: Dirt ranch roads, dirt trails
Best season: Spring and fall
Other trail users: Equestrians
Canine compatibility: Dogs not allowed
Land status: Picchetti Ranch Open Space Preserve
Fees and permits: None

Schedule: Sunrise to a half-hour after sunset daily
Trailhead amenities: Picnic sites, information signboard, winery, restrooms on far side of picnic area
Maps: USGS Cupertino; map in park brochure available at trailhead, online at www.open space.org/sites/default/files/pr_picchetti.pdf
Trail contact: Midpeninsula Regional Open Space District, 330 Distel Circle, Los Altos, CA 94022-1404; (650) 691-1200; www .openspace.org

Finding the trailhead: From I-280 in Cupertino, take the Foothill Expressway exit. Follow Foothill Boulevard, which becomes Stevens Canyon Road, for about 4 miles to the junction with Monte-bello Road near the Stevens Creek Reservoir. Turn right and follow winding Montebello Road about 0.5 mile to the Picchetti Winery. There are two driveways; use the second to access parking for the preserve. GPS: N37 17.691' / W122 05.472'

The Hike

The North Bay's Wine Country gets all the attention, but winemaking has a long history in other parts of the Bay Area. Little Picchetti Ranch, the homestead of Italian immigrants Vincenzo and Secondo Picchetti, preserves a snapshot of that history, with the winery enjoying renewed popularity more than a century after the brothers arrived.

The Picchettis started building on the land in 1882 and began producing wine from grapes grown on the property in 1896. The business took a hit during Prohibition; to make up the losses—and in keeping with the agrarian tradition in the Santa Clara Valley—some of the vineyards were replanted as orchards. But the Picchettis were permitted to produce 400 gallons per year for family use, so winemaking on the property continued unbroken.

▶ In 1872, Vincenzo Picchetti paid $1,500 for his 160 acres of ranchland. In late 2015, the average price of a home on a residential lot in Silicon Valley was nearly $1 million.

Four generations of Picchettis worked the vineyards and orchards, but eventually the ranch grew unprofitable. The Midpeninsula Regional Open Space District acquired the property in the mid-1970s, and

The sun weathers the walls of an old barn and clusters of wine barrels at the historic Picchetti Winery.

the winery and surrounding buildings, including the main ranch house and stable, were refurbished and have been listed on the National Register of Historic Places.

The present commercial Picchetti Winery is leased from the district. If you opt to do a post-hike tasting—highly recommended—check out the bricks in the winery wall in the southeast corner: They slope conspicuously downward, a sign of damage sustained in the 1906 earthquake.

▶ One Picchetti vintage, which can be tasted in the winery post-hike, is made from the "oldest zinfandel vines" in the region. These vines do not need to be watered, as their roots tap water sources far underground.

Beyond the grounds of the winery, the trail's setting blurs the boundaries of industrial, pastoral, and suburban: The Stevens Creek Quarry is front and center in the viewscape to the northeast, and noise from the quarry, as well as from the nearby Sunnyvale Rod and Gun Club, may filter onto the trails. The surrounding hillsides are dotted with massive homes, and the gray shadow of urban sprawl is visible on the Santa Clara Valley floor to the east. But the parklands surrounding the Stevens Creek Reservoir dominate, and signs and sounds of civilization fade away as the Orchard Loop Trail crests a high point and circles around its backside.

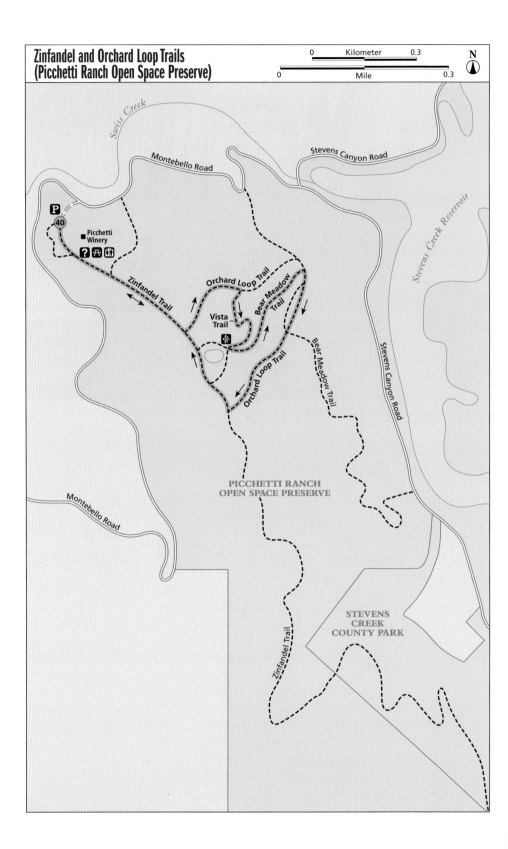

Zinfandel and Orchard Loop Trails
(Picchetti Ranch Open Space Preserve)

Kilometer 0 0.3

Mile 0 0.3

N

Swiss Creek

Montebello Road

Stevens Canyon Road

Stevens Creek Reservoir

P 40

Picchetti Winery

Zinfandel Trail

Orchard Loop Trail

Bear Meadow Trail

Vista Trail

Orchard Loop Trail

Bear Meadow Trail

Stevens Canyon Road

PICCHETTI RANCH OPEN SPACE PRESERVE

Montebello Road

STEVENS CREEK COUNTY PARK

Zinfandel Trail

The trail begins by climbing gently past the picnic area and restrooms. As you leave the winery behind, views from the ranch road open across the Stevens Creek valley and into the Santa Clara Valley. The Orchard Loop Trail breaks left to begin the loop portion of the route, circling the hilltop with the reservoir far below. A short, steep pitch leads up to a picnic site and vista point in a hilltop glade shaded by oaks.

Follow the Vista Trail down to the junction at the pond, little more than a puddle in late season, but still a vibrant habitat. Views on the descent open onto the Stevens Creek drainage, which spills out of the wooded coastal mountains. From the pond, double back to the Orchard Loop via the Bear Meadow Trail, a pleasant ramble with nice views across the Stevens Creek drainage.

Back on the Orchard Loop, descend the ranch road to the junction with the Zinfandel Trail. It's a steady, easy climb past the pond and back to the saddle and trail junction, where you close the loop. Retrace your steps from here to the winery and trailhead.

Miles and Directions

0.0 Start by following the trail past the picnic area, then the restrooms. The route broadens into a ranch road.

0.1 At the junction, stay left on the Zinfandel Trail (no sign).

0.2 At the signed junction, go left on the Orchard Loop Trail. The Zinfandel Trail, where you'll close the loop, continues straight.

0.4 A short, steep pitch deposits you at the junction of the Orchard Loop and Vista Trails. Go right and uphill on the Vista Trail.

0.5 Reach the vista point in a stand of oaks. Follow the path to the left, down toward the pond.

0.6 Arrive at the pond and the signed junction with the Bear Meadow Trail. Check out the marsh and water, then head sharply left down the Bear Meadow Trail. *Option:* You can shorten the loop by connecting with the Zinfandel Trail on the far side of the pond. Turn right on the Zinfandel Trail to return to the winery in a 1-mile loop.

0.9 At the junction with the Orchard Loop Trail, go right. At the Y about 100 yards farther, stay left and downhill on the broad Orchard Loop.

1.0 The Bear Meadow Trail crosses the Orchard Loop, then continues down toward the Stevens Creek Reservoir. Stay straight on the Orchard Loop Trail.

1.2 Climb to the junction with the Zinfandel Trail at a small bridge. Go right on the Zinfandel Trail.

1.3 After passing the pond, pass the junction with the head of the Bear Meadow Trail.

1.4 Close the loop at the first junction with the Orchard Loop Trail. Retrace your steps.

1.6 Arrive back at the winery and trailhead.

41 New Almaden Quicksilver Historic Loop

The remnants of the New Almaden Quicksilver Mine, which delved into one of California's most famous and productive ore bodies, are showcased along this long loop.

Start: Hacienda trailhead
Distance: 7.3-mile loop
Hiking time: 4–5 hours
Difficulty: Strenuous
Trail surface: Dirt roadways, dirt trails
Best season: Spring and fall. Exposed sections of the route can be inhospitable on hot summer days; trails and old dirt roadways may become muddy after winter rains.
Other trail users: Trail runners, mountain bikers, equestrians
Canine compatibility: Leashed dogs permitted
Land status: Almaden Quicksilver County Park
Fees and permits: None
Schedule: Sunrise to sunset daily
Trailhead amenities: Restrooms, trash cans, water, picnic sites, information signboard with maps

Maps: USGS Santa Teresa Hills; Santa Clara County Park brochure and map available at trailhead and at www.sccgov.org/sites/parks/parkfinder/Documents/AQGuideMap.pdf; Historic Trail map and interpretive guide available at trailhead and at www.sccgov.org/sites/parks/parkfinder/Documents/Quicksilver-Brochure-Sm.pdf
Special considerations: Use caution when exploring the historic mining sites, obeying warning signs and staying on the trails (this will also protect you from contact with poison oak). Leave all artifacts on-site for the next visitor to enjoy.
Trail contact: Santa Clara County Parks and Recreation Department, 298 Garden Hill Dr., Los Gatos, CA 95032-7699; (408) 355-2200; www.parkhere.org

Finding the trailhead: To reach the Hacienda trailhead from I-280 in San Jose, take CA 17 south toward Los Gatos to CA 85. Head south on CA 85 to the Almaden Expressway exit. Turn left at the freeway exit, then right onto the Almaden Expressway, and go 4.2 miles to Almaden Road. Turn left onto Almaden Road and follow it for 2.9 miles, through the charming village of New Almaden, to the signed park entrance on the right. The Hacienda trailhead is at the west side of the upper parking area. GPS: N37 10.433' / W121 49.500'

The Hike

Without quicksilver, there would have been no gold. Mercury was critical to extracting the precious metal from deposits in the Sierra Nevada, and to extracting silver from the Comstock Lode in Nevada. The New Almaden Quicksilver Mine was a primary source of the crucial processing material.

For more than 135 years, from the time of Mexican rule in California to 1976, the ore containing quicksilver, called cinnabar, was extracted from these hills. In that time, more than 83 million pounds of mercury were produced.

Those other things that hikers enjoy while on the trail, like views, wildflower blooms, and the chance to see wildlife, are also in evidence along the Historic Trail.

The collapsed schoolhouse at English Camp

Once you hit the high ground, along the Castillero Trail, views open westward onto the Santa Cruz Mountains, including Mount Umunhum, with its distinctive radio-tower topper, and Loma Prieta, namesake of the infamous 1989 earthquake. At Cape Horn Pass, views extend north to the San Jose cityscape and the blue bay beyond. The hills are cloaked in oak woodland, with patches of chaparral on the sunny south-facing slopes. And most of the trails are wide enough for hikers to walk side by side and comfortably pass other trail users.

▶ Well worth the read: Wallace Stegner's classic *Angle of Repose*, an epic love story that begins at the New Almaden Quicksilver Mine.

The loop begins next to the fenced-in display of mining equipment from the Hacienda Reduction Works, which occupied the huge clearing below the upper trailhead parking area. Rusting but still evocative, the enclosure includes a furnace and condensing system, shakers, loaders, fans, and other equipment. This is the second stop on the Historic Trail, which is lined

▶ In addition to historical uses in the extraction of gold from ore and in thermometers, liquid mercury has been used in barometers, batteries, and dental amalgams. Vermillion, a red pigment, contains mercury sulfide. The Ohlone, who lived near the future New Almaden Mine, used the ore, cinnabar, as body paint and later to decorate the nearby Mission Santa Clara.

with numbered markers that correspond to the interpretive guide. To continue on the route, go right on the signed Deep Gulch Trail at the far end of the Hacienda enclosure.

Deep Gulch is pretty much a mining-history-free zone until you near the junction with the trail to English Camp, where you'll pass the tailings pile from the Harry Shaft, which spills down into the ravine. But the setting is cool and, in spring and winter, moist, with water tumbling down the gulch until the hot summer sun dries it out.

By contrast, there's a lot to explore at English Camp: a collapsed schoolhouse, a monument, a church site on a hill. Sun-bleached interpretive signs describe life in the camp, which housed miners from Cornwall, England, and their families. Picnic tables in the shade are perfect for lunch or a snack.

Breaking from the formal Historic Trail route, follow the Castillero Trail, part of the Anza National Scenic Trail and the Bay Area Ridge Trail, up toward Spanish Town, the next stop on the tour. At the crest of the ridge and the junction with the trail to the Hidalgo Cemetery, go right and follow the broad track down to Spanish Town, where the broken windows of the remaining structures look out on incredible views east toward the Santa Clara Valley and west into the Santa Cruz Mountains.

The roadway loops around the back side of the camp and drops to the impressive rotary furnace. In this massive structure, cinnabar was incinerated and the gases condensed into liquid mercury. The fenced-off enclosure also contains a Rossi Retort, which incorporated a "perfect angle of repose" to facilitate the heating and condensing process.

▶ The namesake of the Castillero Trail is Mexican cavalry captain Andres Castillero, who is credited with discovering the New Almaden Mine in 1845.

Back on the Castillero Trail, a flat ramble near the top of the ridge opens to views west of the Santa Cruz Mountains and then out onto the South Bay, an expanse of gray, green, gold, and shimmering blue. At the Bull Run junction, with picnic sites and a water trough for horses, pick up the Mine Hill Trail, which drops into the shade. The short path to the San Cristobal Mine breaks off of Mine Hill; pass through the heavy timbers of the portal and explore. The huge block of granite was used in drilling competitions: The miners at New Almaden would compete with other miners throughout California, according to the trail brochure.

The April Trail breaks off the Mine Hill Trail below the San Cristobal shaft. This side trip leads past the rebuilt powder house—destroyed not by a blast, despite the fact

New Almaden Quicksilver Historic Loop (Almaden Quicksilver County Park)

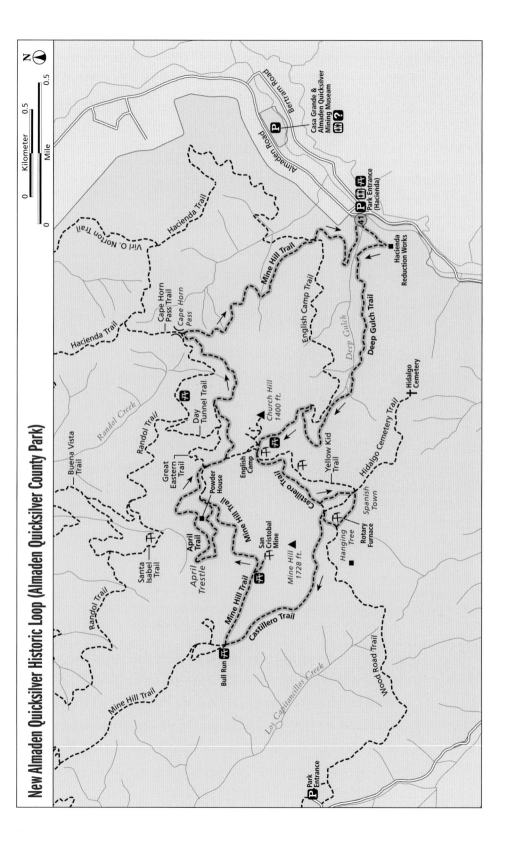

that tens of thousands of pounds of powder were used in the mines each year, but by the Loma Prieta earthquake. The trail proceeds down and around the April Tunnel trestle before climbing back onto the Mine Hill Trail.

Back on the Mine Hill, the descent continues to Cape Horn, where you'll find picnic tables and can enjoy the last of the South Bay views. The Mine Hill Trail turns sharply east. Near the bottom of the mile-long descent, you'll pass two more historic structures: the Almaden Quicksilver chimney, which spewed toxic gases produced by the mining process, and the incline tramway, where as many as one hundred ore cars traveled up and down the mountain, using counterbalance to help control the speed of loaded cars on the downhill run. The route concludes in the Hacienda staging area.

Miles and Directions

0.0 Start by checking out the exhibit of equipment from the Hacienda Reduction Works. The Deep Gulch Trail starts at the far end of the fenced enclosure, passing behind it before heading up into Deep Gulch.

1.1 The broad English Camp Trail is visible through the trees on the other side of the gulch.

1.3 Pass post 3 at the tailings pile.

1.4 At the trail junction, go left and uphill on the English Camp Trail.

1.7 Arrive at English Camp. Explore, then pick up the broad Castillero Trail. *Note:* The formal Historic Trail follows the Yellow Kid Trail, which runs roughly parallel to the Castillero Trail, and is an option that both extends the trail length and adds elevation gain and loss.

2.3 At the junction on the ridgeline, go left onto the Hidalgo Cemetery Trail.

2.4 Arrive at Spanish Town. Enjoy the amazing views, then circle around the back side of the knob on the Yellow Kid Trail.

2.6 Reach the rotary furnace. Continue down the Wood Road Trail for about 0.1 mile to the hanging tree. Retrace your steps to the furnace, then climb the short, steep pitch to the left.

2.9 At the junction with the Castillero Trail; go left on the broad dirt track.

3.2 Pass post 8 and under a fire protection outlet.

3.6 At the trail junction at Bull Run, turn sharply right onto the signed Mine Hill Trail.

3.9 Take the side trail to the San Cristobal Mine. Retrace your steps, then continue downhill on the Mine Hill Trail.

4.4 At the junction, turn left onto the April Trail.

▶ Casa Grande, built in 1854 and used as the home of the New Almaden's mine manager, houses the New Almaden Quicksilver Mining Museum. The museum is open Monday, Tuesday, and Friday from noon to 4 p.m. and on weekends from 10 a.m. to 4 p.m. It is closed Wednesday and Thursday and on Thanksgiving, Christmas, and New Year's Day. Tours are available. For more information, call (408) 323-1107 or visit www.sccgov.org/sites/parks/parkfinder/Pages/Almaden-Quicksilver-Mining-Museum.aspx.

The mouth of the San Cristobal Mine at Almaden Quicksilver County Park

4.5 Pass the powder house.

5.0 Round the switchback that curls around the April Tunnel trestle.

5.4 Meet the Mine Hill Trail at the junction with the Great Eastern Trail. Continue downhill on the broad Mine Hill Trail.

5.7 Pass the trail that breaks right to English Camp, then a second junction with the Great Eastern Trail. Remain on the Mine Hill Trail.

6.2 At the Cape Horn Pass junction, stay right and downhill on the Mine Hill Trail.

7.1 Pass the signed trail to English Camp on the right, and then post 14, for the Almaden Quicksilver Chimney. Continue down on the Mine Hill Trail.

7.2 Pass the site of the incline tramway.

7.3 Arrive back at the trailhead.

A trail leads into the eucalyptus at Sibley Volcanic Regional Preserve.

Appendix: Resources and Further Reading

None of these lists are, by any means, complete. Physical and online libraries and bookstores brim with specialized volumes on San Francisco's history.

Books

Angle of Repose. Wallace Stegner. Penguin Classics, 2000.

Bolinas: A Narrative of the Days of the Dons. Marin W. Pepper. Vantage Press, 1965.

California's Missions. Edited by Ralph B. Wright. Lowman Publishing Co., 1950, 1999.

A Companion to California. James D. Hart. Oxford University Press, 1978.

Discovering Francis Drake's California Harbor. Raymond Aker and Edward Von der Porten. Drake Navigators Guild, 2000.

El Presidio de San Francisco: A History under Spain and Mexico 1776–1846. John Phillip Langelier and Daniel Bernard Rosen. National Park Service, US Department of the Interior, 1992.

Exploring Point Reyes National Seashore and Golden Gate National Recreation Area. Tracy Salcedo-Chourré. Globe Pequot Press, 2003.

Farming on the Edge. John Hart. University of California Press, 1991.

The History and Architecture of the Historic Lifeboat Station. Dewey Livingston and Steven Burke. National Park Service, 1991.

Imperial San Francisco: Urban Power, Earthly Ruin. Gary Brechin. University of California Press, 1999, 2006.

Lands of Promise and Despair: Chronicles of Early California, 1535–1846. Edited by Rose Marie Beebe and Robert M. Senkewicz. University of Santa Clara and Heyday Books, 2001.

The Ohlone Way. Malcolm Margolin. Heyday Books, 1978.

Point Reyes: Secret Places and Magic Moments. Phil Arnot. Wide World Publishing/Tetra, 1992.

Post and Park: A Brief Illustrated History of the Presidio of San Francisco. Stephen A. Haller. Golden Gate National Parks Association, 1997.

San Francisco's Wilderness Next Door. John Hart. Presidio Press, 1979.

Brochures and Articles

"Almaden Quicksilver County Park Historic Trail." Santa Clara County Parks and Boy Scout Troop 446. www.sccgov.org/sites/parks/parkfinder/Documents/Quicksilver-Brochure-Sm.pdf.

"Alum Rock Park: East San Jose's Heart (A Very Brief History)." Judy Thompson. www.nnvesj.org/Archives/ARPHistory.htm#ARP.

"A History Walk of Lake Chabot." Jacqueline Beggs. Alameda Country Historical Society, 1997.

"A Human and Natural History of Stanford's Dish Open Space." Christy Holloway. In *Sandstone & Tile* 35, no. 2 (Spring/Summer 2011). historicalsociety.stanford. edu/pdfST/ST35no2.pdf.

Websites

I referred to a vast number of websites in researching and confirming historical information for this guide. Not all could bee listed here, but these I found to be particularly helpful:

www.parks.ca.gov
foundsf.org
stanford.edu
berkeley.edu
bancroft.berkeley.edu

Index

About the Author

Tracy Salcedo-Choureé has written guidebooks to a number of destinations in California and Colorado, including *Hiking Waterfalls in Northern California*, *Hiking Lassen Volcanic National Park*, *Best Hikes Near Reno–Lake Tahoe*, *Best Hikes Near Sacramento*, *Best Rail-Trails California*, *Exploring California's Missions and Presidios*, *Exploring Point Reyes National Seashore and Golden Gate National Recreation Area*, and *Best Easy Day Hikes* guides to San Francisco's Peninsula, San Francisco's North Bay, San Francisco's East Bay, San Jose, Lake Tahoe, Reno, Sacramento, Fresno, Boulder, Denver, and Aspen. She lives with her family in California's Wine Country. You can learn more by visiting her website at www.laughingwaterink.com.